FOOLS FOR SCANDAL

To Ted + Liz Parkhurst,
with admiration.

Gene Lyons

9 Aug 1996

FOOLS FOR SCANDAL

✦

HOW THE MEDIA
INVENTED WHITEWATER

Gene Lyons

AND THE EDITORS OF
HARPER'S MAGAZINE

NEW YORK

Published by Franklin Square Press, a division of
Harper's Magazine, 666, Broadway, New York, N.Y. 10012

First edition

Library of Congress Cataloging-in-Publication Data

Lyons, Gene, 1943–
Fools for scandal : how the media invented Whitewater /
Gene Lyons and the editors of Harper's magazine.
p. cm.
Includes index.
ISBN 1-879957-52-3
1. Clinton, Bill, 1946– . 2. Clinton, Hillary Rodham. 3. Whitewater Development
Company. 4. Madison Guaranty Savings and Loan Association. 5. Real estate
development—Arkansas. 6. Political corruption—Arkansas. 7. Press and politics—
United States. 8. New York Times. 9. Whitewater inquiry, 1993–
I. Harper's. II. Title.
E886.2.L96 1996
364. 1'68'09767—dc20
94-47455
CIP

Book design by Deborah Thomas.
Cover design by Lorraine Louie.
Edited by Ellen Rosenbush.

Manufactured in the United States of America.
This book has been produced on acid-free paper.

96 97 98 99   10 9 8 7 6 5 4 3 2 1

For my sons, Gavin and Douglas

TABLE OF CONTENTS

ACKNOWLEDGEMENTS

This book could not have been written without the knowledge and generosity of Arkansas journalists. Two deserve special thanks: Ernest Dumas and Max Brantley. Longtime reporters and editors with the *Arkansas Gazette,* they make up a two-man encyclopedia of Arkansas politics. Dumas teaches journalism at the University of Central Arkansas; Brantley edits the *Arkansas Times.* Both indulged my obsession with unfailing good humor.

At the *Arkansas Democrat-Gazette,* editorial-page editor Paul Greenberg, Meredith Oakley, and Jerry Jones saved me from many errors, as did Rex Nelson, John Brummett, Patricia Manson, and Carrie Rengers. Thanks to editor Griffin Smith Jr. for getting me interested in writing for the newspaper, and to publisher Walter E. Hussman Jr.

I am grateful to other Arkansas journalists, including Little Rock AP bureau chief Bill Simmons; Steve Barnes at KARK-TV; Pat Lynch at KARN radio; Deborah Mathis of Gannett Newspapers; former *Arkansas Democrat* editor Bob McCord; Doug Smith, Bob Lancaster, and Leslie Peacock at the *Arkansas Times.* Former *New York Times* New Orleans and London bureau chief Roy Reed and his colleague Robert C. Douglas, both recently retired from the University of Arkansas journalism department, gave invaluable advice.

Thanks also to John Camp and Matt Saal of CNN Special Reports; Stan Crock of *Business Week;* Tom Hamburger of the Minneapolis *Star-Tribune;* Trudy Lieberman of *Consumer Reports;* Joe Conason of the *New York Observer;* Charles Peters and John Meacham of *The Washington Monthly;* Brian Duffy of *U.S. News & World Report;* Jeff Birnbaum of *The Wall Street Journal.* Tim Hackler and Jody Powell of Powell, Tate gave important help to the Harper's National Press Club forum.

Many Arkansans have done their best to educate me about various and sundry topics such as S&L regulation, real estate law, accountancy, investment banking, manic-depressive illness, attorney-client privilege, probable cause, etc. They include Curt Bradbury, Jimmy Moses, Dr. Mark Taylor, Herb Rule, George Campbell, Bill McArthur, Beverly Bassett Schaffer, Archie Schaffer, Warren Stephens, Lee Thalheimer, Governor Frank White, Joe Madden, Judge Chris Piazza, Joe Purvis, Diane Blair, Senator David Pryor, Julie Speed, Fred Harrison, David Criner, Mart Vehik, Joan Vehik, Charles Banks, Brent Bumpers, Summers Matthews, Chris Barrier, Janice Choate, Sharon Bowman, Max Parker, Steve Kirk, Jackson Mott, John Tisdale, and several members of the Psychiatry Department at the University of Arkansas Medical School. My former neighbor, banker, and kitchen debating pal Mike Jones of Mt. Horeb, Wisconsin, was a big help. Any errors or blind spots are all my own doing.

Without *Harper's Magazine* editor Lewis Lapham's faith in my work, the article that inspired this book might not have seen the light of day. Michael Lind did a terrific job editing it. I'm equally grateful for the support of *Harper's Magazine* publisher Rick MacArthur. Jeanne Dubi prodded me along forcefully but gently. Aaron Asher provided crucial structural help. Thanks also to Ellen Rosenbush's editing and to Louisa McCune's diligent fact-checking. Deadline pressure was hard on everybody, but I've never worked in a more amicable, mutually supportive atmosphere.

Closer to home, thanks also to the friends who feigned interest in my ranting and helped me stay calm. My fellow members of the Hillcrest Housewives Club were unfailingly supportive; also my boon companions in the Wattensaw and Central Arkansas Beagle clubs. As always, I owe the profoundest debt to Diane, whom I first followed home to this crazy, cantankerous, wonderful place thirty years ago—and never looked back.

In Darkest Arkansas

I know New Yorkers who have been to Cochin China, Kafiristan, Paraguay, Somaliland, and West Virginia, but not one who has ever penetrated the miasmatic jungles of Arkansas.

—*H. L. Mencken*

The only insecurity I have is the media. Because a misinterpretation by the media is never corrected. They'll misinterpret a quote and say, 'I'm sorry.' But what about the people who read it?

—*Michael Jordan*

✦

Maybe the best way to get a fix on the art of the political smear, Arkansas-style, is to begin with the *Adventures of Huckleberry Finn*. You recall how it goes: rafting down the Mississippi, Huck and Jim took up with two itinerant actors called the king and the duke. Renting a courthouse on the Arkansas shore, the pair couldn't draw but a half-dozen yokels to hear dramatic recitations from *Hamlet* and *Romeo and Juliet*. "The duke said these Arkansaw lunkheads couldn't come up to Shakespeare," Huck tells us. "What they wanted was low comedy—and maybe something ruther worse than low comedy, he reckoned." So the duke posted handbills for a play called *The Royal Nonesuch*. The hook was at the bottom: "Ladies and Children Not Admitted." "'If that line don't fetch them,' says the duke, 'I don't know Arkansaw!'" And fetch them it did, to the absurd spectacle of the king capering about on all fours, naked as a suckling pig and painted to resemble a tie-dyed raccoon. "It would make a cow laugh," Huck swears, "to see the shines that old idiot cut." Plotting revenge, the townsfolk hauled pocketsful of rotten eggs and cabbages to the next night's show—only to have the cunning thespians cut the tie ropes and drift off downriver, free of harm.

Many things have changed here in Arkansas since Twain's novel was published in 1884, but the zest for smutty buffoonery isn't one of them. Temperance crusader Carry Nation, should she return from the grave with her hymnbook and her ax, would find the cultural landscape familiar. Almost everywhere except for a few square miles of Little Rock surrounding the Capital Hotel bar, where out-of-town reporters gather to drink and gossip, the conflict between Sunday-go-to-meeting prudery and honky-tonk raunchiness that typified frontier America until World War II or thereabouts continues unabated.

Given literacy levels among the lowest in the United States, what this adds up to is a populist brand of political warfare that often descends to the level of professional wrestling. In a small, largely rural state with only one real city, it also makes for fantastic—and highly entertaining—gossip. Almost everybody, it seems, has a neighbor whose second cousin knows an old boy who worked on the governor's dentist's car, and *he* says . . .

During the 1990 Arkansas gubernatorial primaries, for example, lurid tales of lust and fornication were widely circulated about three of the four serious candidates—both Republicans, and, of course, Governor Bill Clinton. Only Clinton's Democratic opponent, an earnest good-government type perceived to have no chance, escaped suspicion. There was talk of whores, drunken orgies at duck-hunting clubs, illegitimate children, hush money, even suicides. One Arkansas politician was rumored to have had carnal knowledge of a convicted murderess inside her jail cell. Interracial sex, of course, is a topic of perennial interest. Indeed, it takes some effort to think of an Arkansas politician of note about whom scurrilous rumors *haven't* circulated.

For most Arkansas voters, evaluating this avalanche of smut has always been simple: your candidate is innocent, his or her opponents are probably guilty. The fact that political fault lines here tend to coincide with religious differences—hard-shell denominations to the right, "mainstream" churches to the left—makes it easy to caricature one's enemies as pious hypocrites. Otherwise, it would be tempting to suspect that many Arkansans harbor the secret belief that any politician—or TV evangelist, for that matter—who didn't have some rooster in him couldn't be much of a man.

But who would have dreamed that this stuff could be exported? One of the bitterest ironies of the presidency of native son Bill Clinton has been the marketing and dissemination of slapstick Arkansas political theater to an unexpectedly gullible nation. Prone to be touchy about the caricature of hillbilly squalor associated with the state since territorial days, many here had hoped the Clinton presidency would change things. No longer would Arkansans joke that the state's unofficial motto was "Thank God for Mississippi." After all, the man was a Rhodes Scholar.[1]

But not long after former Arkansas Governor Orval Faubus died in spring 1994, a friend of mine remarked sadly that the Clinton presidency—hailed by euphoric throngs in downtown Little Rock on election night 1992—had turned into the worst thing that has happened to the state since 1957. That year, of course, was the date of Faubus's shameful and futile defiance of President Eisenhower over the integration of Central High School, an act that fixed the image of Arkansas as a bigot's paradise for a generation.[2]

---

[1] In fairness, I should mention that Mississippians are said to refer to a plastic hose for siphoning gasoline as an "Arkansas credit card."

During the 1992 campaign, even seemingly friendly reporters couldn't help but prick Arkansas's thin skin. *Time*'s Margaret Carlson identified Bill Clinton as the "Doogie Howser" of his hometown "and one of the first from the area to go to college." Had *Time* never heard of the Fulbright fellowships? Senator J. William Fulbright was a Rhodes Scholar and president of the University of Arkansas before Clinton was born (not to mention a Razorback football hero). While Clinton was wowing them in grammar school, Fulbright was standing up to Senator Joe McCarthy's red-baiting on the Senate floor. By the time Clinton sought his advice on the draft in 1968, Fulbright was chairman of the Foreign Relations Committee and battling President Lyndon Johnson over the Vietnam War.

[2] In vain did defensive Arkansans point out that the University of Arkansas had accepted black students since 1948, that the Central High crisis began *after* the Little Rock School Board had voted to integrate, and that the *Arkansas Gazette* had won two Pulitzer Prizes for its editorials opposing Faubus's demagoguery. A symbol is a symbol. It's also true that Faubus was re-elected five times, until 1966, when black citizens voting in large numbers for the first time turned him out in favor of GOP moderate Winthrop Rockefeller.

The Central High crisis has served as Arkansas's political and jour-nalistic fault line ever since, and its lingering effects impinge indirectly on the Whitewater story. For from 1957 until the election of Bill Clinton, outsiders who couldn't find the Ouachita Mountains or the Buffalo National River on a map to save their lives knew about 1957—and, therefore, all they thought they needed to know about Arkansas.

To a degree, as Little Rock journalist John Brummett pointed out in *High Wire,* his less than idolatrous book about Bill Clinton, the President's entire political career was founded on the tradi-tional Arkansas worry about what the Yankees think. So the elec-tion-night crowd in 1992 was celebrating a great deal more than a Democratic victory. For native Arkansans, the feeling was almost pal-pable: at last we belong. Even hostile columnists in the Clinton-hating *Arkansas Democrat-Gazette* wrote that his victory had at last "redeemed" the shame of 1957. Then came Whitewater and what Republican House Speaker Newt Gingrich calls "the Clinton scandals." Platoons of reporters arrived from such spotless havens as New York, New Jersey, Maryland, and Washington, D.C., to portray the entire state of Arkansas as a veritable American Transylvania: a dark, mysterious netherworld populated by a mob of ignorant peasants and presided over by a half-dozen corrupt tycoons in collusion with the Clintons as the Count and Countess Dracula. Scarcely a Whitewater story has appeared in the national press that hasn't referred to the state's uniquely "incestuous" links between business, government, and the legal establishment.[3]

So why should you care about Arkansas's hurt feelings? Because you are being duped as surely as Twain's fictional Arkansas rustics who lined up to buy tickets to *The Royal Nonesuch.* Almost everything you may think you know about Bill and Hillary Clinton, the presiden-tial libido, and the couple's allegedly seamy business dealings back in darkest Arkansas—from Gennifer Flowers to the entire Whitewater affair—rests on "facts" that are somewhere between highly dubious

---

[3] Writing in *The New York Times,* veteran Arkansas political reporter Ernest Dumas joked bit-terly that "the word 'incestuous' is coded into the computers of all news media people writing about Arkansas and Whitewater. Press the F1 key and a reflexive sentence will describe the illic-it political and financial culture from which the President of the United States sprang."

and demonstrably false. Far from being the result of muckraking reporting by a vigorous and independent press, what "the Clinton scandals" amount to is possibly the most politically charged case of journalistic malpractice in recent American history.

Of course, "the Clinton scandals" didn't just happen. They are also the result of one of the nastiest and most successful political "dirty tricks" campaigns in recent American history. Aided and abetted by a small group of Arkansas Republicans whose hatred for the Clintons knows no bounds, they originated in a planned, coordinated smear campaign underwritten by right-wing organizations such as Floyd Brown's Citizens United, a California outfit called Citizens for Honest Government, Reed Irvine's Accuracy in Media, and evangelists Jerry Falwell and Pat Robertson. *The American Spectator* magazine, *The Washington Times,* and *The Wall Street Journal* editorial page pitched in enthusiastically. Self-styled "conservative" talk-radio hosts from Rush Limbaugh on down have disseminated hysterical falsehoods to an audience of millions.

But the role of *The New York Times* and, to a somewhat lesser extent, *The Washington Post* in creating and sustaining the Whitewater hoax can hardly be overstated. Having bungled the Whitewater story to begin with, both newspapers' goal for months, indeed years, has been to protect themselves and their damaged credibility. With a few rare but honorable exceptions, the rest of the media pack has obediently followed. [4]

Please understand that apart from a superficial acquaintance with both Clintons shared by thousands of Arkansans, I know none of the characters in the Whitewater saga personally. (My wife gave Clinton a little bit of money and went to Wisconsin for a few days on his behalf as an "Arkansas Traveler" at her own expense. But that's her business.) What little I have written over the years has been mostly critical. Indeed, I cherish a videotape of myself in a short-lived guise as

[4] One irony of the Clinton presidency is that as a centrist and a compromiser, the President has almost no natural allies in the press. With *The Washington Times* and *The American Spectator* flogging the Whitewater story on one side, even *The Village Voice* and *The Nation* joined in the attack. Why? Because while the majority of voters say they're in the middle, most of the passion and all of the good rhetoric are on either end of the ideological spectrum. Once the *Times* and the *Post* committed their prestige to the Whitewater "scandal," there was almost nobody left to question its provenance.

the poor man's Andy Rooney back in 1988 predicting that the governor had won his last election. But it angers me that Whitewater has brought back all the old stereotypes.

It is certainly not the purpose of this book to rebut each and every one of the alleged Clinton smears that have made their way into the public mind. Frankly, not all of them are rebuttable: not only is it logically impossible to prove what *didn't happen* but even Arkansas governors normally conduct their sexual relationships in private. In the famous *60 Minutes* interview that followed Gennifer Flowers's allegations, Bill Clinton pretty much admitted having sinned. How much more the public needs or wants to know is arguable, and will, no doubt, continue to be argued ad infinitum.

But it's worthwhile taking a backward glance at a few of the Clinton "character" stories, if only to demonstrate a fact of life often obscured by the media's pecking order (one that apportions prestige in approximately the same way high school guidance counselors rank colleges). That fact of life is this: where a figure like the President of the United States is concerned, the national media's standards of "proof" are apt to be significantly lower, not higher, than the standards of a newspaper like the *Des Moines Register* or the *Arkansas Democrat-Gazette*. What's more, they're sinking all the time. Because unlike, say, the governor of Iowa or the president of the University of Arkansas, the President of the United States is a national celebrity. And so, of course, is the First Lady. Hence their personal foibles and pecadillos (real or imagined) draw the interest of a vast public that is also panting for revelations about the intimate lives of Clint Eastwood and Tom Cruise. That gets the supermarket rags and tabloid TV shows like *A Current Affair* involved—which, in turn, brings considerable sums of cash into the equation.

Hence a person like Gennifer Flowers, having in 1990 hired an attorney who threatened a libel suit against a Little Rock radio station that broadcast her name in connection with an election-year smear against Bill Clinton, found it very much in her interest to peddle a different story to the *Star*. About $140,000 worth altogether, which, for a fortysomething Little Rock nightclub singer with a $17,000-a-year job, ain't half bad. Same for the Arkansas state troopers who in December 1993 told lurid tales to *Los Angeles Times* reporters and *The*

American Spectator's intrepid David Brock, although their libidinous saga became financially worthless with the telling.

An equally significant factor in the national media's declining standard of proof is today's cable-TV- and talk-radio-driven twenty-four-hour-a-day news cycle. Conservative pundit Fred Barnes, in the course of coming to the remarkable conclusion that President Clinton hasn't been more harshly treated by the press than any other recent president, put it this way in the *Forbes MediaCritic:* "It's true, rumors do slip into news stories more and more. Until recent years, reporters sought to confirm them. If true and newsworthy, the rumors, now confirmed facts, were printed or put on the air. These days, there's a new way of handling rumors: If they're hot, reporters go with them, simply labeling them as rumors. Hold off until confirmation comes through? Forget it. . . . The problem for the public is, after a while, it's difficult to distinguish the rumors from the facts."

Difficult? How about impossible? And try to square Barnes's conclusion that Clinton *hasn't* faced a uniquely hostile press with his main example: Rush Limbaugh's broadcasting to an audience of millions on March 10, 1994, that White House counsel "Vince Foster was *murdered* in an apartment owned by Hillary Clinton, and the body was then taken to Fort Marcy Park." According to Newt Gingrich's favorite talk-show host, a bogus crime scene was then rigged to make Foster's death look like a suicide. Limbaugh repeated the claim several times.

Cautioning the faithful that he was passing on a rumor, Limbaugh got so excited that he fabricated the homicide angle on the spot. The result was a dark mass of conspiracy theories lying just beneath the surface of Whitewater like a submerged log in a swift current—despite four federal investigations and counting, each of which has concluded that Foster died by his own hand due to clinical depression having no relationship to the Whitewater affair.[5]

To my knowledge, Limbaugh has never come clean about the episode. On an April 19, 1994, Whitewater panel discussion on ABC's

---

[5] Indeed, there's a thriving industry in conspiracy theories partly bankrolled by a right-wing philanthropist named Richard Mellon-Scaife and marketed through the auspices of Jerry Falwell, the Michael Reagan program on talk radio, and like-minded organizations. Accuracy in Media continues to buy newspaper ads in major cities allegedly poking holes in this or that aspect of the investigations—allegations long proven to be of no merit.

Viewpoint, he was permitted to falsify his role in the affair without demur from any of the celebrity pundits—Ted Koppel and Jeff Greenfield among them. According to Greenfield, Limbaugh had broadcast the Foster rumor not for its truth content but only as an example of how overwrought some people were getting (although Limbaugh's producer told radio personality Don Imus that the story was a scoop).

I realize that few would call Limbaugh a journalist. Whenever his habit of broadcasting factual absurdities is made an issue, he calls himself an "entertainer" (a very rich and powerful entertainer). But his example serves to highlight a fact of life among the New York/Washington political press so familiar as to be almost invisible: the role of journalist/celebrities, power and money. Consider the well-known examples of Bob Woodward and Carl Bernstein, the *Washington Post* reporters whose courageous reporting helped bring down President Richard Nixon and whose lives were subsequently dramatized in *All the President's Men,* book and film.

Nor is it necessary to topple a president to become rich, powerful, and moderately famous. As James Fallows points out in his fine 1996 book *Breaking the News,* the entire class structure of big-time political journalism has been much altered by the advent of cable TV. "At small newspapers and broadcast stations reporters are paid modestly . . . ," Fallows points out. "But a sizable group of people—thousands—have salaries near $100,000 or above. These are the reporters, editors, columnists, and other journalists connected to broadcast networks, big newspapers, and national magazines. And a significant group— scores, perhaps hundreds, nearly all with connections to TV—have incomes of several hundred thousand dollars and above."

Fallows's point is that journalist/celebrities who achieve six- and seven-figure incomes tend to lose touch with the workaday lives of ordinary Americans. One would have to be quite naive, however, not to recognize the intense pressures on ambitious journalists to put aside their skepticism and tell more (and sometimes less) than they actually know. That the same newspapers, magazines, and TV networks that pay the big bucks tend also to hire Ivy Leaguers straight out of graduate school rather than reporters who have worked their way up through the police beat, city hall, the courthouse, and the state legislature only makes things worse. Every rookie cop and cub reporter used to learn one thing fast: *anybody can say anything about anybody else.* The question is, can they make it stick?

All of which leads us to one final, significant reason why the national media's standard of evidence regarding celebrity politicians is knee-high and sinking fast: *The New York Times* v. *Sullivan,* the 1964 Supreme Court decision that has made it all but impossible for a public figure like the President to win a libel suit against the press. And the bigger and richer the offending organization, the closer to impossible it becomes.

Whatever one thinks of Fred Barnes's conclusions about the hostile welcome to Washington accorded Bill and Hillary Rodham Clinton, it's easy to concur with his prediction: "probably worse still for the next president and the next." On the other hand, it's a reasonably safe bet that the president of the United States who follows Bill Clinton won't come from Arkansas. So before getting down to specifics, there are a few basic things about Bill Clinton's home state that it's important to understand. By far the most significant, I think, is the state's sheer political inconsequence in the Republican scheme of things. Partisans who have sought to demonize the Clintons have had little or nothing to lose.

In terms of simple arithmetic, Arkansas and its paltry six electoral votes have always been the President's greatest political weakness. Remember back during the 1992 campaign, for example, when President Bush couldn't recall where the state was located? Bush dismissively placed the state somewhere between Texas and Oklahoma. Ross Perot, raised in Texarkana—a city whose main street runs along the Arkansas-Texas border—made similar gibes. The GOP ran campaign commercials depicting the state as a wasteland populated largely by buzzards. Even Arkansas Republicans called for apologies.

But the stakes were high. A successful Clinton-Gore presidency had the potential to reverse many of the gains Republicans had made as a result of the Nixon-Gingrich "Southern Strategy" and thus break the GOP's electoral lock on the presidency. Yet the South no longer exists as the political and cultural unit it was during the bad old days of legal segregation. Voters in places like Georgia and Texas don't necessarily cringe to hear an Arkansan mocked as a sleazy, morally corrupt pol from the back end of nowhere. Combine Arkansas's obscurity with its long-standing reputation as a national laughingstock, and almost any absurdity may be said to have happened here. Despite its history of talented, even erudite politicians like Senators J. William Fulbright and Dale Bumpers, what the rest of the country expects out of Arkansas is a shifty redneck.

Conservative agitprop organizations like Floyd Brown's Citizens United set out to provide one. What they couldn't possibly have counted on was the enthusiastic help of the "mainstream" press. On the old-fashioned grounds that none of the ballyhooed "character" charges against the Clintons could ever be proved to any local editor's satisfaction, none of them were ever printed or broadcast inside Arkansas until 1992. Then the *Arkansas Democrat-Gazette* got them from the same place everybody else did—the *Star.*

Another factor in the "Clinton scandals" equation that had enormous local significance was the demise of the *Arkansas Gazette.* Until October 1991, Little Rock had two statewide daily newspapers; a bitter, protracted circulation war spanned almost all of Bill Clinton's time in public office. Having won two Pulitzers during the 1950s for editorials urging opposition to Orval Faubus's racial demagoguery, the *Gazette* had been Arkansas's dominant newspaper since the early 1800s.

Praised, damned, and read by almost everybody, the *Gazette* had long been recognized as one of the South's best newspapers, its idiosyncratic brand of populist liberalism having much to do with the state's seemingly paradoxical politics—a rural, undeniably conservative state that consistently elects moderate to liberal Democrats like Dale Bumpers, David Pryor, and Bill Clinton. But the paper was sold in 1986 to the Gannett chain, which proceeded to tinker with its format, alienating many longtime readers, then gave up in 1991 and sold it again, this time to the locally owned *Arkansas Democrat,* which became the *Arkansas Democrat-Gazette.* The effect upon Arkansas journalism was much the same as if, say, *The Washington Post* folded, leaving only *The Washington Times.* The balance provided by Arkansas's having two newspapers of very different editorial views disappeared. Despite its name, the winning *Arkansas Democrat-Gazette* espouses strict conservative Republicanism. Bill Clinton's political destruction has been its main agenda since memory runneth not to the contrary. During the 1992 campaign, there were days when the *Democrat-Gazette* would run a bitterly critical editorial and as many as four opinion columns denouncing Clinton—although never, it's worth pointing out, as a fornicator and a crook.

Even more significant was the loss of the *Arkansas Gazette*'s staff and institutional memory. With a few exceptions, the state's most experienced and respected political journalists were put out of work. In addition, the *Gazette*'s library and clip files became the property of the winning newspaper's publisher, who has not seen fit to share them with out-of-town reporters (although it's all on microfilm at the public library, and the *Democrat-Gazette* is now on Nexis). The *Arkansas Gazette* had by no means idolized Bill Clinton in either its news coverage or editorial pages; *Gazette* editorial writers tended to admire Clinton's vision of Arkansas's future but often found themselves disappointed by his deal-maker's pragmatism. But the *Gazette,* if it still existed, would have had the experience, the resources, and the inclination to debunk some of the more egregiously absurd stories that began to appear in the national press soon after Clinton became a credible presidential candidate. With several notable exceptions, the *Arkansas Democrat-Gazette* did not.[6]

Arkansas's political insignificance, its remoteness, and the loss of its best newspaper combined to turn the state into a kind of journalistic free-fire zone. Career-minded reporters at the great metropolitan newspapers, magazines, and TV networks didn't need to worry overmuch about burning their sources or earning the contempt of journalists in Little Rock. After Bill Clinton's gone, whether in 1996 or the year 2000, they wouldn't be needing them anymore.

Like any politician, Bill Clinton had accumulated a number of enemies during his five terms as Arkansas governor. Some were ideological, others personal. A few, like Clinton's two-time GOP gubernatorial rival Sheffield Nelson, were both. Nelson also has

---

[6] In fairness, I should point out that almost all of the arguments in this book appeared first in my own column in the *Democrat-Gazette*. Also that I am accorded complete editorial freedom.

a long-standing reputation as a political infighter of exceptional cunning. To pick one example out of a dozen: when Nelson ran in the 1990 Republican primary against his former political beneficiary, business partner, and duck-hunting pal Representative Tommy Robinson, the congressman's medical records somehow ended up on the front page of the *Arkansas Democrat*. Backing Nelson, the newspaper revealed that Robinson had admitted to his doctor that he drank a pint of bourbon a day and relied on Halcion to get to sleep during periods of stress—a medication suspected of inducing agitation and paranoia in some patients. Robinson publicly charged that Sheffield Nelson was behind the leak, but he could never prove it.[7]

Regardless of who gave Tommy Robinson to the *Arkansas Democrat,* there is no doubt that Sheffield Nelson introduced *The New York Times* to Jim McDougal, and hence to Whitewater.[8] During the 1990 general election campaign against Clinton, Sheffield Nelson's team prepared two "attack ads" for radio and TV. Only one got broadcast, and it backfired badly. Clinton had given a speech in which he'd made the fairly unexceptional point that, unlike the U.S. government, the state of Arkansas is forbidden by law from running budget deficits and can't print its own money. It must "raise and spend" all it needs each fiscal year. During the final week of the campaign, Nelson blanketed the state with radio and TV ads featuring Clinton's voice repeating the phrase "raise and spend" like a maniacal parrot. *If that*

---

[7] The meteoric political career of Sheriff, then Congressman, Tommy Robinson is described in my 1993 book *Widow's Web,* which *The Wall Street Journal* editorial page later cited as Exhibit A for its contention that Arkansas is a "congenitally violent place." (Also, I would have thought, a rather funny place, all things considered.) Be it recorded in defense of Sheffield Nelson that on the basis of voluminous evidence, Tommy Robinson's say-so wouldn't be taken by any Arkansas journalist to establish the truth of a statement more controversial than that the sun customarily rises in the east. If Bill Clinton had done no more during the 1980s than stave off the prospect of Robinson becoming governor until the latter's political self-destruction during the House banking scandal of 1992 (he wrote himself 996 bad checks), he would have served Arkansas with distinction.

[8] Regarding Nelson's rivalry with Clinton, it's necessary to understand that there has always been a downside to being an Ivy League smarty-pants in a Southern, rural, intensely populist state. It's the suspicion of "liberal" cosmopolitanism: elitism, religious heresy, and sexual license. Hence the best way to hurt a rival with Clinton's credentials has always been to accuse him of all three. Some who did were true believers whose reasoning ran as follows: Clinton favored health clinics and sex education in public schools; therefore he must be an anti-Christian libertine.

don't fetch them, Nelson must have imagined, *I don't know Arkansaw!* Nelson's campaign had also taped a TV commercial accusing Clinton of adultery and drug abuse but never used it. (In 1992, Nelson told ABC News's Sam Donaldson that he'd had evidence documenting both charges, but he has never produced it.) Clinton, it's been suggested, panicked. Far ahead in the polls, he nevertheless borrowed $50,000, taped spots exposing the sham, and had them broadcast statewide. He won the race easily.

It was also during this election campaign that Arkansas journalists first made the acquaintance of an odd cast of characters later to become familiar to millions of Americans through the combined efforts of the *Star,* a scabrous video called "The Clinton Chronicles," *The New Republic,* and *The Wall Street Journal* editorial page. Their credibility could hardly be more dubious had they floated into Little Rock with a retinue of jugglers and trapeze artists, accompanied by a steam calliope.

For five months in 1988, Larry Nichols had been a $22,500-a-year marketing man for the Arkansas Development Finance Authority (ADFA), the state's centralized bonding agency. Created by Clinton-sponsored legislation in 1985, ADFA's purpose was to serve as a conduit for Arkansas towns and industries to the tax-free municipal bond market, thus helping to attract jobs. Alas, Larry Nichols had a separate agenda. He told people that he was a CIA operative and became involved with The Coalition for Peace Through Strength, an organization headed by retired Army Major General John Singlaub, a one-time associate of Colonel Oliver North. Nichols twice visited Honduras and appeared in videos supporting the Nicaraguan Contras. No problem there. His difficulties began after he took his political activities to work. Instead of coming up with marketing ideas for ADFA, he devoted most of his time at the agency to working on Contra matters. He made 642 long-distance calls at state expense to various Contra leaders and politicians who supported them.

When, in September 1988, the Associated Press learned of Nichols's activities, he claimed that the calls had dealt with bond sales. His supervisors said otherwise; so did the people he'd been phoning. Asked about it in a press conference, Governor Clinton said he'd ordered an investigation. Depending on its outcome,

Nichols would either reimburse the state or be fired. "It looks to me like he could hardly have been doing anything else," the governor said.

A few days later, Nichols was asked to resign. Over the next weeks it was also reported that he faced felony charges in two Arkansas counties for "theft by deception." Nichols had allegedly taken payment from electronics dealers for satellite TV equipment but had never delivered. He avoided prosecution by agreeing to make restitution, but he soon declared bankruptcy and never paid up.

A few weeks before the 1990 contest between Clinton and Sheffield Nelson, Nichols reappeared at a press conference on the steps of the state capitol. He distributed copies of a lawsuit alleging that he'd been wrongly fired from ADFA. The lawsuit also listed the names of five mistresses on whom the governor had supposedly spent Arkansas taxpayers' money. Nichols offered no proof for either allegation. Among the five names on his bimbo list, however, was Gennifer Flowers.

Reporters for both Little Rock newspapers and the AP contacted the women, all of whom denied having had affairs with Clinton. Three threatened libel suits. One who did not was Deborah Mathis, an attractive black *Gazette* columnist and former TV news anchor well known to every reporter in Little Rock for her bawdy, irreverent wit. "Hell no," Mathis told her pals. "But if I did sleep with that fat white boy, he'd still be grinning."[9]

Every media outlet in town came to the same decision: Larry Nichols's allegations couldn't be published. Faxed copies of the lawsuit soon began appearing at smaller newspapers and radio stations all over Arkansas. They, too, refused to touch it. (Copies of Nichols's brief were freely available at Sheffield Nelson's campaign headquarters.) Finally, a conservative talk-show host at a struggling little AM station decided to take a chance. He allowed the list to be read over the air. Almost immediately, the station's owner was delivered a threatening letter from an attorney representing one woman on the list. The incident was never repeated. Callers who tried to bring up the topic on the air got cut off. Four months later, the station received another let-

---

[9] Today Mathis is a syndicated Washington columnist for Gannett newspapers.

ter, this time from Gennifer Flowers's attorney, threatening to sue for defamation and libel. A circuit court judge soon dismissed Nichols's lawsuit for lack of evidence. Nobody in Arkansas heard much of anything from him or Gennifer Flowers until the 1992 presidential primaries.

In January of that year Flowers alleged that she'd had a twelve-year affair with Clinton. The *Arkansas Democrat-Gazette* effectively demolished her credibility. Besides evidently dubbing raunchy remarks into an otherwise innocuous taped phone conversation she'd duped Bill Clinton into having—on the pretext that her apartment had been ransacked in the wake of Nichols's lawsuit—Flowers claimed a degree from a college she'd never attended, membership in a sorority she'd never joined, and jobs she'd never held. A registered Republican, she'd recently worked in the election campaign of a GOP state senator. The Little Rock Excelsior Hotel, where Flowers and Clinton supposedly began their affair in 1979, wasn't built until 1982.

Coincidentally, the only "witness" to buttress Flowers's story had also been Sheffield Nelson's campaign spokesman in 1990. He, in turn, never saw Flowers and Clinton together. Rather, he'd hidden in the shrubbery outside the Quapaw Towers apartment building one day in the late 1970s and seen a "big" car he thought "belonged to someone important"—and might have been Clinton's. Inasmuch as government officials and several state legislators kept apartments in the thirteen-story building, that hardly seemed impossible. Reporters also determined that Clinton never had a car like the vehicle described.

Musicians and nightclub owners in Little Rock who had worked with Flowers described her as an unreliable person who'd boasted of affairs with rich and powerful men in Little Rock and Dallas—but never Clinton. Does it strike you as interesting that Flowers and Sheffield Nelson come from the same hometown (Brinkley, pop. 4,500)? It's Nelson who is a fixture on the nightclub scene where Flowers plied her trade—not Bill Clinton, who, as the product of an alcoholic home, hardly drinks at all.

None of which proves that Bill Clinton never laid a hand on the woman. But it should make a skeptical reporter wonder. Flowers also managed to write an entire book called *Passion and Betrayal* without

specifying a single time and place where she and her illustrious lover
were ever together.[10]

Around the time of the Flowers imbroglio, an uncharacteristically subdued Larry Nichols released a letter to the Little Rock
media. "I want to tell everybody what I did to try to destroy
Governor Clinton," he wrote. "I set out to destroy him for what
I believed happened to me." He apologized to the five women named
in his lawsuit, explaining that unnamed persons had plied him with
rumors about Clinton's personal life—of which he had no independent knowledge.

Not long after Clinton became president, however, Nichols
changed his tune. Soon enough, copies of the almost insanely scurrilous videotape "The Clinton Chronicles" began being mailed to journalists, members of Congress, and conservative talk-show hosts.
Produced by a California outfit calling itself Citizens for Honest
Government, the tape has been widely touted on talk radio, marketed
on Jerry Falwell's *Old Time Gospel Hour,* and sold well over 200,000
copies. How many bootleg copies exist can only be imagined.

The narrator and emcee of "The Clinton Chronicles" is Larry
Nichols. Also assisting with some of the videotape's more lurid charges
is a marginal Arkansas political figure who calls himself "Justice Jim"
Johnson. A former member of the state supreme court and an unre-
pentant Faubus man, Johnson was the state's last openly segregationist
gubernatorial nominee. (He was defeated by Republican Winthrop
Rockefeller in 1966.) Justice Jim's most recent stab at politics was a
futile 1992 effort to persuade voters to reject a measure removing
defunct racist amendments from the Arkansas constitution.

Space does not permit even a cursory rebuttal of the most fantastic
slanders in "The Clinton Chronicles." So reverend an authority as
David Brock, *The American Spectator'*s star reporter, made a great show
of debunking some of the video's more lurid charges in the Winter
1995 edition of the *Forbes MediaCritic.* He reports that the *Spectator'*s

---

10 For what it's worth, Dallas Cowboys owner Jerry Jones, allegedly quite a party animal
himself, bragged to Texas reporters that he'd hired private eyes for Sheffield Nelson who'd
found out about Clinton and Flowers. See *King of the Cowboys,* by Jim Dent, page 211. Funny
they took no photos, isn't it?

office was "flooded . . . with letters imploring me to investigate the allegations." Is President Clinton, as Larry Nichols and Justice Jim Johnson allege, a murdering drug addict? Brock solemnly concludes that he is not. Other deep thinkers on the far right aren't so sure. Witness Floyd Brown's 1992 opus *Slick Willie: Why America Cannot Trust Bill Clinton.*[11] The book, which owes much to information provided by Nichols and Johnson, devotes an entire chapter and appendix to the 1977 suicide of a young woman in South Carolina. Or was Susann Coleman's tragic death a murder, engineered by forces unknown to hide the fact that she was carrying Bill Clinton's love child?

Brown's evidence? An anonymous letter and the fact that the unfortunate woman had once enrolled in a University of Arkansas law school class Clinton taught. "I'm sure when she went to Professor Clinton's class she was the center of attention," Brown writes ominously. "She was one of only about a half dozen women in the room of 100 men." With their lurid speculations, Brown and his star investigator David Bossie contrived to smear a half-dozen innocent bystanders—one a Little Rock poet who "admitted" composing an elegy to the dead woman. Bossie submitted to Brown a report describing the poet as "two-faced" and a "pathological liar," who—wouldn't you know?—"did admit knowing Bill and Hillary Clinton." The First Lady, it seems, taught Sunday School at the poet's church.

In the course of their quest for truth, according to a July 13, 1992, CBS News report, Brown and his henchmen peered into people's windows, invaded hospital rooms, and misrepresented their motives and identity. Their conclusion: "As long as her family refuses to enlighten the public as to its knowledge of the facts of that sad winter day, we won't know why this woman, seven months pregnant, had her head blown off. . . . And who was the father of that unborn child? These questions remain unanswered, but Bill Clinton's hirelings are working day and night to keep them a mystery."[12]

---

[11] Head of the arch-conservative Citizens United, Brown is also the creator of the Willie Horton attack ad of the 1988 Bush-Dukakis race. Even the Bush campaign denounced Citizens United operatives as "the lowest forms of life."

[12] Before Citizens United unmasks me, I must confess that I, too, taught Susann Coleman, an intelligent and gracious woman, in an eighteenth-century English literature course at the University of Arkansas–Little Rock.

Such farcical episodes would ordinarily not bear recounting, except for two things: other less lurid but equally absurd charges made by Larry Nichols against the President would later be taken very seriously by *The New Republic, The Wall Street Journal,* and also, there's reason to believe, *The New York Times.* Keep Citizens United gumshoe David Bossie in mind too. Presently an aide to Senator Lauch Faircloth (R., North Carolina), he was recently described in *Newsweek* as "a ready resource for journalists covering Whitewater. He provides documents and points them toward leads."

Enter now investigative reporter L. J. Davis, who came to Little Rock in early 1994 for *The New Republic* to look into alleged conflicts of interest involving former Governor Clinton and his wife. The result of Davis's investigation became the magazine's April 4, 1994, cover story, entitled "The Name of Rose."

In essence, Davis portrayed Clinton's governorship and the Arkansas legal and financial community as a cozy conspiracy in what he described as a "Third World" setting—a sort of deep-fat-fried Gambino family. "With the stroke of a pen and without a visible second thought," Davis wrote, "then-Governor Bill Clinton . . . gave life to two pieces of legislation inspired by his wife's boss [i.e., the Rose Law Firm]—revising the usury laws and permitting the formation of new bank holding companies."

In fact, Arkansas usury laws were revised as follows: In 1982, Republican Governor Frank White got the legislature to place a constitutional amendment on the general election ballot replacing the state's restrictive 10 percent interest limit. He campaigned for it vigorously. Every bank, car dealer, and large retail merchant in the state supported the change. Needing the support of organized labor, which opposed the change, White's opponent, Bill Clinton, sat on the fence. Clinton won the election, but the amendment passed without his help, leaving Arkansas with one of the most restrictive usury laws in the country—5 percent above prime—when most states have no usury laws at all. Clinton never touched it, and White returned to his banking career.

Davis also wrote darkly of a 1985 Arkansas law permitting state-chartered banks to open branches in more than one county.

"Worthen [National Bank]," he wrote, "could not have been brought to life without [Clinton's] government." Clinton, *The New Republic* alleged, also favored Worthen by making it "a major depository of the state's tax receipts," in gratitude for which Worthen awarded the Rose Law Firm its lucrative legal business.

But Worthen existed as a *federally chartered* bank holding company called FABCO (First Arkansas Bankstock Corporation) long before Clinton took office. Nor did the governor award Worthen state deposits; then the state's largest bank, Worthen had been the major depository since before Bill Clinton was born. (State law apportions such deposits among competing institutions.) As for the Rose Law Firm, it had been Worthen's chief counsel for *fifty* years.[13]

Davis's main focus of conspiracy is the mighty Stephens Inc. investment banking empire and Clinton's role in stuffing its coffers with illicit bond money through ADFA, Larry Nichols's old agency. (Not surprisingly, Nichols was one of Davis's key sources.) Now, historically speaking, the influence of Stephens Inc., one of the largest off–Wall Street investment banks in the United States, on Arkansas finance and government can hardly be overstated. But for *The New Republic,* a magazine, by the way, that at the time employed no fact-checkers, to assert that Bill Clinton made the Stephens family rich makes about as much sense as arguing that Chase Manhattan's David Rockefeller owes it all to Mario Cuomo. From World War II until the end of the Faubus era in 1966, the Stephens family ran Arkansas like a company store. But to rational minds, the story of the last two decades has been the steady waning of the Stephens influence inside Arkansas—even as their wealth and power increased everywhere else.

Since 1978, the principal agent of that decline has been Bill Clinton. Nevertheless, L. J. Davis speculated that "the intimate connection between Rose, Stephens Inc. and the governor's office may help explain how the Stephens family made a vast amount of money when its most visible enterprises were doing no such thing." The secret to the family's prosperity, he intimated, "seems to reside in the unusual way Bill Clinton's state dealt with Stephens Inc.'s old specialty, government bonds."

---

[13] Worthen has since been sold to Boatmen's Bank of St. Louis.

Taken together, the value of Stephens Inc. comprises just under 7 percent of the Stephens family's $1.7 billion net worth. Besides owning vast reserves of natural gas in Arkansas, Colorado, Oklahoma, and Texas, the family until the early 1990s had huge soft-coal reserves in Montana and Wyoming, gas and electric utilities, telecommunications and newspaper holdings, banks, and scores of other enterprises all over the planet. In addition, family patriarch Jack Stephens is a card-carrying Republican, a big George Bush supporter who has bankrolled virtually every Clinton challenger except Sheffield Nelson. Over the last decade, Stephens Inc.'s underwriting fees on bonds issued by *all Arkansas government agencies combined* totaled $2.1 million—less than 1/2 of 1 percent of the firm's total revenues. Arkansas state government business brings in roughly $1 out of every $8,000 of Stephens family income in any given year. This is why knowledgeable people in Little Rock regard the puffed-up self-importance of L. J. Davis and the rest of the "Yankee carpetbagger press," as he put it, as a bitter joke.

Be that as it may, a buck is a buck to Stephens Inc., which is why Davis got the whole ADFA story (courtesy of Larry Nichols) spectacularly backward. As a matter of fact, since Clinton's establishment of the state bonding authority in 1985, Wall Street firms like Paine Webber and Merrill Lynch became bigger players in Arkansas bond underwriting, and the income that Stephens Inc. derived from the state's government and industrial bonds has declined. That is precisely why Stephens fought the new agency tooth and nail in the Arkansas legislature. As they see it at Stephens Inc., Bill Clinton cost them millions of dollars. *The New Republic* couldn't have gotten the story more inside out and upside down had L. J. Davis been handed the text of his article by Elvis himself. Which turned out, in a manner of speaking, to be something close to what did happen.

Within days of his article's appearance on the newsstands, a March 23, 1994, editorial titled "Censored in Arkansas" appeared in *The Wall Street Journal*. In it, the editors breathlessly announced that while researching his daring article, Davis had been coldcocked by an unknown assailant in his Little Rock hotel room. He'd awakened several hours later with a lump on his head. "The room door was shut and locked," the *Journal* reported. "Nothing was missing except four 'significant' pages of his notebook that included a list of his sources in Little Rock." Warned by a mystery phone call that his life would be in danger the closer he approached "the red zone," Davis beat it back to New York. He told reporters his doctor thought the lump on his head had been caused by a small, blunt object.

The *Journal* castigated its pussyfooting rivals for going far too easy on the nefarious Bill Clinton and the thugs who worked for him. "The respectable press is spending too much time adjudicating what the reader has a right to know," editors complained, "and too little time with the old spirit of 'stop the presses.'"

The suggestion that President Clinton was in the habit of employing hoodlums in Little Rock who assaulted inquisitive reporters aroused the curiosity of the *Arkansas Democrat-Gazette,* where nobody had ever heard of such a thing. Within days, the newspaper tracked down Davis's assailant: a half-dozen or so straight gin martinis. It seemed that during the same four hours on Monday, February 14, that Davis reported having spent face down on the carpet in the foyer of his Little Rock hotel room, he'd actually spent seated upright on a barstool in Filibuster's, an appropriately named joint. At least that was what the hotel barkeep said, and Davis's bar tab supported that account.

Undaunted, the *Journal* editorialists plugged away, portraying the President's native state as a dark, malevolent, hellish world—and flailing away at Stephens Inc. as if it were Murder Inc. Almost everything on the newspaper's editorial page concerning Arkansas has been of similar ilk. Indeed, some have questioned why my own work has been so harshly critical of *The New York Times.* Hasn't *The Wall Street Journal* editorial page run amok on the topic of Whitewater for weeks and months at a time? Indeed it has. But where the *Times* is concerned, one can discern a glimmer of hope, an occasional hint of intellectual honesty. As the L. J. Davis example shows, however, the *Journal*'s editorial page is a hopeless case. Paul Greenberg, the *Arkansas Democrat-Gazette*'s conservative Republican editorial-page editor, has put it more succinctly than I ever could. "Just mention Arkansas or the Clintons to *The Wall Street Journal*'s Bob Bartley, editor and gentleman, and his eyes narrow, his suspicions burgeon, his paranoia blooms like a mammoth magnolia . . . and all systems are wildly Go! Soon his sleuths descend on Arkansas to send back eye-witness imaginings. Result: It's not always easy these days to distinguish an editorial in the once staid *Journal* from a lay-out in the old *Police Gazette*."[14]

Then, in the January 1994 issue of *The American Spectator,* appeared David Brock's infamous "Troopergate" article, in which a couple of hard-drinking Arkansas state cops told reporters lurid tales of Bill Clinton's alleged sexcapades. The article is indispensable to a connoisseur of Arkansas political mischief. Making small pretense of objectivity, and pausing to admire his sources' manly physiques, Brock gleefully passes on every scurrilous accusation troopers Larry Patterson and Roger Perry could dream up. Some are so screwy it's hard to imagine that even the troopers expected to be believed. Others cast more doubt on their own character and judgment than on the President's.

A reporter who believes that any governor could get away with sending state cops out to solicit women like roadies at a rock concert—much less get away with it for *twelve years*—will probably believe anything. Where was the curiosity and skepticism of the crackerjack reporters to whom these tales were narrated? Even the troopers' inability to affix a single date and time to any of Clinton's alleged indiscretions—thus making it impossible for him to defend himself—failed to faze them. For example, how did troopers Patterson and Perry know, as they related, that the Clintons fought bitterly about sex? Supposedly they eavesdropped electronically. And how were they sure that Bill Clinton and a certain trollop had sex one night in a pickup truck on the grounds of the Governor's Mansion? Again, because they supposedly trained a security camera on the truck and watched on TV. (Arkansas reporters who asked for a demonstration

---

[14] An Australian TV crew visiting Little Rock shortly after the L. J. Davis fiasco told Ernest Dumas and me that colleagues in the Washington press had warned them to be careful. They should assume that operatives for Stephens Inc., which owns the Capital Hotel, had their telephones tapped. Anything they said could get back to the White House. They could also count on being tailed by Clinton operatives. In response to our incredulity, they insisted that that was exactly what they'd been told.

After the Australians had been in Arkansas almost a week, I asked them what they now thought about the idea that Clinton (or anybody else in Arkansas) had a secret police force capable of monitoring the press. They laughed heartily. "Couldn't organize a pissing match in a brewery," one said.

couldn't see a thing.) Sworn law enforcement officers, the troopers also told Brock that they'd tracked down the spurned mistress of one of Clinton's Republican opponents and tried to bribe her into unmasking the father of her bastard child. All despicable acts, and possibly illegal.

In TV interviews, the *Los Angeles Times*'s William Rempel, whose sanitized version of the troopers' tales was the first to be published nationally, rolled his eyes skyward to express the unutterable tedium of spending month after month in backward Arkansas. Yet it apparently never occurred to him or his colleagues to check their sources' credentials. CNN's position seemed to be that since any sane woman would deny having a love affair with Clinton, the troopers' story was unverifiable—thus relieving them of any responsibility to try. That's what makes *The American Spectator* version of the story so useful. In effect, Rempel and his colleagues had served as censors, filtering out the improbable and absurd aspects of the troopers' braggadoccio and passing on only what they could prove, which in the end was almost nothing.

It took the Little Rock bureau of the Associated Press, by contrast, only about twenty-four hours to learn that in 1990 Patterson and Perry had wrapped a patrol car around a tree at 3:00 A.M. one morning. To keep their jobs, they swore to their superiors that they had been completely sober and doing public business—inducing a female trooper who'd been along for the ride to cover for them. In a subsequent civil lawsuit, the two troopers swore under oath that they'd downed a half-dozen whiskeys apiece at the Bobbisox Lounge before the accident. The Little Rock cop who wrote up the accident report apparently had looked the other way because they were brother officers. Next it turned out that visitors' logs that Patterson and Perry alleged Hillary Rodham Clinton ordered to be destroyed—ostensibly to hide Gennifer Flowers's visits—had never, in fact, existed.

The troopers had lied for money once. Why would any reporter think they wouldn't do it again? In the end, what "Troopergate" amounted to was that Bill Clinton had made a long-distance call from Virginia to a Little Rock woman at what most people would think an unusual hour. She told reporters he was talking her through a personal crisis. Maybe so, maybe not. Why is it your business or mine?[15]

Of course, the granddaddy of all the wildly inaccurate stories to come out of Arkansas during the Clinton presidency has been Whitewater. No sooner had the trooper farce begun to play out in December 1993 than the celebrity pundits on the TV talk-show circuit took to demonstrating their tough-mindedness by regretting its tawdriness but predicting that the Whitewater "scandal" would really bring the President woe. Led by indignant editorials in *The New York Times* and *The Washington Post,* the clamor began to build in December 1993 for President Clinton to appoint a special prosecutor to investigate himself. Republicans smelled blood. Business was soon booming again at Little Rock's Capital Bar.

Which makes it all the more troubling, to use Senator Alfonse D'Amato's favorite word, that the most noteworthy thing about Whitewater too has been the shameful performance of a credulous, scandal-mongering press. Having helped to create Whitewater through incompetent, mendacious reporting to begin with—as this book attempts to prove in some detail—*The New York Times* in particular has done just about everything in its substantial power to flog the issue.

From its dimmest origins in *Times* reporter Jeff Gerth's March 8, 1992, article about the Clintons' ill-fated land deal, the Whitewater "scandal" has worked as follows: Tipped off by an interested party, a reporter, editorial writer, columnist, or Republican politician conceives a theory of what *must* have happened in a given set of circumstances—most often circumstances altered by ignorance or suppression of inconvenient facts. The theory gets stated as a rhetorical question: Did the Clintons do X, Y, or Z? Next is an insinuation: it sure

---

[15] Paula Jones's sexual-harassment lawsuit grew out of *The American Spectator* article. What few people have noticed is that either she or the troopers haven't told the truth. (More likely both.) Jones initially filed her lawsuit because Brock's article said she'd announced herself dazzled by Governor Clinton's lovemaking and volunteered to be his permanent squeeze. She now says he made unwanted advances. Clinton says it never happened. The trooper who pointed out the governor's hotel room to Jones—not Perry or Patterson—says she asked him if she could meet Clinton and that he never saw her go inside. Paula Jones's family doesn't believe her story. Why should anybody else?

looks as if they must have done it. Then, a conclusion: of course they did it, the cunning rascals. Eventually, theory metamorphoses into pseudo-fact: they did it. All without anything remotely resembling proof having been offered. When evidence to the contrary comes along, it's shoved aside, minimized, or suppressed, a new theory is created, and the entire press pack goes whooping off down yet another trail. If they were rabbit hounds, you'd have them gelded as house pets.[16]

To the practiced eye, the *Times* coverage of Whitewater has followed this pattern with almost comic regularity. Such are the realities of American journalism, moreover, that when the *Times* commits itself to a scandal involving the President of the United States, the rest of the media invariably follow. Partisan political operatives and opportunistic opponents, meanwhile, get a free ride.

Sociologically speaking, as James Fallows says in *Breaking the News,* "political-journalistic Washington functions much like a big high school, with cliques of popular kids, the nerds, the rebels, the left-outs and so on. To be on TV is to become very quickly a cool kid. Friends call to say they've seen you. People recognize you in stores. Whether people agree or disagree with what you said (or whether they even remember), they treat you as 'realer' and bigger than you were before." In such a climate, conformity flourishes and rumors proliferate. Mere accuracy yields to semi- or uninformed speculations. With journalists aspiring to become TV personalities and six-figure incomes at stake, it's less a matter of how plausible and/or factual a given accusation against a politician may be, and more a matter of the status and effrontery of the accuser.

Let's examine a more recent case in point: *Times* columnist William Safire's famous "congenital liar" attack on Hillary Clinton in January 1996. To anybody with more than a passing familiarity with

[16] As a breeder of beagle hunting and field-trial dogs, this metaphor comes naturally to me. I own a hound named Leon who has an exceptionally "cold" nose, meaning he's often able to detect the scent of rabbits when other dogs can't. Alas, Leon also has poor judgment. On a bad day, he's capable of loudly baying his way—alone and ignored by the pack—down scent lines so old that the rabbits who left them may exist only in the form of coyote scat. Due to his habit of babbling about nothing, my friends call Leon "The Journalist."

Whitewater, Safire's charges were silly. "Why the White House conceal-ment?" Safire asked. "For good reason: The [Rose Law Firm billing] records show Hillary Clinton was lying when she denied actively repre-senting a criminal enterprise known as the Madison S. & L."

In fact, the First Lady has never denied representing Madison. At an April 22, 1994, press conference largely devoted to Whitewater, Mrs. Clinton was asked how her name ended up on the bottom of a letter addressed to Arkansas Securities Commissioner Beverly Bassett Schaffer. Her answer filled the better part of a full column in the April 23 edition of, yes, *The New York Times.*

In essence, the First Lady answered that a young associate at the Rose Law Firm by the name of Rick Massey had a friend at Madison Guaranty—struggling like virtually all S&Ls in the mid-1980s. Massey and Madison executive John Latham had an idea how the S&L could improve its capital net worth by selling preferred stock. Hillary knew Madison's CEO, Jim McDougal, whom the law firm had represented in the past. So she agreed to pitch McDougal the business. "I did that," she told reporters, "and I arranged that the firm would be paid a $2,000-a-month retainer. And that was ordinary and customary. That would be billed against, unlike retainers at some really big law firms that if you pay the retainer they keep it, no matter whether they do any work for you. This was really an advance against billing. . . . The young attorney, the young bank officer did all the work, and the let-ter was sent. But because I was what we called the billing attorney—in other words, I had to send the bill to get the payment made—my name was put on the bottom of the letter. It was not an area that I practiced in. It was not an area that I really know anything, to speak of, about." Mrs. Clinton then went on to describe in considerable detail the fate of the preferred stock idea.

So had the First Lady, as Safire alleged, lied about representing Madison? Not at all. Indeed, her long-lost billing records, when they finally emerged before the Senate Whitewater Committee later that month, confirmed her account. So did the testimony of her former associate Rick Massey—although that's not what you read in *The New York Times* or any of the newspapers and newsmagazines promoting the Whitewater "scandal."

What did Safire think had been the First Lady's motive for allegedly lying and hiding her records? "By concealing the Madison billing records two days beyond the statute of limitations," he charged, "Hillary evaded a civil suit by bamboozled bank regulators." But, in fact, the Rose Law Firm had signed an agreement waiving the statute of limitations. The only thing Mrs. Clinton appeared to have gained in the matter of the missing billing records was embarrassment.

Suffice it to say that Safire's entire "congenital liar" column is of approximately the same degree of accuracy from beginning to end. The *Arkansas Democrat-Gazette,* which normally syndicates Safire, declined to run it. But after President Clinton threatened to punch the famous columnist in the nose, the paper ran a somewhat censored version. Editor Paul Greenberg, the Pulitzer Prize–winning editor who stuck Clinton with the nickname "Slick Willie," told readers he'd found it necessary to edit Safire in order to "check some of his wilder swings, and generally clean up his invective here and there." Translation: an Arkansan who might think it futile to file a libel suit against *The New York Times* might not be so hesitant to take on the *Democrat-Gazette.*[17]

The point here is to illustrate how celebrity trumps accuracy in political journalism almost every time. Safire's column did provoke a bit of hand-wringing here and there, allowing the *Times* columnist to make self-deprecating jokes about his own chutzpah, but in all the tumult and shouting attendant upon the piece, did anybody bring the columnist up short on *factual* grounds? Certainly nobody of remotely equivalent status. It simply isn't done.

"The most sacred cow of the press," the late George Seldes used to say, "is the press itself." Reporters who pore over politicians' words with the rapt attention of an IRS auditor scrutinizing a bookie's tax return—searching out inconsistencies, gaffes, flip-flops, anything they can call "news"—recoil in horror at their own work getting anything like the same treatment. Hence Whitewater.

It will be objected that I have failed to acknowledge the distinc-

---

[17] Greenberg billed the 1982 election between Clinton and GOP Governor Frank White as "Slick Willie vs. Godzilla." Considering White's pop-eyed demeanor and his signing of Arkansas's infamous 1981 "Creation Science" law mandating the teaching of fundamentalist theology in biology classes, the description struck most readers as harder on him than on Clinton.

tions among a columnist like Safire, *The New York Times* editorial page, and its news columns. Very well, then, I acknowledge them. Safire's "congenital liar" piece is indeed an extreme case. Readers understand both his partisanship and penchant for overstatement, and learn to make allowances. But I would also argue that absent typographical cues, many readers would find those distinctions increasingly hard to make. Nor can readers easily defend themselves against ostensibly "objective" news stories with hidden agendas.

As to the personalities and motives involved, I have little interest and no opinion. Having bungled the Whitewater–Madison Guaranty S&L story in the first place, the *Times* found itself in the position of a bookkeeper who'd "borrowed" a couple of thousand from petty cash and, finding himself unable to return it, had two choices: own up and face the music or borrow more cash, head to the race track, and play the trifecta. For whatever combination of reasons, *Times* reporters and editors opted to gamble. In so doing, the newspaper's coverage fell captive to Republican partisans with a vested interest in promoting scandal. The rest of the media obediently followed.

Since the tale's premises were faulty, however, as time passed the Whitewater story line failed to advance in a comprehensible manner. Narrative tension proved difficult to sustain. Rather than coming closer, the crisis point kept receding ever farther into the distance. Reporters capable of summarizing ten centuries of Balkan history in a few terse paragraphs pronounced themselves stymied by a $220,000 real estate deal in the Ozarks.

Anybody who tried to pitch "Whitewater" to a Hollywood producer would find the task impossible. In Alfred Hitchcock's terms, Whitewater had no "MacGuffin"—no smoking gun, no 18 1/2–minute tape erasure—merely an endlessly shifting list of accusations and rhetorical questions. Very often they were questions the media had forbidden itself to answer, inasmuch as that couldn't be done without revealing not merely the huge gaps in the story's premises but the manner in which they came to exist.

One result has been a flourishing market in conspiracy theories of varying degrees of nuttiness. Another has been widespread bewilderment among the public as to what Whitewater is even about in the simplest sense. Arkansas journalists who have taken it upon themselves to keep up with the constantly expanding, ever shifting "scandal" have grown accustomed to getting calls from bewildered TV producers from around the world—New York, London, Sydney, Tokyo—who can't get a handle on Whitewater and seek local expertise. One has often been tempted to sing them a few verses of the old rugby ballad about "the Wah-wah Bird"—a mythical beast that flies in tighter and tighter concentric circles until vanishing into what the song calls "the orifice of his fundament," then complains about his inability to see in the dark.

Whitewater Deconstructed

It is like a church lit but without a congregation to distract you, with every light and line focused on the high altar. And on the altar, very reverently placed, intensely there, is a dead kitten, an eggshell, a bit of string. . . . It is a leviathan retrieving pebbles. It is a magnificent but painful hippopotamus resolved at any cost, even at the cost of its dignity, upon picking up a pea which has got into a corner of its den . . .

—*H. G. Wells on the novels of Henry James*

◆

The Great Whitewater Political Scandal and Multimedia Extravaganza is now on the verge of entering its fourth smash year. One would gather that the American republic teeters on the brink of constitutional crisis. The dread "gate" suffix of Nixonian legend has been applied. Melodramatic charges of bribery, corruption, cover-up, even of suicide and murder fill the air (although at the time of this writing the focus has shifted to "improprieties" in Washington). There has even been some loose talk of presidential impeachment. All this over a failed $220,000 dirt-road real estate deal up in Marion County, Arkansas, and a savings and loan flameout that cost taxpayers a lousy $65 million—the 196th most costly S&L failure of the 1980s, nationally speaking, and one that accounted for about 7 percent of the roughly $1 billion tab bankrupt institutions ran up in the state. How much corruption, after all, was apt to be found in a development whose roads remained unpaved some six-teen years after Bill and Hillary Clinton invested in it? For the longest time, it was hard for most Arkansans to take all the belly-aching over Whitewater and Jim McDougal's Madison Guaranty very seriously.

Then how did we get there from here? Well, it all began with a series of much-praised articles by investigative reporter Jeff Gerth in *The New York Times*: groundbreaking, exhaustively researched, but not particularly balanced stories that combine a prosecutorial bias and tactical omission to insinuate all manner of sin and skul-duggery. Accompanied by a series of indignant editorials, Gerth's work helped create a full-scale media clamor in December 1993 for a special prosecutor. Absent the near-talismanic role of the *Times* in American journalism, the whole complex of allegations and suspicions subsumed under the word "Whitewater" might never have made it to the front page, much less come to dominate the national political dialogue for months at a time. It is all the more disturbing, then, that most of the insinuations in Gerth's reporting are either highly implausible or demonstrably false.

So let us return briefly to the 1992 primary season. By early March, candidate Bill Clinton had survived both Gennifer Flowers's allegations of sexual hanky-panky and the controversy over his draft status to finish a strong second in New Hampshire. Clinton had won big in Georgia, and with six Southern primaries coming up on Super Tuesday, March 10, he appeared poised to seize momentum for good. If anybody was going to deny Clinton the Democratic nomina-tion, something would have to happen soon.

On Sunday, March 8, 1992, Jeff Gerth's initial Whitewater story appeared on the *Times*'s front page. The distortions began with the headline: CLINTONS JOINED S&L OPERATOR IN AN OZARK REAL ESTATE VENTURE. This headline was misleading, because when Bill and Hillary Clinton entered into the misbegotten deal to subdi-vide and develop 230 acres along the White River in 1978, Jim McDougal wasn't involved in the banking or savings and loan businesses at all. He was a career political operative—a former aide to Senators J. William Fulbright and John L. McClellan.

McDougal had done quite well for himself (and Fulbright) invest-ing in the inflation-fueled Ozarks land boom of the Seventies. But it wouldn't be until five years later—by which time the Whitewater investment was already moribund—that he bought a controlling interest in Madison Guaranty. In the interim, Bill Clinton had completed his term as Arkansas attorney general and been elect-ed governor in 1978, served a stormy first term, lost a re-election bid to Republican Frank White, then defeated White in a come-back bid in 1982. On her part, Hillary Rodham Clinton had gone to work at the Rose Law Firm in 1977, gave birth to Chelsea in 1980, and begun chairing her husband's education reform com-mission in 1983. McDougal, meanwhile, had worked briefly as a Clinton aide in 1979, bought control of a small bank in Kingston, Arkansas (pop. 200), in 1980, and lost an election of his own—a quixotic 1982 bid to defeat Representative John Paul Hammerschmidt in heavily Republican northwest Arkansas. (Hammerschmidt had beaten Clinton in 1974.) McDougal and his wife, Susan, had achieved minor local celebrity due to a series of unintentionally hilarious, cornpone TV ads for a McDougal subdivision called Maple Creek Farms. During the intervening five years, the Whitewater project—amply publicized in Arkansas news-papers at its inception—had manifestly failed to develop. It was in 1983 pretty much what it remains today: a handful of mobile homes and modest frame dwellings scattered along county-maintained gravel roads in a beautiful but fairly remote part of the Ozarks.[1]

---

[1] Coincidentally, a friend and I own a fifteen-acre fishing camp along Crooked Creek no more than a fifteen-minute canoe float from Whitewater. We bought it in the early Eighties in the fervent hope that the area would never develop during our lifetimes. So far we're closer to being right than Jim McDougal. The problem with the Whitewater site, from a developer's point of view, is that it's on the wrong side of the White River. The only road in and out is Arkansas Highway 101, narrow, steep, and curvy even by Ozarks standards. It's roughly a half-hour drive from Whitewater to Flippin (pop. 1,100), the nearest town with a grocery store and bait shop—and until 1994 required crossing a one-lane bridge over Crooked Creek. Good-paying jobs in the area are scarce. The nearest town with a hospital and a golf course—assum-ing Whitewater hoped to attract retirees—is the Baxter County seat of Mountain Home, roughly forty-five minutes away. Marion County, where Whitewater is located, is also dry (no alcoholic beverages). Had Whitewater been located on the Baxter County side of the White River, prospective buyers would have been afforded the same views and the same terrific trout fishing without quite the same isolation. Nor would it have required an hour's round trip to buy a six-pack.

If less than crucial to understanding the Whitewater saga, such details do help illuminate why the initial *Times* story troubled most Arkansas reporters. Take Gerth's murky lead sentence: "Bill Clinton and his wife were business partners with the owner of a failing Savings and Loan Association that was subject to state regulation early in his tenure as Governor of Arkansas, records show." While technically factual, Gerth's lead appears calculated to obscure at least as much as it reveals. A simple narrative chronology—adding the "when" to the "who" and the "what"—would have made the Whitewater deal look far less suspicious. After all, how could Bill Clinton have known in 1978 that McDougal would buy a controlling interest in an S&L in 1983? How could either man have anticipated the great S&L meltdown of the 1980s? Having failed to guess the future, what should the Clintons have done with their Whitewater investment? Could a buyer have been found in, say, 1984 to relieve them of their share of a losing proposition? What ethical questions might *that* have raised ten years later? These are the kinds of questions reporters are supposed to ask themselves before raising the scandal flag.

Simple narrative, however, eluded Gerth at every turn. So did a lot of key facts. "The Clintons appear to have invested little money," Gerth wrote, "so stood to lose little if the venture failed, but might have cashed in on their 50 percent interest if it had done well." In reality, the couple had put $220,000 in borrowed money at risk.[2] Gerth also made enough of an issue of the Clintons' mistaken deduction of Whitewater loan payments from their income taxes to make a skeptic wonder if a *New York Times* reporter could really be innocent of the fact that investing borrowed money is more expensive than putting down cash.

Although it is true that a line-by-line exegesis of the 1992 *Times* article reveals a fair number of details that enable a careful reader to cast doubt on its premises—a few vaguely worded sentences more than twenty paragraphs from the top, for example, hint at the Whitewater deal's actual time sequence—these details did little to alter the article's accusatory tone. And newspaper

---

[2] The Clintons ultimately lost, as the world now knows, about $42,000.

readers shouldn't have to be textual exegetes. Most readers—
including the *Times*'s own editorial writers and columnists, as we
shall see—read Gerth's story to mean exactly what its headline
implied: that *as governor,* Clinton had entered into a "sweetheart
deal" with an S&L wheeler-dealer for whom he could do big favors.

L
ike many investors, Jim McDougal had been lured into the S&L
business after 1982 by Reagan-era reforms intended to fix the
problems caused by runaway inflation. One of the most concise
descriptions of what eventually went wrong was written for the
Miami Herald by financial writer Mollie Dickenson:

> Numerous banking experts say that only about 100 S&Ls, out of the
> 4,000 existing in 1980, were operated fraudulently. But all thrifts were in
> crisis by 1980 because Federal Reserve-imposed high interest rates (topping
> out at 21.5 percent by 1981) forced thrifts to pay unprecedented interest
> rates to keep their depositors from fleeing to uninsured, but liquid, money-
> market accounts. Meanwhile, thrift income was locked in to long-term, low-
> interest home mortgage payments. They were hemorrhaging.
>
> From 1980 to 1982, Congress and the Reagan administration took
> numerous bipartisan steps to help S&Ls survive—allowing them to pay com-
> petitive interest rates, to make riskier, higher-returning investments, and to
> increase insurance coverage for accounts from $40,000 to $100,000. . . .
>
> But from 1982 to 1985, as the deficit soared and the Fed kept interest
> rates high, the administration, under Vice President George Bush's deregu-
> latory "Task Group," deregulated S&Ls administratively with ideological,
> free-market abandon, further removing investment restrictions on thrifts,
> and actively promoting the founding of hundreds of new thrifts. At the
> same time, the administration cut the regulatory budget. . . .
>
> This lethal combination attracted some rogue operators into the indus-
> try; it also encouraged ethical but inexperienced operators to invest in
> unfamiliar territory, but neither in the numbers the public was led to
> believe. Compounding the problem, generous 1982 tax incentives to invest
> in commercial real estate began to cause tremendous over-building. When
> they were repealed in 1986, even made retroactive, real estate values plum-
> meted, including, of course, the new commercial real estate holdings of
> S&Ls.

Whether Jim McDougal was a rogue or a naif, as of this writing his fate remains in the hands of special prosecutor Kenneth Starr, and his guilt or innocence of charges not involving the Clintons is beyond the scope of this book. In retrospect, it's clear that McDougal had bought the institution at precisely the wrong time. And although Gerth wrote that McDougal quickly built Madison "into one of the largest state-chartered associations in Arkansas," it was actually relatively small: among thirty-nine S&Ls listed in the 1985 edition of Sheshunoff's *Arkansas Savings and Loans,* Madison ranked twenty-fifth in assets and thirtieth in amount loaned.

Nevertheless, the institution soon got into trouble. Like many another S&L operator in the early 1980s, McDougal faced a paradoxical situation: Madison had to grow or die. He chose to gamble, competing for brokered deposits by paying out far higher interest than Madison's loan portfolio was bringing in, and trying to cover the difference with speculative real estate investments. Along the way, McDougal made loans to several prominent Democrats—although Bill Clinton, it's worth pointing out, was not among them.

Jeff Gerth's original 1992 story narrated the now familiar tale as follows:

> After Federal regulators found that Mr. McDougal's savings institution, Madison Guaranty, was insolvent, meaning it faced possible closure by the state, Mr. Clinton appointed a new state securities commissioner, who had been a lawyer in a firm that represented the savings and loan. Mr. Clinton and the commissioner deny giving any preferential treatment. The new commissioner approved two novel proposals to help the savings and loan that were offered by Hillary Clinton, Governor Clinton's wife and a lawyer....
>
> It was also in 1984 that Madison started getting into trouble. Federal examiners studied its books that year, found that it was violating Arkansas regulations and determined that correcting the books to adjust improperly inflated profits would "result in an insolvent position," records of the 1984 examination show.
>
> Arkansas regulators received the Federal report later that year, and under state law the securities commissioner was supposed to close any insolvent institution.

As the Governor is free to do at any time, Mr. Clinton appointed a new securities commissioner in January, 1985. He chose Beverly Bassett Schaffer ...

In interviews, Mrs. Schaffer, now a Fayetteville lawyer, said she did not remember the Federal examination of Madison, but added that in her view, the findings were not "definitive proof of insolvency."

In 1985, Mrs. Clinton and her Little Rock law firm, the Rose firm, twice applied to the Securities Commission on behalf of Madison, asking that the savings and loan be allowed to try two novel plans to raise money.

Mrs. Schaffer wrote to Mrs. Clinton and another lawyer at the firm approving the ideas. "I never gave anybody special treatment," she said.

Madison was not able to raise additional capital. And by 1986 Federal regulators, who insured Madison's deposits, took control of the institution and ousted Mr. McDougal. Mrs. Schaffer supported the action.

Gerth's story has been praised in the *American Journalism Review* as containing 80 to 90 percent of what the press knows about Whitewater today. Rival reporters did complain, though, that they found it hard to follow. What it lacked, they said, was a "nut paragraph" summing up what the Clintons had done wrong and why it was important. The insinuations behind Gerth's story, on the other hand, couldn't have been much clearer. They may be summarized as follows: When his Whitewater partner and benefactor Jim McDougal got in trouble, Bill Clinton dumped the sitting Arkansas securities commissioner and appointed a hack, Beverly Bassett Schaffer. He and Hillary then pressured Bassett Schaffer to grant McDougal special favors—until the vigilant feds cracked down on Madison Guaranty, thwarting the Clintons' plan. When dragged into the open by the intrepid Gerth, the aforementioned hack denied complicity in events she'd forgotten. This, then, is the Received Version of Whitewater as it first took shape in the pages of *The New York Times*. The problem is, it bears almost no relation to reality.

Consider, for example, Gerth's treatment of the appointment of Beverly Bassett Schaffer as Arkansas securities commissioner in his March 8, 1992, article: "After Federal regulators found that Mr. McDougal's savings institution, Madison Guaranty, was insolvent, meaning it faced possible closure by the state, Mr. Clinton appointed a new state securities commissioner . . ." The clear implication is that *in response* to a Federal Home Loan Bank Board report dated January 20, 1984, suggesting that Madison might be insolvent, Clinton in January 1985—a full year later—installed Bassett Schaffer for the purpose of protecting McDougal.

In reality, the timing of Bassett Schaffer's appointment had nothing to do with the FHLBB report, which there's no reason to think Clinton knew about. (FHLBB reports are strictly confidential, and the Clintons had no financial stake in Madison Guaranty, although that, too, has been obscured.) The fact is that Bill Clinton *had* to find a new commissioner in January 1985 because the incumbent, Lee Thalheimer, had resigned to reenter private practice. Appointed by Republican Governor Frank White and kept on by Clinton, Thalheimer says he told Gerth this in an interview and describes the *Times* version as "unmitigated horseshit."

Bassett Schaffer strenuously insists that to this day she has never met McDougal, never heard Bill Clinton mention his name, does not believe he influenced her appointment—and told Gerth so in writing. She had actively sought the job from the moment she learned that Thalheimer was quitting (he confirms recommending her to Clinton). She herself had volunteered in Clinton's 1974 congressional campaign and had worked for him full time on the Arkansas attorney general's staff while in law school. Her brother, Woody Bassett, also a Fayetteville attorney, is a personal friend and longtime supporter of Bill Clinton's.

The claim that Jim McDougal was behind Bassett Schaffer's appointment rests entirely on the word of McDougal himself, a manic-depressive whose lawyer filed an insanity plea in a 1990 bank-fraud trial in U.S. District Court, in which he was found not guilty. In his original 1992 article, Gerth acknowledged McDougal's medical history but described him as "stable, careful and calm." Subsequent mention of those difficulties all but vanished from *The New York Times*—despite the fact that the supposed recipient of Bill Clinton's largesse was bankrupt, destitute, and living on Social Security disability payments. Also unmentioned was that McDougal has long since recanted his accusations against Clinton and taken to blaming the whole mess on Republican partisans in the Resolution Trust Corporation.

Nor had the former state regulator taken refuge in a weak memory. Remember Gerth's statement that "Mrs. Schaffer, now a Fayetteville lawyer, said she did not remember the Federal examination of Madison, but added that in her view, the findings were not 'definitive proof of insolvency.'" Gerth now concedes that they talked for hours. Bassett Schaffer recalls being puzzled by *The New York Times*'s interest in Madison Guaranty—not merely the smallest of Arkansas S&Ls taken over by the feds but one her office dealt with sternly.[3] Oddly, Whitewater never came up in Bassett Schaffer's interviews with Gerth. She says she'd never heard of the place until she read Gerth's story in the *Times,* and there is no reason to doubt her. The S&L had no money at risk in the deal; nor is the Whitewater investment ever mentioned in FHLBB examination reports about Madison's plight. (Like many small states, Arkansas conducts no independent audits, relying entirely on private accountants and federal bank examiners.)

In any event, Bassett Schaffer felt that Gerth had a shaky grasp of the facts and an accusatory tone. To clear the air, she reviewed her records on Madison Guaranty, then wrote Gerth a detailed thirteen-page memo on February 25, 1992. Another telephone interview followed, then a second, five-page memo on February 28—more than a week before Gerth's first article appeared. She directed him to specific documents at the Arkansas Securities Department, documents he ignored.

But did Bassett Schaffer help McDougal anyway? Did the Arkansas Securities Department, as Gerth asserts, have proof of Madison Guaranty's insolvency in early 1985? Did Bassett Schaffer have the legal authority to shut it down? Consider the allegation that Madison was insolvent and Bassett Schaffer failed to act. True, the

---

[3] Among other things, Bassett Schaffer believes that the 1990 federal bank-fraud charges against McDougal came at least in part because she encouraged the FBI to investigate Madison Guaranty.

1984 FHLBB report did argue that Madison Guaranty had overestimated its profit from contract land sales—not including Whitewater—by $564,705. According to the report, "Correcting entries will adversely effect [*sic*] net worth and result in an insolvent position." But is this legal proof of insolvency? Hardly. In the first place (although Gerth neglected to point this out), the title page of the document from which the *Times* reporter took the one brief passage he cited stipulated that it had "been prepared for supervisory purposes only and should not be considered an audit report." In her memos, Bassett Schaffer had emphasized that the 1984 report—the one Gerth claimed she didn't remember—"merely discusses the potential effect that certain adjustments *might* have *if* they were made. They were not made."

In fact, federal auditors later accepted Madison's position on contract land sales.[4] Indeed, on June 26, 1984, six months after the report the *Times* cited, and six months *before* Bassett Schaffer took office, Madison Guaranty's board of directors met in Dallas with state and federal regulators. They agreed to enter a formal "Supervisory Agreement" with the FHLBB that spelled out detailed legal and accounting procedures designed to help the S&L improve its financial position. In a letter dated September 11, 1984, the FHLBB gave Madison formal approval of a debt restructuring plan that "negate[d] the need for adjustment of $564,705 in improperly recognized profits" and dropped all references to insolvency. Arkansas officials also called Gerth's attention to an independent 1984 audit that also refuted Madison's insolvency. In his story, the reporter neglected to mention either document.

The Arkansas Securities Department's power to close ailing S&Ls was mostly theoretical anyway. Bassett Schaffer's office had no plenary power to shut S&Ls and seize their assets. State law required that a petition be filed and a public hearing held before an elected chancery judge. Nor did Arkansas law make any provi-

---

[4] Transactions in which the buyer needs no down payment and the seller keeps the deed until the tract is paid for—a common means of selling undeveloped real estate in the South and West. If the buyer defaults, the seller retains ownership and treats the payments as rent. In early efforts to flog the Whitewater story, *Time* magazine found contract land sales highly suspicious.

sion for paying off depositors of bankrupt institutions. That duty belonged to the Federal Savings and Loan Insurance Corporation. Bassett Schaffer had little choice but to follow its lead.

To anybody who knows anything about the S&L collapse, the very idea of vigilant Republican-appointed federal regulators doing their best to shut down rogue S&Ls while Arkansas officials schemed to keep them open is ludicrous. "The FSLIC," Bassett Schaffer wrote Gerth, "did not want management tipped off as to the timing of a seizure, and the mere filing of a public petition . . . might well have created a panic among depositors and a run on the institution. . . . Certainly, it was critical to maintaining public confidence in the insurance fund that FSLIC be prepared to accept the receivership. We all agreed that any receivership should be handled under federal law and, of course, that meant that the FHLBB and FSLIC controlled the timing."

Bassett Schaffer urged the *Times* reporter to interview the federal regulators in charge of Madison. There's no indication that Gerth ever did. "I know what they're alleging," says Walter Faulk, then director of supervision for the FHLBB in Dallas. "That here is a person [Bassett Schaffer] who was given a job and in return did favors for Hillary Rodham Clinton. I know that was not the case. We acted in unison all along. I never saw her take any action that was out of the ordinary. Nor, to be perfectly honest, could she have gotten away with anything if she did. To my knowledge, there is nothing that she or the governor of Arkansas did or could have done that would have delayed the action on this institution."

The *Times*'s March 8, 1992, article came as a revelation to Bassett Schaffer in more ways than one. She learned of Whitewater and the Clintons' business ties with Jim McDougal for the first time. More than that, she was stunned by Gerth's opportunistic version of events. She threatened, but later reconsidered, filing a libel suit; as a public figure, her chances of winning were small, and the expenses would have been ruinous. "I provided you with a detailed account in writing of the facts," she wrote Gerth bitterly. "This information was ignored and, instead, you based your story on the word of a mentally ill man [McDougal] I have never met and documents which you admitted to me on the telephone on February 26, 1992, were incomplete." She got no reply until the fall of 1993, when Gerth and Stephen Engelberg wrote two more Whitewater articles that pointed the finger of suspicion even more clearly in her direction. Information she'd freely provided the reporters was taken out of context and given a prosecutorial spin.

By late 1993 the stakes had grown incontestably higher. Bill Clinton was President of the United States. One L. Jean Lewis, an investigator with the ostensibly neutral Resolution Trust Corporation, had filed a series of criminal referrals involving the Clintons and apparently leaked them to Gerth and Susan Schmidt of *The Washington Post*. Right-wing outfits like Citizens United had begun to churn out what Trudy Lieberman in the *Columbia Journalism Review* called "a steady stream of tips, tidbits, documents, factoids, suspicions and story ideas for the nation's press."

Following *The Washington Post*'s October 31, 1993, revelation that the RTC had made criminal referrals naming the Clintons to the Justice Department, Gerth and Engelberg weighed in with lengthy articles on November 2 and December 15. The first dealt mainly with the still-unsubstantiated claims of Municipal Judge David Hale that Bill Clinton had pressured him commit federal bank fraud by lendimg $300,000 to Jim McDougal's wife, Susan.

The David Hale presented to its readers by the *Times* was devoid of all locally distinguishing characteristics. Hale was never a Clinton intimate but a lowly municipal court judge (misdemeanors and preliminary hearings only). He owed his job not to Bill Clinton but to Republican Governor Frank White, who appointed him during his 1981–82 term.[5] Like all Arkansas judges, he's since been re-elected every two years. Because Hale is deemed a gutless wonder by local prosecutors and criminal-defense attorneys, his excuse that Bill Clinton made him do it has

---

[5] Some in the press persist in identifying Hale as a "Clinton-appointed" judge. But Frank White actually signed a bill creating the judgeship. The law specifically exempted Hale from a provision in the Arkansas constitution that forbids appointed judges from seeking election to the same job. Suffice it to say that Hale, in his capacity as municipal judge, disgraced himself and his oath of office by making blatantly illegal and unconstitutional rulings.

provoked hilarity in Little Rock. Did Clinton also urge Hale to set up thirteen dummy companies with the same mailing address, lend himself Small Business Administration funds earmarked for "socially or economically disadvantaged" entrepreneurs, then default? Gerth and Engelberg's story left out all the good bits.

Elsewhere the November 2 *Times* piece was pretty much a rehash of the original 1992 article, with a few characteristically misleading tidbits added for emphasis. "By 1983, Mr. McDougal's bank was in trouble with Arkansas regulators. The state's banking commissioner, Marlin S. Jackson, ordered the bank to stop making imprudent loans. Mr. Jackson, a Clinton appointee, said in an interview last year that he told Mr. Clinton at the time of Mr. McDougal's questionable practices." Left out of the anecdote, however, was the punch line. What Jackson had told the *Los Angeles Times* (which also turned the tale inside out but did give fair context) was that what had worried him was the Bank of Kingston's habit of making loans to prominent Democrats and major corporations outside its geographical area—among them Bill and Hillary Clinton. The governor, Jackson said, had urged him to ignore politics and be the "best banking commissioner in the country." Jackson had acted, indirectly resulting in the Clintons' own note being called.

But the real bombshell was Gerth and Engelberg's December 15, 1993, story, which all but accused both Clintons, Jim McDougal, and Beverly Bassett Schaffer of criminal conspiracy to keep Madison Guaranty afloat regardless of the cost. The article was a masterpiece of innuendo. Not only was Bassett Schaffer's appointment depicted as a corrupt favor to McDougal but "over the next 18 months up to the point where Federal officials removed Mr. McDougal, the new regulator took no significant action against Madison, even as she was moving vigorously against another failing institution with similar problems." That would have been the Guaranty Savings and Loan in Harrison, Arkansas, a $450 million institution that was closed in 1985. Ironically, Gerth and Engelberg knew about this case only because of Bassett Schaffer's own well-meaning help. She had cited the example of the Harrison S&L to illustrate her point that federal regulators called the shots. "In 1985, at our urging," she'd written Gerth eighteen months earlier,

> the FHLBB seized state-chartered Guaranty S & L in Harrison, Arkansas. The institution sued the State, the FHLBB and FSLIC claiming that FSLIC could not take over the institution unless the state regulator first went to state court to appoint a receiver. The Eighth Circuit Court of Appeals upheld our actions, and found that federal law pre-empted state law ... in the case of any conflict. The ruling in this case influenced our later decisions not to proceed with receivership without the concurrence of the FHLBB and FSLIC.

Such subtleties, however, eluded *Times* reporters seeking a Byzantine backwoods conspiracy.

But the allegation in Gerth and Engelberg's December 15 account that has shown the most staying power involves a supposed quid pro quo involving Hillary Rodham Clinton. It centers on an April 1985 political fund-raiser Jim McDougal held, and the suspicion that he may have shoved some funny money into Bill Clinton's campaign coffers. "Just a few weeks after Mr. McDougal raised the money for him," the *Times* noted darkly, "Madison Guaranty won approval from Mrs. Schaffer, Mr. Clinton's new financial regulator, for a novel plan to sell stock."

Now, what made Madison Guaranty's plan "novel" is hard to say. It was not unusual for state-regulated S&Ls in 1985 to issue stock. Even so, the adjective, with its implication of wrongdoing, has recurred mantra-like in virtually every Whitewater roundup article since. On the day before the planned Clinton fund-raiser, the *Times* pointed out, senior officials from Madison met with FHLBB regulators in Dallas and discussed a plan to issue preferred stock. You might wonder why, if federal auditors had supposedly pronounced Madison Guaranty insolvent in 1984, they were discussing a stock issue in April 1985, but mere logic fades when the press has a political quarry like the First Lady caught in the crosshairs. "The search for new capital," Gerth and Engelberg continued,

> took Madison to the offices of Mrs. Schaffer, who had the ultimate authority to approve any such stock sale. One of the lawyers employed by Madison

to argue its case before the state regulators was Mrs. Clinton.

Within weeks, Mrs. Schaffer wrote a letter to Mrs. Clinton giving preliminary approval to Madison's stock plan.

The sale never went forward. But this fall, the [RTC] asked the Justice Department to examine a number of Madison's transactions, and Federal officials say the state's approval of the stock plan was among the matters raised by investigators.

Again, not quite accurate. Regardless of Hillary Rodham Clinton's motives, for her to have ventured anywhere near Madison in any capacity would have been a damn fool thing to do. But the fact is that the First Lady didn't "argue" anything "before the state regulators." Nor did anyone. There were no hearings held and no formal application filed. Rather, her name appeared at the bottom of a letter written by a junior member of the Rose Law Firm expressing the opinion that it would be permissible under state law for Madison Guaranty to make a preferred stock offering.

After studying the applicable statutes and consulting with her staff, Bassett Schaffer agreed. "Arkansas law," she wrote in a two-paragraph letter dated May 14, 1985, "expressly gives state chartered institutions all the powers given regular business corporations . . . including the power to authorize and issue preferred capital stock."

Arkansas statutes also contain a so-called wild-card clause, which explicitly grants state-regulated thrifts all the rights and powers allowed other S&Ls by federal regulators. The securities commissioner had issued the narrowest sort of ruling. She hadn't approved the scheme at all; she'd merely said that it was *legal.* Had she ruled otherwise, Madison Guaranty would have had no difficulty finding a judge to reverse her.

In subsequent actions, Bassett Schaffer confronted the S&L with a Catch-22 of sorts. Before the state would allow the actual registration and sale of preferred stock, she informed Rose Law Firm attorneys, the S&L would have to meet more stringent federal and state net-worth requirements. Since the whole *point* was to improve Madison's net worth to begin with, the S&L never filed an application. Far from rolling over for the First Lady, Bassett Schaffer stifled the Madison proposal in its infancy while permitting stronger thrifts to improve their capital positions by offering stock options.

Nor was the matter kept secret from federal regulators. "I saw no favors done," insists Walter Faulk, the official charged with the FHLBB's oversight of Madison. "I saw a regulatory opinion issued that I would have issued too. We were urging all the institutions that needed capital to raise it any way they could. Madison's board was talking about going public. Knowing that they would have to meet SEC regulations—disclosure, due diligence, and so forth—it's highly unlikely that they could get any of it sold to informed investors. But 'Is it permissible?' is a very different question from 'Can we get it done.'" Once again, *The New York Times* had alleged scandalous deeds without interviewing any of the federal regulators. Bassett Schaffer had told Jeff Gerth the whole story in writing more than eighteen months earlier. Once again, the reporter had treated her version and that of her former colleagues in the Arkansas Securities Department as if they did not exist.

Soon after the December 15 piece appeared, an NBC-TV crew led by Citizens United operative David Bossie attempted an ambush interview of Bassett Schaffer outside her Fayetteville office after she'd refused to speak with them. Her husband snapped Bossie's photograph and sent it to the weekly *Arkansas Times,* which ran a sympathetic interview. In the article, Bassett Schaffer complained about her treatment by *The New York Times.* "The tone is very aggressive and suspicious," she said. "The attitude has been 'Prove the negative, defend yourself . . .' Why is Jim McDougal's word better than mine?"

A remarkably touchy Gerth phoned the *Arkansas Times* editor to complain about the paper printing such things. Didn't he know that these people were criminals?

By all accounts, it was apparently sometime in 1985 that McDougal's manic-depressive illness began to manifest itself. Frantic to save both Madison and the real estate empire he'd built around it, he appears to have succumbed to grandiose delusions of his own financial wizardry. Among the diagnostic criteria for the disease in the DSM-IV, the *Diagnostic and Statistical Manual of Mental Disorders* of the American Psychiatric Association, are "expansiveness, unwarranted optimism, grandiosity, and poor judgement [which] often lead to . . . activities such as buying sprees . . . foolish business investments," and so forth. Unknown to regulators at first, McDougal began shifting money from one account to another in a scheme of dizzying complexity.

McDougal was outwardly flush and brimming with self-confidence when he hosted the April 1985 fund-raiser in the lobby of Madison's Little Rock headquarters to help Bill Clinton retire a $50,000 campaign debt. (It was the fact that the fund-raiser was held a bit more than a month before Hillary's law firm approached the Arkansas Securities Department about the "novel" stock offering that aroused the *Times* reporters' suspicions—and also the suspicions of the RTC investigators who were leaking documents to the *Times* in 1993.) But if McDougal had shoved any questionable money in the Clintons' direction—either through Whitewater or the fund-raiser—the Arkansas Securities Department sure found an odd way to reward him. No sooner did Bassett Schaffer receive the FHLBB's 1986 report on Madison than she recommended stringent action. On July 11, 1986, she and a member of her staff flew to Dallas to meet with FHLBB and FSLIC regulators for a showdown with Madison's board. McDougal himself was not invited.

"At the meeting," she'd written Jeff Gerth in February 1992, "we jointly confronted the Board with the findings of self-dealing and insider abuse. . . . The Board was presented with a Cease and Desist Order that, among other things, called for the Board to fire Jim McDougal and other family members. (A copy of the Order is in the files of the Arkansas Securities Department.) It was a long and confrontational meeting. The Madison Guaranty Board members and their lawyers appeared stunned."

McDougal was stripped of authority, and Madison Guaranty agreed to another Supervisory Agreement that essentially left Arkansas officials, as Bassett Schaffer wrote, "to babysit the institution until FSLIC found some money to pay off depositors. In 1987, we received an annual audit for calendar year 1986 reflecting that Madison Guaranty was insolvent. Shortly thereafter, we asked that the institution be transferred to the FSLIC on the ground of its insolvency. There can't be anyone left in America who doesn't know by now that FSLIC was dead broke in 1986. Madison Guaranty was the least of their problems. Further, since Jim McDougal had been removed from the institution, there was little harm done in letting it sit, as did hundreds of others, while new management searched for ways to salvage its worthless assets."

Bassett Schaffer's registered letter strenuously urging the FHLBB and FSLIC to shut down Madison Guaranty and two far larger Arkansas S&Ls was dated December 10, 1987. Fifteen months later, following the 1988 elections and the inauguration of President George Bush—a politician with S&L problems even closer to home—federal regulators finally got around to taking action.

There is not the slightest evidence, then, that Bassett Schaffer inappropriately delayed taking action against Madison Guaranty. When I asked Gerth in 1994 about the discrepancies and omissions in his reporting, he stood his ground, alternately argumentative and defensive, and did not wish to be quoted. He argues, for example, that he never literally wrote that Jim McDougal had *in fact* gotten Bassett Schaffer the job, merely that he'd claimed to. Her denial struck him as beside the point. In other instances, he pleads limitations of time and space.

The perception Gerth most resents, however, is the one most talked about in Arkansas: his reliance on the hidden hand of Sheffield Nelson—Clinton's 1990 Republican gubernatorial opponent. The *Times* reporter insists that Nelson did no more than give him Jim McDougal's phone number and later introduce him to Judge David Hale, whose defense attorney is Nelson's associate. Nelson, the Republican nominee for Arkansas governor again in 1994 (he was defeated badly by Democrat Jim Guy Tucker), tends to be coy about his role. But he has given other reporters a thirty-eight-page transcript of an early 1992 conversation between himself and McDougal, who was embittered by what he then saw as Clinton's abandonment.

Indeed, Jeff Gerth, Sheffield Nelson, and *The New York Times* go back many years. As long ago as 1978, Gerth wrote an exposé about Nelson's mortal foes, billionaire natural-gas moguls and investment bankers Witt and Jack Stephens. What made Gerth's piece significant was its timing: shortly before a Democratic primary in which the Stephenses' nephew, U.S. Representative Ray Thornton, was eliminated in a three-man race for the U.S. Senate. Thornton had nothing to do with his uncles' business dealings. Gerth, however, had told local reporters he'd uncovered a scandal that would knock Thornton out of the race. Most observers thought the *Times* article did swing just enough votes in Fort Smith—where the Stephens brothers owned a gas-distribution company that was paying them at a better rate than other gas-royalty owners—to keep Thornton out of a runoff election eventually won by Senator David Pryor.

A few more highlights from Sheffield Nelson's political biography may help underline his motives for helping reporters portray the Clintons in the worst possible light. Hired as Witt Stephens's personal assistant out of college, Nelson was later installed as CEO of Arkansas-Louisiana Gas Co. (Arkla), controlled by the Stephens family and the state's principal natural-gas utility. (It was his subsequent refusal to use Arkla pipelines to carry gas from other Stephens-owned companies to buyers east of the state that eventually provoked a lifelong blood feud of Shakespearean malevolence.) Until 1989, Nelson was a Democrat, impatiently biding his time until the end of the Clinton era. He even raised funds for Ted Kennedy's 1980 presidential campaign in Arkansas. From 1986 to 1988 he served as Clinton-appointed chairman of the Arkansas Industrial Development Commission. But when it became apparent that Clinton would run again in 1990, Nelson became a Republican. He prevailed in a remarkably nasty 1990 gubernatorial primary against his own longtime pal, U.S. Representative Tommy Robinson. (Robinson's campaign, naturally, was funded by Stephens interests.) Bill Clinton then proceeded to defeat Nelson 58 percent to 42 percent in the general election.

Clinton owed his 1990 triumph in part to the fact that his Public Service Commission conducted an inquiry into a business deal involving a friend of Nelson's named Jerry Jones. It seems that back when Nelson was CEO of Arkla, he'd overridden the objections of company geologists and sold the drilling rights to what turned out to be a mammoth gas field in western Arkansas to Arkoma, a company owned by Jones, whom Nelson had brought onto Arkla's board of directors. The price was $15 million. Jones found gas almost everywhere he drilled. Two years after Nelson's departure, Arkla paid Jones and his associates a reported $175 million to buy back the same leases as well as some other properties. Jones then bought the Dallas Cowboys and won three Super Bowls. The election-year probe of the Arkla-Arkoma deal resulted in millions of dollars of refunds to rate payers. It also earned the President a permanent spot on Sheffield Nelson's enemies list. The result, it's been no exaggeration to say, has been Whitewater.

The talents of investigative reporters now poring over Whitewater documents might be better spent looking into another McDougal real estate venture. Sheffield Nelson and Jerry Jones put up a reported $225,000 each in return for a 12.5 percent share of McDougal's ill-conceived luxury retirement community on Campobello Island, New Brunswick, Canada. It was New Deal Democrat McDougal's odd conceit that wealthy vacationers and retirees would be moved by sentimental memories of Franklin Delano Roosevelt's summer retreat (remember *Sunrise at Campobello?*) to purchase lots on an island that is in fact damp, cold, foggy, and remote. The Campobello project not only failed but helped pull Madison down with it. Gerth and the *Times* have left that aspect of the Madison Guaranty story unexplored—even though, unlike Whitewater, the name of Campobello Properties Ventures is mentioned prominently and repeatedly in the very FHLBB examination report that Gerth quoted in his original March 8, 1992, article. Also unlike Whitewater, the Campobello project *did* put a big chunk of Madison Guaranty's scant capital at risk—some $3.73 million, to be exact, at a time when the FHLBB examiner contended that the S&L was actually $70,000 in the hole.

At last report, that particular picturesque stretch of Canadian coastline belonged to the Resolution Trust Corporation. Nelson and Jones, however, actually made a profit. In 1988, the FHLBB, then supervising Madison Guaranty's assets, bought the boys out for $725,000—leaving them a profit of $275,000. No doubt there's a plausible explanation, although William Seidman, chief of the FDIC and the RTC at the height of the S&L crisis, told the *Fort Worth Star-Telegram* that "I can't believe it. It's an extraordinary event. It smells. It could be legit, but I doubt it." Gerth says the Campobello deal holds no interest for *Times* readers.

Meanwhile, the same faults that mar Jeff Gerth's reporting on Whitewater—misleading innuendo and ignorance or suppression of exculpatory facts—also showed up in the *Times*'s accounts of Hillary Rodham Clinton's 1978 commodity trades and her husband's dealings with Tyson Foods. In the Gerth version, as in pulp fiction, it is all terribly simple and terribly suspicious: attorney Jim Blair helped Hillary turn $1,000 into $100,000; in return, Tyson Foods reaped a bonanza in direct and indirect benefits. "During Mr. Clinton's tenure in Arkansas," Gerth wrote near the top of his front-page account, "Tyson benefited from a variety of state actions, including $9 million in government loans, the placement of company executives on important state boards and favorable decisions on environmental issues." Chicken mogul Don Tyson was himself portrayed as a major Clinton supporter and fund-raiser, one whose close ties to the President had "been a subject of debate for years in Little Rock and [which] became an issue during the 1992 Presidential campaign."

The alleged $9 million in loans were the linchpin of an otherwise revealing but unsensational story, the implied quid pro quo for old pal Blair's generous tips to Hillary—in return for which his then-client, now-employer was portrayed as having reaped a veritable bonanza from the state of Arkansas. Following Gerth's report, the incriminating $9 million figure appeared everywhere. The *Times* itself weighed in with a March 31 editorial called "Arkansas Secrets," attacking the "seedy appearances" of Bill and Hillary Clinton's "extraordinary indifference to . . . the normal divisions between government and personal interests." The same editorial went on to deride what it called "The Arkansas Defense," supposedly the argument that "you cannot apply the standards of the outside world to Arkansas, where a thousand or so insiders run things in a loosey-goosey way that may look unethical or even illegal to outsiders." Nor had the *Times* editorial writers been the only ones to scold the Clintons for succumbing to the lax moral climate of the President's native state. The *Baltimore Sun* opined that the First Lady's adventures in the cow trade "certainly [don't] smell right, especially considering that [Jim Blair] represented a giant, influential agri-business firm in Arkansas that later received what seemed to be favors from Gov. Clinton." *Newsweek*'s Joe Klein spoke of the President's "multiple personality disorder," involving a moderate Clinton, a liberal Clinton, and "the likely suspect in the Whitewater inquiry, a pragmatic power politician who did whatever necessary to get and keep office in Arkansas . . . granting low-interest loans to not very needy business interests, who in turn contributed generously to his political campaigns. This Clinton snuggled up close to the Arkansas oligarchs, the bond daddies and chicken pluckers—and never quite escaped the orbit of the shadowy Stephens brothers, Witt and Jackson."

Now, Witt Stephens has been dead for years; Jack Stephens is a Reagan Republican who has bankrolled nearly every Clinton opponent (except Sheffield Nelson) from day one. Otherwise there's just one problem: the $9 million loan never existed. Especially attentive readers of *The New York Times* may have noticed an odd little item in the daily "Corrections" column on April 20, 1994:

> An article on March 18 about Hillary Rodham Clinton's commodity trades misstated benefits that the Tyson Foods company received from the state of Arkansas. Tyson did not receive $9 million in loans from the state; the company did benefit from at least $7 million in state tax credits, according to a Tyson spokesman.

Gerth blames a chart misread on deadline. But was the *Times* embarrassed? Hardly. In the journalistic equivalent of double jeopardy, *Times* editors, having convicted Hillary Clinton on a spurious charge, decided she was still guilty, but of a *new* charge: helping Tyson Foods to $7 million in tax credits. No sooner had Hillary Clinton held her April 22, 1994, press conference on

Whitewater-related issues than the *Times* scolded that the First Lady's performance had been smooth but cleverly evasive. Particularly suspicious, an April 24 editorial found, were her dealings with Jim Blair, "a lawyer for Tyson Foods, a large company that was heavily regulated by and received *substantial tax credits* from the Arkansas government." [My emphasis] And people call the President slick!

The truth is far less lurid. The $7 million in investment tax credits Tyson Foods claimed against its Arkansas state tax bill after 1985—that is, between seven and fourteen years *after* Hillary's commodity trades—were never Bill Clinton's to bestow or withhold. Rather like the child-care expense credit on IRS Form 1040, they are written into the state's revenue code. *All* qualifying corporations claim them, friend or foe. To earn them, Tyson invested some $300 million in plants and equipment, creating, the company claims, roughly 4,000 jobs. But Clinton couldn't have prevented the company from claiming the credits had the investments brought no jobs at all.

True, the Clinton administration did sponsor the 1985 law that created the tax credits. It did so under strong pressure from International Paper, which threatened to take its processing plants elsewhere unless Arkansas matched tax breaks available from other states—a potentially severe economic blow to the already poor southern half of the state. Far from being unique to Arkansas, state investment tax credits are now the rule from sea to shining sea. During the same week the *Times* made its lame correction, Tyson announced the opening of a new plant in Portland, Indiana. According to a press release by Indiana Governor Evan Bayh, the state provided some $9 million in economic incentives—more than Tyson got from Arkansas during Bill Clinton's six terms.

More than mildly shocking, however, given the stakes, was the *Times*'s failure to check with either Tyson or whatever Arkansas state agency supposedly made the loans. Admittedly, that would have been hard, since Arkansas has no laws permitting or prohibiting the lending of such sums to a thriving Fortune 500 corporation. But when Arkansas reporter Ernest Dumas called around, all parties promptly and vigorously denied the allegation. Nor had they spoken to anybody from *The New York Times.*

Elsewhere, nearly every detail cited as evidence of shady connections between the Clintons and Tyson Foods in the *Times*'s March 18, 1994, front-page story got the familiar Gerth treatment. Besides the imaginary $9 million in loans, Gerth cited several other suspicious transactions, among them a bitter court battle, in which Clinton "failed to take any significant action," over polluted groundwater in the town of Green Forest and a pair of seemingly tainted appointments—including naming a Tyson veterinarian to the state Livestock and Poultry Commission, and Jim Blair himself to the University of Arkansas board.

Once again, the national press has tended to take *The New York Times*'s word for it and to pore over Mrs. Clinton's cattle trades with a high-powered magnifying glass. But what if it's all nonsense? What if despite the Clintons' and Blairs' close and enduring friendship—which the *Times* acknowledged—almost everything else in the story relative to the governor and Tyson Foods was as inside out and upside down as Gerth's version of the Madison Guaranty story?

And so it was: Reappointing a Tyson veterinarian to the Livestock and Poultry Commission? Clinton's guilty as charged. Except that the fellow happens to be the state's ranking expert on chicken diseases, the prevention and treatment of which is the commission's principal task. An objective account of the court battle would have revealed that the city of Green Forest was a defendant in the same lawsuit. Bill Clinton was not. Officials of the Arkansas Department of Pollution Control and Ecology testified for the plaintiffs against Tyson Foods. As for naming Jim Blair to the University of Arkansas board? Well, it's quite an honor, and Blair can undeniably score great Razorback tickets. Otherwise, where's the scandal? At any rate, Blair wasn't a Tyson employee back when he and Hillary did their cattle trades. He was in private practice as one of Fayetteville's most prominent corporate attorneys, representing banks, trucking companies, insurance firms, and poultry interests.

To anybody who knows Arkansas politics, Bill Clinton's running feud with the chicken and trucking lobbies was one of the two or three most persistent stories of the 1980s (another being his ongoing battle with Stephens family interests). Far from selling out to trucking and poultry when he first became governor in 1979, Clinton instantly made them bitter enemies—an enmity that persisted at varying degrees of intensity until he left Little Rock for Washington.

Back in 1978 when Hillary did her commodity trading, poultry needed Clinton a lot more than Clinton needed poultry. With Governor David Pryor and U.S. Representatives Jim Guy Tucker and Ray Thornton fighting it out for the vacant seat of Senator John L. McClellan—who had died in 1977—the Democratic gubernatorial nomination, tantamount to election in Arkansas, was all but Clinton's for the asking. Clinton met with representatives of the poultry industry in the summer of 1978 and assured them he understood the prospects for growth. But they wanted help with their single major need—lifting the 73,280-pound weight limit on Arkansas highways to conform to the 80,000-pound loads allowed by most states. Tyson Foods and other poultry and agricultural interests argued that the light loads put them at a competitive disadvantage. But the state's Highway Commission, a constitutionally independent agency beholden to no governor, opposed lifting the weight limit. Clinton promised the poultry producers that he would remain neutral, and that if the legislature passed the 80,000-pound limit he would sign it. That was good enough for Tyson and the rest to support Clinton against weak opposition.

Shortly after Clinton's inauguration, however, the poultry folks got a surprise. There was their buddy Bill up on the dais at a press conference with Highway Director Henry Gray flatly denouncing the 80,000-pound limit. Yielding to the special interests, Clinton allowed, would just tear up Arkansas highways. Twice the Arkansas Poultry Federation set up meetings with the young governor to patch things up. Clinton stiffed the chicken moguls both times—sending an aide to a Fort Smith meeting in his place and later letting Don Tyson and the rest cool their heels in his conference room for an hour and twenty minutes while he chatted with a state senator. Led by Tyson himself, the poultry officials stalked out—

vowing to have no more to do with the governor. By all accounts, Tyson and Clinton didn't speak to each other for years.

In 1980, poultry, trucking, and other shipping interests all but unanimously backed Republican Frank White in his upset win over Clinton. (Tyson himself contributed small amounts to both campaigns.) After White delivered on his pledge to fight for the 80,000-pound limit, they supported him against Clinton once more in his failed 1982 re-election bid. Although a lifelong Democrat, Don Tyson led the industry in gifts to White in 1982.

So when would Clinton have delivered the quid pro quo for lawyer Blair's 1978 cattle trading tips? Well, not upon returning to office in 1983. Governor White had won a temporary victory for the truckers, but the law expired. By 1983 Arkansas was the only state with the lower truck weight limits. Clinton and the Highway Commission finally capitulated on the 80,000-pound limit. But against strong opposition, Clinton pushed through an unusual "ton-mile" tax on eighteen-wheelers—scaling the fee to the weight and distance they drove on Arkansas highways. (In keeping with tradition, a profile of Clinton in *The New York Times Magazine* by Michael Kelly omitted the political context and cited the same fight as evidence of Clinton's spinelessness.) The ton-mile tax was eventually thrown out by the U.S. Supreme Court after a five-year legal contest.

Nothing Clinton did or failed to do during his five terms as governor succeeded in winning him the trust or support of the poultry industry. And in the legislature, the poultry and trucking industries fought virtually every Clinton initiative. With the exception of a broadly popular 1 percent sales tax increase in 1983, they beat back one Clinton education proposal after another. On a famous occasion in the mid-1980s, the enmity became so intense that an Arkansas Poultry Federation lobbyist and a Clinton legislative aide had a shoving match in a hallway outside the state House of Representatives.

Indeed, it was Clinton's anger at the poultry growers and the Stephens interests after they combined to beat back a half-cent education sales tax in 1987 that provoked him to create a statewide "blue-ribbon" panel to write Arkansas's first meaningful ethics and disclosure law. After the selfsame "special interests" gutted the thing during a special session, Clinton dissolved the legislature, put the new standard on the ballot as an initiated act, campaigned for it hard, and won.

Don Tyson did throw in with the governor on one notable issue during Clinton's last go-around with the Arkansas legislature. A charter member of the so-called Good Suit Club—a group of wealthy bankers and businessmen like Tyson and Wal-Mart's Sam Walton who met informally to encourage educational reform—he endorsed Clinton's plan to levy a 1/2 of 1 percent increase in the corporate income tax to benefit community technical colleges, helping the bill win the necessary three-fourths vote. Somebody quick call Gerth at *The New York Times* and notify the special prosecutor. Something tells me they're fixing to load those technical colleges up with poultry science courses.

All of this raises the *really* interesting question at the heart of the Whitewater affair: Why—with representatives of the vaunted national press camped out in Little Rock for weeks at a time, squinting over aged public documents and pontificating nightly at the Capital Bar—has nobody blown the whistle on Gerth and *The New York Times?* There are several reasons, ambition and fear among them. It's always safest to run with the pack, and editors who invest thousands on a scandal don't normally want to hear that there's no scandal to be found. In this post-Watergate, post-everythinggate culture, few reporters wish to appear insufficiently prosecutorial—particularly not when the suspects are the President and his wife. By definition they've got to be guilty of something; it may as well be Whitewater.

Prove Your Innocence

Something is out there, and we haven't got it yet.
—*Senator Frank Murkowski (R., Alaska)*
Special Committee to Investigate Whitewater Development
Corporation and Related Matters
February 27, 1996

✦

When the dust and feathers finally settle after the great Whitewater pecking party," I wrote in an *Arkansas Democrat-Gazette* column in August 1994, "chances are the press will blame Hillary." As predictions go, this one's held up pretty well. Witness the huge stir accorded the belated discovery of the First Lady's lost Rose Law Firm billing records, climaxing in her melodramatic summons to appear before Whitewater independent counsel Kenneth Starr's Washington grand jury. Finding no smoking gun to justify the carnival of speculation, innuendo, fuzzy logic, political opportunism, and just plain bad reporting that had characterized Whitewater from the start, editorial-page inquisitors were apt to conclude that had the First Lady allowed her husband to release all the documents back in 1993 when *The New York Times* and *The Washington Post* began to clamor for them, none of the rest needed to have happened.

Just about every Arkansas reporter I know agreed. Had the White House dumped two pickup loads of Whitewater documents on the doorsteps of the *Post*'s and the *Times*'s Washington bureaus that winter, the "scandal" would have ended before spring. Probably, indeed, within a couple of weeks. In the long run, reporters tell themselves, the news media tend to be self-correcting. Competition makes it so. Hence also in the long run, a kind of rough justice is eventually achieved. It's a delusion, of course, but a comforting one to which most journalists subscribe.

As to the President and First Lady, however, just about the last thing that strikes the national press is the first thing that strikes most Arkansas reporters—friend, foe, or skeptical observer: that is, how very unlikely it seems that Bill and Hillary Clinton would go in the tank for such trivial amounts of money. Whatever their character flaws, nothing known about the couple indicates that they would break the law for profit. That Clinton served five terms as Arkansas governor untouched by financial chicanery amid a newspaper war that brought down several lesser politicians strikes many here as significant.[1]

Does it come under the heading of special pleading or hometown favoritism, moreover, to observe that the Clintons are arguably the least wealthy couple to occupy the White House during this century? Probably even Harry and Bess Truman were well-off by comparison. The First Family had a healthy income at the time Bill Clinton took the oath as President of the United States, but they owned no real estate, not even a home; their only automobile was a 1986 Olds Cutlass. Apart from the perpetual-motion machine of his political ambition, whatever else makes Bill Clinton go around it's clearly not cash.

Demonstrably more interested in money than her husband, Hillary Rodham Clinton also impressed most who dealt with her over the years as entirely too fond of her own sense of propriety to stick a FOR SALE sign on it. Work aggressively to sell a client's story? Of course: Hillary Clinton was a corporate litigator. But if you had it in mind to commit a felony that had the potential to compro-

---

[1] During Little Rock's newspaper war, many scalps were taken. Even minor financial corruption brings great public wrath. Attorney General Steve Clark, a Clinton ally, was caught by the *Arkansas Gazette* padding his expense account for costly dinner dates. As a result of the newspaper's efforts, Clark was tried, convicted, and eventually sued for repayment. There's no reason to imagine that reporters would have covered for Bill Clinton.

mise her and her husband's political ambitions? Hillary Clinton would be just about the *last* person in Arkansas you'd want to let in on the secret. She'd cut you off at the knees. Even when Jim McDougal was on the edge of losing his reason, his actions indicate, he always understood that much.

But let's ignore Hillary's status as cartoon archetype—Superwoman vs. Ultrabitch, and all that. Merely for the sake of argument, let's assume that the First Lady is a normal human being prone to normal human emotions. Then let's examine how those emotions may have factored in to her presumptively bad decision not to release all those boxes of Whitewater documents to the press back in December 1993.[2]

Almost any way you look at it, 1993 was a dreadful year for the woman. Did she and her husband achieve a lifelong ambition by moving into the White House? They did. But there's simply no way Hillary could have been prepared for the jolt of becoming a national symbol as universally known as Elvis or Michael Jordan, her privacy gone forever. As First Lady of Arkansas, it was possible for her to have an independent career, to drive herself and Chelsea to the video-rental store, to dine out with friends without being mobbed, to walk down the street in San Francisco, New York, or Washington as freely as anybody else. Never again.

Then in April, Hillary lost her father, Hugh Rodham, who lingered in a Little Rock hospital for a couple of weeks before dying of a stroke. By all accounts, father and daughter had always been

---

[2] No doubt the *funniest* example of deep thinking on the Hillary's-a-bitch theme had to be a "psychological portrait" by Camille Paglia in the March 4, 1996, issue of *The New Republic*. Entitled "Ice Queen, Drag Queen," it portrayed Hillary as "man-woman . . . bitch goddess" and "the drag queen of modern politics."

I can't decide which is my favorite among Paglia's brilliant insights. Is it that Hillary was attracted to her husband in the Yale Law School lounge because his "exotic, rural, sensually sweet and ripe watermelons were a symbol of freedom, fruitfulness and abundance"? Bill Clinton, see, "was Female Man, whose boyish androgyny seemed to promise . . . an escape from the sexist past." Or is it Paglia's retrospective analysis of a Wellesley College commencement address Hillary had given in 1969? Had she really berated GOP Senator Edward Brooke over Vietnam, her ostensible topic? Not likely. Paglia deduced more profound forces at work, to wit: "a visceral response to the invasion of her all-women's school by a glamorous, lordly male." And how do we know this? Because in 1972 Senator Brooke "sauntered elegantly down the Capitol steps" and displayed to Paglia *herself* "a distinctly roving eye."

close. Three months later, her close friend Vince Foster killed himself in a Washington, D.C., park. Rumors and conspiracy theories began to circulate almost immediately. Despite no credible evidence, those insinuations quickly slithered their way into the respectable press by the now familiar route—crackpot newsletter to the London *Sunday Telegraph* to *The Wall Street Journal* editorial page to the world.

Then, at Christmas, after she learned that her husband's mother was stricken with the breast cancer that would kill her within a month, came the Arkansas state trooper smear. Putting aside the personal betrayal and the press's unprecedented assault on her marriage, let us recall that of the many raunchy tales troopers Larry Patterson and Roger Perry cooked up for *The American Spectator* and the *L.A. Times,* some of the most humiliating concerned her. Hardly had this sordid episode played itself out, moreover, than the high panjandrums on the nation's editorial pages and TV talk shows began to insist that, *to prove their innocence,* the Clintons turn over every scrap of paper in their possession—tax returns, Whitewater documents, canceled checks, bonus pizza coupons, Hillary's Girl Scout cookie receipts, the lot.

"It may be that there is nothing damaging or even embarrassing in them," conceded an editorial in *The New York Times* on December 23, 1993. "Indeed, in an angry interview . . . in which she defended her husband against recent allegations about his private life, Mrs. Clinton said she was 'bewildered' about the continuing interest in the Clintons' relationship with Mr. McDougal and Whitewater." The editorial went on to cite the suspicions of "Federal investigators" that McDougal had gotten favorable treatment from Arkansas regulators at Governor Clinton's behest. "But surely another reason," the *Times* thundered, "lies in the White House's ongoing evasions over the past two years. That alone has left the impression that there's something untoward in these files. There is only one way to tell: Hand them over."

And to whom? Why, to the press, of course, those high-minded guardians of public morality. Specifically, to the very *New York Times* reporters whose inept, accusatory articles had created the Whitewater "scandal" in the first place. Better than anybody else at the White House, Hillary Rodham Clinton was in a position to understand how misleading (at best) the *Times* articles had been. As billing attorney for the Madison Guaranty account, she knew perfectly well that Arkansas regulators had cut Jim McDougal no slack. Far from doing her or the Rose Law Firm any favors, Securities Commissioner Beverly Bassett Schaffer had stuck it to their client.

Exactly what else the First Lady knew about *The New York Times*'s shabby treatment of Bassett Schaffer isn't the point. The two were never friends; they hadn't spoken for years.[3] Hillary certainly knew that regulators had removed the McDougals from Madison Guaranty in July 1986; also that Jim McDougal had within a month of that event been hospitalized. She knew that the McDougals had divorced, and that Jim was living alone and broke. Thanks to the newspapers, she also knew that McDougal had made a number of rash allegations that were not merely false but silly. That the Clintons *hadn't* lost money on their Whitewater investment, for example. "I could sink [that] quicker than they could lie about it if I could get in a position so I wouldn't have my head beaten off," McDougal claimed in a widely quoted excerpt from a tape-recorded talk between himself and Sheffield Nelson. "And Bill knows that."

McDougal's claim was absolute nonsense, of course, as subsequent investigation proved. The fact is, the Clintons had lost more than $42,000. Indeed, McDougal had sent them and their accountant a letter summarizing Whitewater's losses as long ago as 1986 (although that letter would itself eventually prove inaccurate, if not purposefully deceptive).

[3] When I first interviewed Bassett Schaffer and her husband early in 1994, they were angry and bewildered over the White House's failure to defend her against *The New York Times.* They believed that a sharp rebuttal would have compelled the press to examine the abundant factual record. At roughly the same time, evidence presented to the Senate Whitewater committee showed, President Clinton was scribbling notes to aides wondering if Bassett Schaffer would defend *him.* Aides considered sending an emissary to Arkansas to talk things over with her. But they feared that somebody would make an issue of it, and chickened out.

In late 1993, Bassett Schaffer's husband had encountered White House aide Bruce Lindsey at a Razorback basketball game that the President attended and vented his anger. Sure enough, during Whitewater committee hearings in December 1995, Senator Alfonse D'Amato did his best to put a conspiratorial spin on the meeting—conducted in front of 20,000 spectators and a statewide TV audience.

Another widely reported episode was McDougal's foolish tale about how Bill Clinton had jogged into his office one sweltering summer day in 1984, complaining of poverty and asking to have Hillary put on a $2,000-a-month retainer, "whimpering" that he needed that amount to supplement his paltry $35,000-a-year salary. Like many of McDougal's stories, its real purpose was to emphasize his own vast power and influence. The press, however, interpreted it as *prima facie* evidence of corruption. Viewed with an ounce of skepticism, McDougal's story made little sense. It wasn't until April 1985, after all, almost a year after the alleged meeting between the governor and the banker, that Hillary came to negotiate the retainer agreement with Madison Guaranty. She was by then a star litigator at the Rose Law Firm—one of the state's most prestigious. Her income that year from her law practice alone was $55,000. Together, the Clintons reported income of $102,500. Considering that they enjoyed free room and board at the Governor's Mansion, and few debts apart from Whitewater, they weren't doing half bad. Not by Arkansas standards, anyway.

Moreover, most people understand—even if poor McDougal had forgotten—that law firms share among the partners any profits after expenses. Given the Rose Firm's size and its monthly billings (about $800,000 in 1985), if Hillary pocketed $20 a month out of Madison Guaranty's $2,000 retainer, it would have been a lot. RTC investigators ultimately dismissed McDougal's allegation for that very reason. As necessary, however, the press feigns the credulousness of a child. This particular shuttlecock was still being batted about as late as February 1996. An editorial in the left-leaning weekly *The Nation* essentially proposed indicting the First Lady for perjury because her version of how she came to represent Madison Guaranty differed from what McDougal had told reporters.

Also consider the press's handling of *The Washington Times*'s December 1993 "revelation" that Whitewater-related legal files had been removed from Vince Foster's office a few days after his death and handed over to the Clintons' personal lawyer. At the time of Foster's suicide, let us recall, there *was* no Whitewater investigation, or even the rumor of one. So where in the world did reporters *think* the Clintons' papers were going to go?

Just because your lawyer dies, regardless of how, it doesn't mean that every piece of paper in his office is delivered to the police. And certainly not to newspaper reporters. Who would entrust anything ticklish to an attorney if it did? This is called lawyer-client privilege, and it's fundamental to our system of justice. The fact that Foster was a government employee made things a bit trickier, but ultimately made little difference. One of his first jobs as the President's lawyer had been to set up a blind trust for the Clintons' assets. The simple fact is that investigators who entered Foster's office in search of a suicide note on July 22, 1993, not only had no reason to examine the Clintons' personal files but had no legal right. Every lawyer and investigator who testified at subsequent Senate hearings on the matter agreed: to search the files would have required a subpoena, which could have been issued only after a federal judge found "probable cause" that evidence bearing directly upon Foster's death would be found inside.

"Probable cause," moreover, isn't mere suspicion of the kind whooped up by Rush Limbaugh and the editors of *The Wall Street Journal*.[4] It's got to be based on compelling evidence. Again, the Senate testimony would be unanimous: none of the investigators who looked into Foster's death so much as considered seeking such a subpoena. There was never a particle of evidence to indicate why they should. Hence it follows that there was also no logical reason, amid the shock and sorrow of Foster's death, for an experienced lawyer like Mrs. Clinton to worry about the contents of those files—almost no matter *what* was in them. Any other conclusion can proceed from only the sheerest kind of speculation.

White House counsel Bernard Nussbaum made the point succinctly in a speech to the New York Bar Association. "After a lawyer's death," he said, "a client's files in a lawyer's office belong

---

[4] "Until the Foster death is seriously studied," *Journal* editors wrote after being disappointed by the results of the first of four investigations, "a Banquo's ghost will stalk the Clinton administration." Apparently finding reason for suspicion in the First Lady's decision to visit her mother, *Journal* editors scrutinized her exact movements. "Mrs. Clinton's plane landed on July 20 at 7:30 P.M. Central Time, or shortly after Mr. Foster's body was discovered at Fort Marcy. The visit was something of a surprise." (Actually, it wasn't. She was in Little Rock to attend an Arkansas Children's Hospital function.) The connection between these events was left to the reader's imagination.

to the client. . . . The personal files in Foster's office belonged to the President and First Lady. And so they were sent to the First Family, which promptly transferred them to its personal counsel. When the Whitewater matter did erupt in the press five months later," he added, "every request of the Department of Justice or the Independent Counsel for documents was honored. . . . The documents were preserved, as was the right to claim privilege. That right, as I said, was never exercised."

But none of that prevented *The New York Times* from importing the literary conventions of the spy thriller into the paper's coverage. Quoting unidentified "federal law enforcement officials" on December 22, 1993, David Johnston wrote that "although they had *no way of knowing the precise nature of the files,* the documents contained in them *could prove relevant* to two inquiries under way at the Justice Department. [My emphasis] One involves the circumstances of Mr. Foster's suicide, which the President has described as a result of profound depression whose nature had escaped the recognition of Mr. Foster's colleagues and might never be fully understood. The other concerns the collapse of an Arkansas savings and loan association that was owned by James McDougal."[5] In a December 26 editorial, the *Times* described as terribly suspicious President and Mrs. Clinton's possession of *their own legal files,* "presumptuously spirited from the office of the deputy White House counsel, Vincent Foster, following Mr. Foster's suicide."

Newsweek's Michael Isikoff summed up the press pack's mentali-

---

[5] When not hyperventilating over Vince Foster, *Times* reporters are capable of fine reporting about suicide. Witness sportswriter Ira Berkow's 1995 piece on the seemingly inexplicable death of a high school honor student and star football player in Maine. Berkow quoted Dr. Thomas Jensen, a psychiatrist who had interviewed the young man's friends.

"'They told me that it seemed no one really knew what Scott's feelings were, that he seemed to hide them behind his striving for perfection,' said Jensen. 'He always seemed too good to be true to them—that he was so driven, so focused on his goals. And when you are depressed, you could have a million things going right for you but if one thing is wrong, the depressed person completely loses perspective. And he focuses on that one negative thing, and he convinces himself that suicide is the only option. In psychiatric terms, it is called cognitive distortion. And we treat it effectively with medication and psychotherapy.'"

To anybody who has read independent counsel Robert Fiske's June 30, 1994, report, or spoken to any of Vince Foster's family and friends, Berkow's article couldn't be more on target.

ty in a PBS interview with Charlie Rose in July 1995. "Whitewater started to take off as an issue in December 1993 [with the news] that Whitewater documents were *spirited out of Foster's office in the hours after his death by top White House aides.* [My emphasis] ... No single allegation seemed more troubling or suspicious than to somehow link Foster's death to Whitewater. You know, is there any possibility that he was so worried about Whitewater that he killed himself because he was so fearful about some damaging disclosure? Or is it even worse than that? Some people believe that Foster was murdered, even though there's really no evidence of that."

Of course, some people also believe in leprechauns, sex perverts from outer space, and Pat Robertson's ability to alter the path of hurricanes through prayer. Indeed, Robertson continues to flog the conspiracy theory of Foster's death on *The 700 Club.* It only underscore's Isikoff's irresponsibility to point out that his remarks were made in July 1995, *more than a year after* independent counsel Robert Fiske's report ruling that there was no evidence linking Foster's death to Whitewater.

In short, the high-dollar press handled the question of Foster's files almost exactly as most in the media had initially dealt with the Arkansas state trooper smear, which was then in progress: censoring the more absurd conspiracy theories being cooked up by every nutty right-wing organ but tiptoeing up to throw fuel on the bonfire all the same. These reverend authorities were the very ones demanding the right to pore through the Clintons' private business records in order to assess their moral worthiness. "Hand them over," *The New York Times* had commanded in the tone of a vice cop addressing a pimp. So Hillary Rodham Clinton apparently got her back up and said, in effect, "Not if they bind me hand and foot and pitch me into the Potomac in a blizzard."

And so, in effect, they did. In early January 1994, the White House arranged to have the Clintons' Whitewater records subpoenaed by the Justice Department in a manner openly calculated to make them available to investigators but shield them from the press. The media went wild. "These clumsy efforts at suppression are feckless and self-defeating," chided the *Times.* "The White House's attempts to maintain political control of the investigation into

President and Mrs. Clinton's real estate dealings in Arkansas are swiftly draining away public trust in their integrity."

The Washington Post joined the chorus a few days later. "Someone said the other day that Washington may now have reached the state-of-the-art point of having a cover-up without a crime." By failing to come clean, the *Post* continued, the White House had managed only "to make it appear as if the Clintons have something to hide."

It was left to *Time* magazine to reduce the matter to its essence. Where did Whitewater fit, columnist Michael Kramer wondered, among the "jumble of disturbing impressions" of President Clinton? He summarized the media's suspicions in what may be the quintessential Whitewater paragraph. Let's count the "maybes," shall we? Whitewater, Kramer opined, is "different—*or could be*—because the wrongdoing (*if there was any*) *may have involved* abuses of power while Clinton was serving as Governor of Arkansas. On the other hand, Whitewater too is from the past. So *even if* the worst *were proved*—and *no one yet knows* what that is—the offense *might not warrant* impeachment." Then came the clincher: "How is it possible," Kramer wanted to know, "that two respected lawyers like Bill and Hillary Clinton don't possess a paper trail capable of *proving their innocence*?" [My emphasis]

Had *Time*'s resident inquisitor plagiarized Kafka's *The Trial* or Orwell's *1984*? No. Here is an American political journalist, ostensibly at the top of his game, demanding with absolute solemnity that the President of the United States and his wife prove themselves innocent of charges he could not himself define. And what the rest of the media had decided was this: By failing to roll over and expose their throats and underbellies, the Clintons were "acting guilty." They had committed the unpardonable sin of allowing their disdain for the press to show in the most public possible way. And for that, they would pay and pay.

But was it possible that Hillary Rodham Clinton also knew, or suspected, things about the Whitewater deal that she didn't want the press to know? It was almost certain. In the late 1980s, Hillary had been forced to take over the day-to-day operations from the then-hospitalized Jim McDougal in order to straighten out the

Whitewater Development Company's affairs and file its tax returns. She had sought (though never got) power of attorney, and what she found in Jim McDougal's books must have caused her real concern. The company's records were absolutely chaotic. Property taxes, in some instances, hadn't been paid for years. The owner of a lot Mrs. Clinton had financed personally had gone into bankruptcy. She had never been notified, and the Whitewater Development Company had made no payments on the note. The corporation's state franchise fees hadn't been paid for several years. "Some time within the next three weeks," Hillary's accountant had written her in December 1989, "we will call the realtor on White Water Estates to try to establish what assets, liabilities, income and deductions the corporation has, and whether or not a tax return has been filed or is required. We decided that the corporation does not need to be liquidated since it still holds land and note receivables [*sic*] on the land sold."

Even worse, it was clear that, for reasons of his own, Jim McDougal had concealed from the Clintons the true status of Whitewater from mid-1984 onward. Why? Several reasons present themselves, all conjectural. But it certainly seems to be no accident that McDougal's silence on Whitewater coincided almost exactly with the 1984 FHLBB examination report detailing Madison Guaranty's financial plight—the very one Jeff Gerth dealt with so creatively in his Whitewater reporting. Judging by his actions, it's clear that McDougal didn't want *anybody* to realize just how shaky Madison Guaranty and its real estate subsidiary, Madison Financial, had gotten to be. Not even the S&L's employees, some of whom were left holding the bag for considerable sums when Madison Guaranty crashed, or its board of directors—and certainly not Bill and Hillary Clinton.

Today, the facts are all there to see in the Pillsbury Report, a $3.6 million study done for the Resolution Trust Corporation by the eminently Republican San Francisco law firm of Pillsbury, Madison & Sutro. "Through May 1984," they found, "the project had lost money, and the venturers had been forced to advance money to cover these losses. The amounts advanced, however, had been modest and the venturers' respective advances had been relatively even. After May 1984, this changed."

The report treats only as a footnote another elementary aspect of the Whitewater story that has been bungled by the media: "The press often refers to the McDougals and the Clintons as 'partners' in Whitewater. Whitewater was a corporation, not a partnership. Hence, they were 'shareholders.'" The distinction is crucial to understanding the Clintons' seeming passivity about their investment. If they had been partners, the Clintons would have had to file a Whitewater tax return each year; as shareholders, they didn't. That was Jim McDougal's job. They trusted him to do it. Their own profits or losses could be determined whenever the corporation closed its books. No doubt it would have been wiser for the Clintons to have kept a closer eye on Whitewater. But wouldn't it also have been wiser for newspapers like the *Times* and the *Post* to have their business reporters explain to editors the differences between a partnership and a corporation? If *Business Week* got it right, why didn't the *Times?*

But back to 1984. It was also during that year that McDougal's frantic financial juggling act began. "More and more," the Pillsbury Report says, "the McDougals lacked the money to pay their personal debts, so increasingly they transferred money between entities they owned or controlled to cover their obligations to third persons." One of those entities was Whitewater. Back in 1993, however, when the press began to freak out over Whitewater, the Clintons had no access to much of the information now available in the Pillsbury Report. Hillary, her lawyers, and accountants had seen the Whitewater books, but they hadn't seen the books of the ten or more other McDougal-owned corporate entities that had accounts at Madison Guaranty, nor those of Madison Financial. Unlike the investigators, the Clintons had no subpoena power. Hence what fiscal shenanigans McDougal might have gotten himself into as things began to fall apart in 1984–86 and his mental health began to deteriorate, the Clintons couldn't have known with much more exactitude than the editors of *The New York Times.*

Even so, any halfway fair appraisal of what the Clintons *did* know about Whitewater in early 1994 stands conventional wisdom on its head. To put it bluntly, *it wasn't the McDougals who got shafted in the deal, it was the Clintons.* As managing partner of the project, McDougal ruined it—just as he ruined almost everything else he touched during the period. The evidence is incontrovertible, though it does have to be dug out of the Pillsbury Report by careful reading. Alas, that requirement seems to have excluded almost everybody in Washington.

Here's what happened: Facing a cash-flow problem in May 1985, McDougal chose not to involve the Clintons. How could he? He'd been commingling funds and juggling the books from upward of ten other companies he controlled for more than a year. The basic goal appears to have been to pay off as much collateralized debt as he could—thus preserving his assets—and replace them with "non-recourse" loans, many from his own S&L. Those loans he may have expected to repay at his leisure, after the crisis had passed.

McDougal basically gave away the store. He sold all of Whitewater's remaining lots (twenty-four of the original forty-four) to one Chris Wade, the realtor charged with marketing and selling the development. The asking price for twenty-three of those twenty-four lots, according to a "Whitewater Estates" inventory list dated November 1984, had been $191,550. In return for the land, Wade agreed to assume $35,000 of the $96,000 still owed by the Clintons and McDougals on the original 1978 loan that had financed the project. (Wade was so slow to pay that the bank was still charging the Whitewater Development Company interest on the money until 1992.) In fact, one of the reasons Whitewater had a cash-flow problem was that it had paid the same Chris Wade a total of $28,000 in 1985 for what is still something of a mystery. In 1985, the realtor had succeeded in selling exactly one Whitewater lot and had sold a total of four since 1982.

McDougal also accepted from Wade a 1979 Piper Seminole airplane, supposedly worth $35,000.[6] McDougal promptly pressed the Piper Seminole into service as Madison Guaranty's official corporate aircraft. It's not recorded that the S&L paid leasing fees

[6] According to a February 7, 1994, article in *The New York Times.*

to Whitewater; it simply used the plane for free. Eventually, the Pillsbury Report says, McDougal sold the Piper to himself. The price is not listed or where the money came from. Nor, for that matter, where it went. Along with the McDougals' luxury cars, it was merely another grandiose perk.

"The need for the bank debt payments is fairly obvious," notes the Pillsbury Report, "but the rationale for the payments to Wade and [his company] Ozarks Realty is less clear." The ethics of a realtor buying at fire-sale prices properties he had failed to sell retail are questionable at best. Wade basically walked away with half the company for the price of that airplane.

"May 1985 marked more than the end of another fiscal year," the report notes. "It also marked the end of Whitewater as a project. By the end of May, the land was gone; all that remained was debt and notes receivable that did not generate enough cash to service the debt. The Company would continue to exist but there was never again any prospect that it might turn a profit."

Maybe Whitewater would have failed anyway. But what's absolutely clear is that McDougal deliberately kept the Clintons in the dark. It was in April 1985, let us recall, that McDougal put the Rose Law Firm on retainer and hosted a political fund-raiser for Bill Clinton at Madison Guaranty headquarters in downtown Little Rock. Perhaps he had a guilty conscience.[7] It wasn't until Hillary Clinton took over management of the Whitewater Development Company that she would learn Whitewater had been all but formally defunct for four years. Due to the work she had done putting the doomed company's affairs in order, however, she certainly knew that more than $134,000 had been deposited into the Whitewater account between 1984 and 1986 from other McDougal-owned companies. Similar amounts had been paid out, much of it to individuals and companies having nothing to do with their investment in the Ozarks. The legitimacy of those transactions couldn't be guessed by the evidence at her dis-

[7] According to Bill and Hillary Clinton's sworn, written interrogatories, which neither the Pillsbury Report nor the RTC has challenged, McDougal never told them anything about any of these transactions.

posal. Some of them, however, must have looked very odd indeed.

A single example should suffice: In October 1986, three months *after* Jim McDougal had been forced out of Madison Guaranty by state and federal regulators, the Whitewater Development Company bought 810 acres of land outside Little Rock (roughly 175 miles south of Whitewater itself) from International Paper. The deal had been negotiated in March. "At the time," according to the Pillsbury Report, "the McDougals told International Paper that they were the sole owners of Whitewater, with Jim being the president and Susan the secretary."

International Paper financed the deal. As earnest money for the $550,950 purchase, McDougal wrote a $25,000 personal check. The money came directly from the proceeds of a $300,000 loan from David Hale to Susan McDougal. (This is the same loan that Hale later told reporters Governor Bill Clinton had pressured him to make.) The remaining $275,000 went to pay off other McDougal debts having nothing to do with Whitewater. Yet no sooner had the property been acquired, according to the Pillsbury Report, than "Jim McDougal, acting on behalf of Whitewater as its president, conveyed the 810 acre International Paper parcel from Whitewater to [another McDougal company] Great Southern Land; the deed was recorded on December 15, 1986. These documents did not relieve Whitewater of the mortgage; they did, however, remove the asset."

In the meantime, McDougal had written the Clintons two letters, in November and December 1986—their first communications regarding Whitewater in almost two years. He led off with the good news that all the remaining lots had been sold in 1985. But he made no mention of the fire-sale prices or that the buyer had been the realtor who was supposed to be acting as their agent. He added that the corporation's losses came to approximately $90,000, but added that he wanted "to be able to take advantage of the $90,000 loss for tax purposes since Susan and I have in large measure contributed to the company the funds necessary to cover the losses."

McDougal enclosed a stock transfer proposing that the Clintons hand over their share of Whitewater—ostensibly to spare them the public embarrassment of being involved in a losing venture. In effect, he was offering to buy their share of the corporation for half the amount of the losses—that is, for $45,000. Since the Clintons had contributed at least $36,000 to Whitewater, that may not have looked like too bad a deal. But there was a hitch: Whitewater still owed almost $100,000 to Citizens Bank in Flippin, which wouldn't agree to release the Clintons. (This is not surprising, since McDougal's ouster from Madison Guaranty had been covered in the Little Rock press.)

"Nowhere in the letter," the Pillsbury Report notes tartly, "was there any reference to the International Paper deal, which had closed the previous month." McDougal subdivided the tract and dubbed it Lorance Heights; much of it was located in piney woods south of Little Rock. By 1988, forty-eight disgruntled buyers filed suit against Great Southern Land, alleging a failure to pay property taxes, blacktop the roads, and provide natural gas service as promised. International Paper sued for nonpayment of the mortgage. In March 1989, the company won a $478,000 judgment against Whitewater; it remains unsatisfied.

The Clintons knew nothing about the International Paper deal. "Their signatures," notes the Pillsbury Report, "do not appear on the relevant documents. McDougal's letters to them do not mention the transaction. The transaction did not benefit Whitewater or the Clintons; in fact, it left Whitewater with a large mortgage but no corresponding asset, and eventually it led to litigation and the entry of a judgement against Whitewater." (Incidentally, there is no evidence in the Pillsbury Report to suggest that either Clinton knew David Hale had lent Susan McDougal anything. Considering how the $300,000 was used, it is all but certain Jim McDougal kept that a secret too.)

So it's not too fanciful to imagine that had knowledge of McDougal's little International Paper–Lorance Heights deal fallen into the wrong hands at the wrong time, it could have done Bill Clinton's political career great damage. Anybody but a politician would have sued both McDougals and realtor Chris Wade—although both were bankrupt by the time the truth began to emerge in 1989.

What further nasty surprises might lie amid the tangled thicket of McDougal's finances? Hillary Clinton couldn't possibly have known, but probably she didn't want to find out about them in the newspapers. Yielding to political necessity, the White House asked Attorney General Janet Reno to appoint an independent counsel in January 1994, and handed the Whitewater files over to the Justice Department. If there had to be a Whitewater investigation, the Clintons had evidently concluded, let it be a proper one, conducted by professionals who knew the law, not by a baying pack of media hounds whose zeal for scandal was exceeded only by their moral arrogance and intellectual dishonesty. But was stonewalling the media back in January 1994 bad politics? Put it this way: that the policy didn't work out too smoothly doesn't make it the wrong decision. Things could very easily, all things considered, have been far worse.

Meanwhile, the real Whitewater craziness was taking place in Kansas City. By early 1994, the regional office of the Resolution Trust Corporation had begun to resemble bureaucratic warfare at its deadliest. The agency's normal operations appear to have ground to a halt as colleagues investigated and spied on one another. Charges and countercharges zipped back and forth by fax and e-mail. Accusations of political bias, purge, and cover-up filled the air.

The proximate cause of all the trouble was a previously insignificant RTC investigator of decidedly conservative views named L. Jean Lewis, who had taken it upon herself to topple the President of the United States. An FBI agent who dealt with her during this period would later testify that she'd made dramatic pronouncements to him about altering the course of history. Lewis's bureaucratic enemies alleged that a book was in the works, but Lewis later denied this under oath. Alas, one big problem with this grand scenario was that Lewis was, on evidence, barely competent to do her job. She was neither a lawyer nor a CPA, and she'd had no meaningful law enforcement experience. What she did have was a zealot's rashness and inability to comprehend facts at odds with her preconceived ideas, and an amazingly selective memory. Lewis was also dogged and cunning. She soon had reporters and eager Republicans eating out of her hand.

In essence, Jean Lewis's job at the RTC was that of a glorified bank teller: to sift through the records of failed S&Ls, looking for signs of fishy transactions to pass on to the FBI. Her Whitewater adventures began in direct response to Jeff Gerth's March 8, 1992, reporting in *The New York Times,* which she assumed to be the gospel truth. Her boss told her to check it out.

After poring over Madison Guaranty's records for a couple of months, Lewis got all excited. Following Gerth's lead, she focused on the six months before Arkansas Securities Commissioner Beverly Bassett Schaffer had supposedly acted on Madison's behalf in May 1985. Finding evidence of Jim McDougal's fiscal shenanigans everywhere she looked, Lewis jumped to a big conclusion: everybody in Arkansas who had ever done business with Madison Guaranty was part of a big conspiracy, including the Clintons. She simply assumed that whatever appeared to benefit McDougal also benefited them. No other possibilities appear ever to have crossed her mind.

On July 15, 1992, Bill Clinton formally became the Democratic presidential nominee. On September 2, Lewis filed a "criminal referral" with the FBI and the U.S. Attorney in Little Rock naming the McDougals—and as "possible witnesses" Bill and Hillary Clinton, Arkansas Lieutenant Governor Jim Guy Tucker, and former Senator J. William Fulbright.

RTC referrals normally took months to process. But Lewis was in a hurry. Within days, she began to pester Little Rock FBI agents with demands for action. When they stopped returning her calls, she left a taunting message with agent Steve Irons's receptionist on September 9. "Have I turned into a local pariah," Lewis asked, "just because I wrote one referral with high-profile names, or do you plan on calling me back before Christmas, Steven?????" Irons would later testify that he did so only to tell her tactfully to back off.

When Lewis showed up at Irons's Little Rock office on September 18, he told her that due to the referral's sensitivity, no action was likely to be taken on it before the election. She warned him that RTC officials in Washington knew of her referral and expected action—which was not true. Much to Lewis's eventual chagrin, Irons took contemporaneous notes. She would later deny under oath having had any such discussions until December 1992.

Lewis then began hounding aides to Little Rock U.S. Attorney Charles Banks, a Reagan appointee who had brought federal bank-fraud charges against McDougal two years earlier. Banks, too, would eventually testify to several contacts between Lewis and his office that she had denied under oath.

Ironically, Lewis's repeated calls caused others to question her judgment and motives. On October 7, the FBI's Little Rock office sent a teletype to national headquarters pointedly critical of Lewis's referral. It noted that Jim McDougal had been tried and acquitted in 1990, and added that the RTC's "supposition that other persons benefitted does not appear to be factually support-ed by the details that follow." Evidence that the Clintons profited from McDougal's machinations was nonexistent; the likelihood that they knew about them was described as highly implausible. The facts, the FBI concluded, indicated that "McDougal was in charge of [Whitewater] records . . . and does not suggest the Clintons had access to checking account statements that would have reflected the questionable transactions at the time." Evidently Lewis had also submitted as "evidence" newspaper arti-cles whose contents could not be verified.

On October 16, U.S. Attorney Banks wrote the FBI formally rejecting Lewis's referral on the same grounds. "While I do not intend to denigrate the work of RTC," Banks added, "I must opine that after such a lapse of time the insistence for urgency in this case appears to suggest an intentional or unintentional attempt to intervene into the political process of the upcoming presidential election. You and I know in investigations of this type, the first steps, such as issuance of grand jury subpoena for records, will lead to media and public inquiries of matters that are subject to absolute privacy. Even media questions about such an investigation in today's modern political climate all too often pub-licly purports [sic] to 'legitimize what can't be proven.' For me personally to participate," Banks continued, "in an investigation that I know will or could easily lead to the above scenario . . . amounts to prosecutorial misconduct and violates the most basic fundamental rule of Department of Justice policy. I cannot be a party to such actions."

By February 23, 1993, Jean Lewis's work had also been subjected to withering analysis by Mark MacDougal, a career trial lawyer in the Fraud Section of the Department of Justice. Not very gently, MacDougal pointed out that Lewis appeared to have no grasp of federal banking law. Contrary to her assumptions, moving cash from one account to another within the same bank hardly constituted the crime of "check-kiting" (hours of subsequent congressional hearings on the topic notwithstanding). Lewis's referral, he concluded, "does not provide . . . factual allegations sufficient to establish the elements of any of the criminal statutes used in the prosecution of bank fraud cases."

But Little Rock FBI agents had an even more basic problem with Lewis's efforts. By wasting their time on Madison Guaranty, RTC investigators were overlooking two far more significant Arkansas S&L failures: the $833 million collapse of First Federal Savings, and the $650 million nosedive of Savers Savings. The Little Rock office emphasized that both "are believed to have much greater prosecutive potential than Madison Guaranty," and urged Lewis and her colleagues to get on the stick.[8]

Under anything resembling ordinary circumstances, that should have been the end of it. Lewis herself had prepared a 1991 memo listing Madison Guaranty as the thirteenth most important S&L failure in Arkansas—third from the bottom. But for reasons that remain unclear, nobody ever told Lewis that her referral had been found deficient. Imagining the worst, she and her immediate supervisor, Richard Iorio, went on the warpath.

---

[8] Ironically, the arrival of independent counsel Kenneth Starr put an effective end to all other S&L investigations in Arkansas. There were simply no available FBI agents left to do the work. The statute of limitations expired and the RTC went out of existence without another criminal charge being filed.

Jean Lewis testified in Senate hearings that she'd submitted a criminal referral on First Federal Savings in 1991. She also denied that FBI agents had pressed her about the matter. Sworn testimony and numerous teletypes and memos back and forth among the respective agencies contradicted her on both counts.

On October 6, 1993, Lewis sent a very odd e-mail message to Iorio, with copies to two other colleagues. Completely unbidden, she wanted it known, *Washington Post* reporter Susan Schmidt had shown up on her doorstep. She'd heard Schmidt out, Lewis reported, administered a brisk scolding, and sent her away empty-handed. "My parting comment," Lewis contended, "was 'When you contacted me last Thursday, I told you that I had no comment, and made every effort to be polite in doing so. What you have done this evening is the most unprecedented breach of professional courtesy that I've ever witnessed, so I will say this one more time, and one more time only. Do not contact me again at my office, or my home. I have no comment on your investigation and will not answer any of your comments. Do not waste any more of my time or yours.'"

The term for such memos is "covering your ass." Lewis added that judging from Schmidt's questions, the reporter had by some nefarious means put her hands on a copy of the 1992 criminal referral, and meant to pursue the story. She appended a list of questions Schmidt had asked, among them the role of the late Vince Foster in the Whitewater affair and "If I was frustrated that my 'work product was stymied and roadblocked at certain federal levels.'" Schmidt also informed her that the indefatigable Jeff Gerth was back on the story. "I thanked her for the heads up," Lewis concluded.

Schmidt's article revealing the existence of RTC criminal referrals involving the President and First Lady appeared on the front page of *The Washington Post* on October 31. Within a week, RTC officials removed Lewis from the Madison probe and gave her another assignment. She kept working on Madison anyway.

By fall 1993, Jeff Gerth was offering Arkansas reporters piles of confidential banking records detailing the dealings of Governor Jim Guy Tucker with Madison Guaranty. *The New York Times,* he explained, had little interest in so obscure a figure. Gerth never named his source, but he did say that she worked for the RTC regional office in Kansas City.

At most law enforcement agencies, passing out confidential financial documents to the press would have constituted a firing offense. But the Kansas City leaker knew the score. Anybody who raised a stink was apt to be charged with a cover-up by *The New York Times*. Furthermore, whenever the *Times* and *Post* cited anonymous "federal investigators" as their Whitewater sources during the period, it was almost certainly L. Jean Lewis and her pals.

Ignoring the FBI's repeated attempts to persuade the RTC to investigate Arkansas S&L failures almost twenty times larger, Lewis and her colleagues had worked on almost nothing but Madison during 1993. RTC time sheets showed that the Kansas City sleuths devoted 2,608 hours to Madison in 1993 and exactly none to the $833 million First Federal Savings collapse. In 1994, they spent 2,458 hours probing Madison, exactly none on Savers Savings. Politics, they would later testify, had absolutely nothing to do with it.

Judging by stacks of e-mail and memos she wrote, Lewis spent much of her time trying to determine the fate of her initial 1992 referral. Who was covering up? Soon after chasing *The Washington Post* from her door, Lewis ran her referral by Paula Casey, the new Democratic U.S. Attorney in Little Rock. Casey, too, turned it down, citing the analysis by the Justice Department and her Republican predecessor, Charles Banks.[9]

Now Jean Lewis had her villainess. The Clinton administration, she decided, was engaged in a systematic cover-up. In the interim, Lewis prepared nine more criminal referrals regarding Madison. But when she and Iorio submitted the new charges on October 1, 1994, their boss, a career government lawyer named Julie Yanda, demanded an "unprecedented" legal review. That requiring such reviews had been national RTC policy for several months, Lewis cared not a fig. Nor did Iorio. Both would later testify that Yanda's action constituted "obstruction of justice"—a felony. (Always good for a sound bite, Senator Richard Shelby, an Alabama Republican, used the word "conspiracy.")

When Lewis's new referrals did come back from RTC lawyers seven days later, they were filled with impertinent questions. Why, for example, were some persons named as suspects when on the face of the supporting documents they appeared to be victims of

---

[9] A former law student of Bill Clinton's, Casey would ultimately recuse herself.

fraud? But Lewis and Iorio forwarded the new referrals without alteration. Then they set themselves the task of identifying those responsible for the cover-up. On January 17, 1994, Lewis bought herself a microcassette tape recorder and a stack of blank tapes. She and Iorio began to take their colleagues aside for little chats about Whitewater. More than one had the uneasy feeling that they were being surreptitiously taped.

On February 2, 1994, an attorney named April Breslaw visited Kansas City from the Washington office of the RTC. Weeks earlier, the Clinton administration had bowed to pressure and agreed to the appointment of Whitewater independent counsel Robert Fiske. Jean Lewis's ten criminal referrals were already in his hands.

Breslaw was a career employee who worked for the civil side of the RTC. Her job had nothing to do with criminal prosecution. Her task in Kansas City was to decide whether there was anybody worth suing in the Madison debacle to recover lost money. Jim McDougal, for instance, clearly was not. He had no assets worth pursuing. But was there anybody directly responsible for the S&L's collapse who did?

Although she wasn't supposed to be working on Madison Guaranty anymore, Jean Lewis knew who *she* thought should be sued: Bill and Hillary Clinton. So she and Iorio made it a point to get Breslaw into Lewis's office. During their talk, she would later testify in excruciating detail, Lewis noticed that an eight-year-old tape recorder on her desk had mysteriously switched itself on. It malfunctioned often, she said. Lewis decided not to tell Breslaw that the tape recorder was on. Then she steered the conversation around to Whitewater.

Lewis told Breslaw flatly that she believed Whitewater caused a loss to Madison. She cited a 1985 payment from Whitewater to a firm that had done work on a different McDougal property. It struck Lewis as terribly suspicious. "It made no sense to me, April," she said. "Why would they zap Whitewater $30,000 for an engineering survey on property that Whitewater had no technical or legal ties to that we could find?"

A less zealous investigator might have wondered if McDougal had been playing it entirely straight with the Clintons. But no such hypothesis could dent the hard shell of Lewis's zeal. Breslaw expressed lawyerly skepticism. "It's that kind of crap . . . ," she began. "I mean, I don't know if it gets us to any of it or not. Because obviously this money could go into Whitewater and then come out of Whitewater. So what you end up with, net, at the end, is still a question mark.

"I think if they can say it honestly," Breslaw continued, "the head people, Jack Ryan and Ellen Kulka [RTC officials in Washington], would like to be able to say Whitewater did not cause a loss to Madison. We don't know what [independent counsel] Fiske is going to find, and we don't offer any opinion on it. But the problem is, nobody has been able to say [to] Ryan and Kulka, 'Sure, say that. . . .' I'm sorry to ask the same questions I'm sure that others have asked. Did Whitewater cause a loss to Madison? How could we get a more definitive answer?"

In context, any fool can see that Breslaw is expressing a bureaucratic truism. Would the RTC prefer not to investigate the President of the United States? Of course it would. Breslaw would later testify that she hadn't met Ryan and Kulka at the time her remarks were secretly taped. Lewis herself admitted that she couldn't prove anything either way. "If you want me to sit here and give you unequivocal answers to whether or not Whitewater caused a loss," Lewis conceded, "I can't do it. All I can tell you is that . . . yes, *I believe* that Whitewater caused Madison a loss."

Sensing Lewis's drift, Breslaw sought to reassure her. "They're looking for what they can say," she said, "and I do believe they want to say something honest. But I don't believe at all, and I don't want to suggest at all, that they want us to move to certain conclusions. I really don't get that feeling. But there are answers they would be happier about, because it would get them, you know, off the hook. And that would be it about Whitewater."

If only Lewis had the subpoena powers of the FBI, she lamented, she could provide Breslaw with that answer. But alas, she did not. Five days later, on February 7, the RTC made the decision to hire the firm of Pillsbury, Madison & Sutro to answer those questions once and for all. To April Breslaw's apparent relief, the matter was out of her hands. But her own adventure in Whitewater had not yet begun.

A few weeks later, the myth of L. Jean Lewis, GOP Joan of Arc, was born. On March 24, 1994, Representative Jim Leach of Iowa took the floor in the U.S. House of Representatives. His announced theme was "the arrogance of power—Machiavellian machinations of single-party government." He compared Bill Clinton's Arkansas to Huey Long's Louisiana.

Leach, whom *Newsweek* described as "an Iowa moderate who radiates Main Street Republican probity," denounced the Clintons for having gone into business with what he called "a budding S&L owner." He asserted that Jim McDougal had "provided virtually all the money; the Governor-in-the-making provided his name." Leach asserted that, contrary to the Clintons' claims, they had clearly not lost money. Armed with confidential RTC documents slipped to him by Jean Lewis, he affected, like her, to believe that every nickel that passed through the Whitewater account had gone straight into their pockets.

Even *Newsweek*'s account of Leach's speech noticed that he "put up a fragile case for his first allegation." But the charge that drew the most play was what the magazine called "disturbing evidence for [Leach's] charge of political interference." Most persuasive, *Newsweek* thought, "was a sheaf of notes from Jean Lewis, the criminal investigator who led the Madison inquiry in RTC's Kansas City, Mo. office. She charged that superiors in Washington pressed her to ignore evidence that the Clintons' Whitewater venture played a significant role in draining Madison's accounts. Most telling was Lewis's account of a Feb. 2 meeting in which RTC attorney April Breslaw told her the agency was under pressure to conclude that Whitewater did not contribute to Madison's losses. 'She felt like they wanted to be able to provide an "honest answer,"' Lewis quoted Breslaw, 'but that there were certain answers that they would be happier to get because it would get them off the hook.'"

Reading the *Newsweek* account, you can almost hear the panting. Weeks and months of pulling the affair apart piece by damning piece seemed to lay ahead. On the House floor, Leach was even less equivocal. "Courageously," he said, "Kansas City investigators refused to allow Washington RTC objections to change the content of the referrals they sent in the second week of October 1993 to the Justice Department. Courageously, Kansas City investigators refused to back the position that Madison's losses were unrelated to Whitewater. . . . Fact: on February 2, 1994, the day [then Treasury Secretary] Roger Altman briefed the White House on Madison Guaranty, RTC senior attorney April Breslaw visited the Kansas City office and said that Washington would like to be able to say that Whitewater caused no losses to Madison. Kansas City employees protested that this was not the case."

When she learned about Leach's charges, Breslaw would later testify, she was stunned by Lewis's betrayal. And bewildered. She knew she'd said no such thing. But even if she'd had a bias about Whitewater, what would have been the point of pressuring Jean Lewis? Lewis's criminal referrals had already gone to the independent counsel.

Lewis had had absolutely no role in deciding whether or not to sue the Clintons. Breslaw had asked her to provide definitive evidence, but she couldn't. Five days later, the whole thing had been dumped into the collective laps of a law firm whose senior partner was Jay Stephens, former Republican U.S. Attorney for the District of Columbia under Reagan and Bush. The White House had bitched and moaned about Stephens's partisanship. Surely it was all a bitter joke.

If so, few of Jean Lewis's colleagues in Kansas City were amused. By August 1994, they'd compiled a list of grievances against her and Richard Iorio. After a two-week preliminary investigation by employee-relations types out of Washington, the matter was referred to the RTC's inspector general.

Included among the allegations regarding Lewis were:

*Improper disclosure of confidential documents;

*Secretly tape-recording conversations with RTC employees;

*Maintenance of confidential documents at home, rendering them inaccessible to RTC staff;

*Frequent use of government equipment for personal gain.

The allegations against Iorio included:

*Allowing Lewis to withhold information and documents regarding Madison from RTC lawyers;

*Allowing Lewis to neglect her assigned cases and continue working on Madison;

*Failure to take action regarding Lewis's leaks of confidential documents;

*Condoning Lewis's secret recordings of colleagues.

No wonder RTC senior officials in Washington agreed to place the pair on administrative leave pending a full investigation.

Enter independent counsel Kenneth Starr. GOP partisans had become disillusioned with preliminary conclusions reached by independent counsel Robert Fiske. A longtime prosecutor and a Republican, Fiske had issued a June 30, 1994, report concluding that Vincent Foster's death had been a tragic suicide and nothing more—a blow to conspiracy theorists everywhere. Fiske's report indicated that friends and family said that Foster had been despondent over "mean-spirited and factually baseless" editorials attacking him in *The Wall Street Journal*—but had mentioned Whitewater to nobody. (The *Journal* promptly jumped on Fiske and hammered him day after day.) Fiske had also concluded that while Clinton appointees at Treasury, Justice, and in the White House ought to have known better than to discuss the RTC's Whitewater probe, they'd attempted no cover-up and violated no laws. Information had moved up the bureaucratic ladder; nothing to speak of had moved back down.

Not only was Robert Fiske reaching conclusions Republican partisans didn't want to hear; he was moving too fast. If Whitewater was going to be kept cooking until the 1996 elections, something would have to slow it down. On August 5, 1994, a three-judge panel of the U.S. Court of Appeals removed Fiske and appointed Kenneth Starr, the former solicitor general under President Bush. The justices found no fault with Fiske but determined that his appointment by Attorney General Janet Reno could suggest the *appearance* of bias. Inasmuch as Reno herself had said so in initially resisting the idea of an independent counsel, the White House could hardly complain.

Unlike Fiske, Starr was something of a political activist; he'd recently volunteered to write an *amicus* brief in support of Paula Jones's sexual-harassment suit against the President. His law firm represented the Bradley Foundation, proud underwriter of *The American Spectator,* publisher of the 1994 Arkansas state troopers smear. His Chicago law firm, Kirkland & Ellis, it later emerged, had quit representing the Republican National Committee only two days before Starr's appointment. And although Starr had been a judge, he had no experience as a prosecutor.

Some Democrats did question Starr's objectivity, particularly after it was revealed that David B. Sentelle, the presiding judge of the panel, had lunched with his own political patrons, North Carolina Senators Jesse Helms and Lauch Faircloth, shortly before appointing Starr. Five former presidents of the American Bar Association took issue with the manner of Starr's selection. Even *The New York Times, mirabile dictu,* pronounced Starr's appointment "fatally tainted." The editors argued that he should resign. But the new independent counsel ignored them, and the controversy quickly died down. Like a barking dog at a fence, the press tends to shut up when people don't pay it any mind.[10]

Sure, Starr was in a tricky position. After all, if he could indict, or at least humiliate, Bill and Hillary Clinton, he'd become a big dog in the GOP hierarchy. If he couldn't, then some on the right were bound to call him a traitor. But early reports cast the man as the straightest of arrows; partisan, yes, but too principled to let ideology interfere with his duty.

Soon enough, Starr had begun to accumulate a number of "Whitewater" guilty pleas. A real estate appraiser admitted back-dating appraisals to make it appear to regulators that Madison Guaranty's loans had been properly documented. A college professor who had been an aide to Bill Clinton in 1979–80 agreed to a misdemeanor plea of falsifying a loan application. (He'd borrowed money for one purpose and used it for another.) A real estate agent who had sold (and bought) Whitewater lots con-

---

[10] All this, moreover, took place before *The Washington Monthly* revealed that Judge Sentelle's wife had taken a job in Senator Faircloth's Washington office.

fessed to concealing assets in a bankruptcy proceeding. Little Rock Municipal Judge David Hale pleaded guilty to swindling the Small Business Administration out of more than $2 million, then disappeared for almost two years at government expense—presumably in exchange for testifying that Bill Clinton made him do it. None of these revelations had any relationship to Whitewater or the Clintons, but they kept the press speculating that Starr was working his way up the ladder.

The Whitewater-related guilty plea that drew the most notice early on was that of Associate Attorney General Webster L. Hubbell. Hubbell was not only the number-three man in the Justice Department but Hillary Clinton's law partner and the President's golfing pal. Caught bilking his own clients and law partners of close to $500,000, Hubbell was turned in by the Rose Law Firm itself.

Hubbell's disgrace was no doubt an embarrassment and a bitter personal blow to the Clintons. But they were the victims, not the perps. To me, Hubbell got off easy. Previously the owner of a fine reputation in Little Rock, had he burglarized his law firm for 1 percent of what he took by deception, he could have ended up doing hard time in an Arkansas penitentiary. A far more unpleasant way to pay for one's crimes, let me assure you, even than being grilled by Senator Alfonse D'Amato.

For all the huffing and puffing, however, Starr didn't seem to be getting anywhere for much of his first year in Little Rock. Indeed, in political terms, his single most decisive act was one the press hardly noticed: he asked the RTC to turn over its internal investigation of L. Jean Lewis and Richard Iorio to the independent counsel. The agency was only too happy to comply. It even offered the independent counsel Lewis and Iorio's services, at RTC expense. Then Starr turned the whole thing inside out. Lewis's and Iorio's actions would no longer be the focus of the probe. Rather, he opened a grand jury investigation *of the officials who had brought charges against them.* According to an investigative article in *The Nation* by Joe Conason and Murray Waas, these very RTC officials were *at the exact same time* engaged in settlement negotiations in a multimillion-dollar lawsuit against Starr's

Chicago law firm, Kirkland & Ellis. (Unlike Robert Fiske, Kenneth Starr had elected *not* to give up his private practice during his tenure as independent counsel. He continued to represent clients and to draw an estimated $1-million-a-year income from the firm.)

Days before formal negotiations began, Starr turned the Whitewater grand jury loose on the RTC—specifically on Jack Ryan and Ellen Kulka, then the agency's acting head and chief counsel, respectively. Readers may recall that it was to Ryan and Kulka that RTC attorney April Breslaw had referred in her tape-recorded talk with Jean Lewis. It was also Ryan and Kulka who had reviewed the preliminary evidence of Lewis and Iorio's alleged misbehavior and ordered them suspended with pay, pending investigation. The same two Washington officials who would have the final say on any settlement between the RTC and Kirkland & Ellis. There's no evidence that Ryan and Kulka allowed Starr's intimidation to affect their judgment. But the RTC wanted to settle for $1 million; it ended up accepting $325,000.

Federal prosecutors are forbidden to practice law on the side. U.S. attorneys can't have any outside sources of income *at all.* The independent counsel law does allow it, but does that make Starr's action any better? A more blatant abuse of prosecutorial powers can hardly be imagined. Mrs. Clinton and the Rose Law Firm would have been slow-roasted over a fire of shredded billing records for anything resembling Starr's actions.

Kenneth Starr and L. Jean Lewis have something else in common too: the conservative Landmark Legal Foundation in Kansas City. Landmark has represented Jean Lewis through her travails free of charge—including her dealings with Starr. They also represent Paula Jones. Landmark, in turn, is partially bankrolled by another of Starr's clients, the Bradley Foundation—bankroller of *The American Spectator.* And the Bradley Foundation has also reimbursed the state of Wisconsin for work done on a "school choice" case by Starr and his law firm. Getting dizzy? There's more. The Landmark Legal Foundation is involved in the Wisconsin case too, *on the same side.* And people say Arkansas is an incestuous world.

Next thing you know, the Republicans took both houses of

Congress in the 1994 elections. It didn't take the Psychic Friends Network to predict that the GOP would do its best to turn C-SPAN into The Whitewater Channel. In late summer of 1995, House and Senate Republicans debuted two new programs more or less simultaneously: Senator Alfonse D'Amato's committee, which would do its best to exploit as much political benefit as possible from events surrounding Vince Foster's suicide, and the L. Jean Lewis show, produced and directed by Iowa Representative Jim Leach.

True, a small glitch had developed in the scenario some months earlier. A detailed, apparently well-sourced article appeared on the front page of *The Wall Street Journal* on February 22, 1995. Written by Ellen Joan Pollock and Viveca Novak, the article's headline read: CAPITAL SECRET: THERE MAY BE LESS TO WHITE-WATER CASE THAN MEETS THE EYE. Persons expecting high drama when independent counsel Starr presented the results of his inquiry, the *Journal* warned, were apt to be disappointed. "Indeed," they wrote, as "Starr moves ahead with his investigation and refines his legal case, what is most noteworthy is how many of the biggest Whitewater headlines appear to be heading toward the cutting-room floor. . . . A blow-by-blow account of the various charges involved in the Whitewater scandal," the *Journal* added, "shows that at this point, investigators have found little evidence to support many of the sexiest, most publicized allegations."

What happened next was exactly what happens when a turkey hunter slips through the woods before dawn and sits stock still at the base of a pin oak. Everything went silent for a little bit, then the cacophony began again. Nobody prominent in the Washington media mentioned the *Journal* article. Nobody attempted any follow-ups. Nobody at *The New York Times,* nobody at *The Washington Post, Time, Newsweek,* or the TV networks. For all the impact Pollock and Novak's article had, they may as well have hollered down a well.[11]

---

[11] Readers of *Harper's Magazine* who read my October 1994 article "Fool for Scandal: How the *New York Times* Got Whitewater Wrong" may have been less surprised by Pollock and Novak's reporting than many *Journal* readers. Its findings were supported by several other reporters at an October 25, 1994, forum at the National Press Club sponsored by the magazine and broadcast on C-SPAN. (The text of the forum is reproduced in the Appendix to this book.)

A bit more than a month before Whitewater hearings were scheduled to begin in July, Kenneth Starr indicted Arkansas Governor Jim Guy Tucker. The charges involved an allegedly sham bankruptcy proceeding connected to Tucker's acquisition of cable-TV franchises in Texas and Florida. Tucker had taken out an SBA-guaranteed loan from David Hale—funds for which, as a Vietnam-era veteran, he was legally eligible, and which he had repaid in full.

The indictment had no relationship to Whitewater, Madison Guaranty, or the Clintons. At the time of the allegedly suspect transactions, Tucker was a private businessman and attorney. Longtime political rivals, he and Bill Clinton were closer to being enemies than friends. Every Arkansas reporter knew that. Their mutual dislike had been acknowledged for years. They had never had any private business transactions. While it's "certainly true in the narrow sense that nothing in Tucker's indictment relates to the President," conceded an editorial in *The Wall Street Journal*, "it's equally certain that the indictment paints an unflattering picture of the political and business atmosphere that nurtured the President . . ."

A former state prosecutor and U.S. congressman, Tucker claimed that Kenneth Starr's motives were purely political. The independent counsel, he said, had indicted him simply because he couldn't indict Bill Clinton. He vowed to fight what he called a Republican "witch hunt" until the end. Given Tucker's well-known love of a scrap, Arkansas reporters believed him.[12]

On the eve of congressional hearings, *The Wall Street Journal* reported on June 26 that "a long-awaited report on the collapse of Madison Guaranty Savings and Loan corroborates most of

[12] Like the McDougals', Jim Guy Tucker's guilt or innocence is beyond the scope of this book. His lawyers argued that the first two counts of the three-count indictment resulted from fabrications by David Hale. The form of the third count had many Little Rock defense attorneys scratching their heads. Tucker and his co-defendants were not accused of bankruptcy fraud or tax evasion but of *conspiring* to evade taxes—an unusual way to draw up an indictment. It's a tactic that allows hearsay testimony by the likes of Hale but doesn't require prosecutors to prove that Tucker actually made any illicit gains. Tucker's lawyers contended he'd used bankruptcy to clarify a muddled ownership situation. He'd acquired a cable-TV company only to be faced with a lawsuit from an individual claiming a part share. The company was put through bankruptcy as a means of redistributing its assets; all claims were paid in full. As in all cases of its kind, the devil is in the detail.

President and Mrs. Clinton's assertions about their Whitewater real estate investment." A preliminary report submitted to the RTC by Pillsbury, Madison & Sutro, wrote Ellen Joan Pollock, "shows that the Clintons were passive investors in Whitewater Development Corp. and weren't involved in its financial transactions until 1986. . . . That is significant because of allegations that funds transferred from Madison to Whitewater before 1986 contributed to the thrift's collapse." The report also verified the amount lost by the Clintons on their investment.

"The investigators did find," the story added, "that Mr. McDougal and his former wife, Susan, bore more of the risk and financial burden than the Clintons. Many people who have studied the affair have wondered why." Pollock's story made it clear that the Pillsbury Report drew no final conclusions as to liability for Madison's losses. It was nevertheless a potentially severe blow to the Jean Lewis–Jim Leach version of Whitewater.

Four days later, *The Washington Post* came to the rescue with a jumbled article standing the matter on its head. That the Clintons had spoken truthfully about Whitewater was deemed no longer significant. The *Post* zeroed in on the McDougals' putatively greater losses. Readers had to sift through nine long paragraphs of implied accusations before coming upon this: "The report supported the Clintons' contention that they lost money and were basically passive investors. They did not sign checks or receive much financial information. In eight years, they wrote or received fewer than 20 letters about Whitewater."

But to fully restore the President and First Lady to the status of leading suspects would require the efforts of Jeff Gerth and Stephen Engelberg. It took them almost three weeks to parse the Pillsbury Report in a manner consistent with *The New York Times*'s company line. No word of the report's existence, much less its findings, appeared in the newspaper until Sunday, July 16.

Even by Gerth's standards, the article was a masterpiece of innuendo and disinformation. Not a syllable about McDougal's slipshod, deceptive management of Whitewater appeared. It took the *Times* a full twenty-four paragraphs to get around to mentioning that the report "explicitly supports the Clintons' oft-repeated assertion that they were 'passive investors' in Whitewater and had little role in its financial management until 1988." The *real* significance of the Pillsbury Report, the *Times* assured its readers, was that their partner had shielded "the Clintons to an extent far greater than previously reported, from paying their half of Whitewater's losses. From 1980 to 1986, that partner, James B. McDougal, advanced the Whitewater venture the $100,000 it needed to avoid a messy default on its bank loans, while the Clintons, half-owners of the corporation, contributed nothing, the report says."[13]

Now consider page 61 of the Pillsbury Report, dated April 24, 1995: "To summarize, through May 31, 1984, the Clintons had advanced cash of $35,970 to Whitewater, while the McDougals, and entities they controlled, had advanced $47,331. These totals do not include bank debt that they had personally obligated themselves to pay (e.g., Mrs. Clinton's $30,000 Madison Bank loan . . .); it focuses solely on the cash actually advanced."

As Gerth and Engelberg's article later concedes, the Clintons did indeed lose $42,192 in Whitewater. That McDougal's financial high jinks had been calculated to cover *his* butt rather than the Clintons' appears never to have crossed the reporters' minds. The *Times* even went so far as to quote McDougal's deceptive November 14, 1986, letter offering to relieve the Clintons of their share in the company. But, like the S&L owner himself, Gerth and Engelberg neglected to mention his bargain-basement sale of Whitewater's

---

[13] Neither the Pillsbury Report nor any of the zillions of media accounts give any final figures for how much the McDougals lost on Whitewater. Because any and all advances to the Whitewater Development Company from McDougal-controlled entities stopped after Hillary Clinton stepped in to run the company after 1986, the RTC had no interest in the matter. Hence the Pillsbury Report simply doesn't address it. Under Hillary's management, the corporation paid its back taxes and fees, bought and sold a property from a deceased buyer's bankrupt estate, and repaid its remaining loans. What remained of the company was then sold to Jim McDougal in 1992 for $1,000.

Vincent Foster warned his clients that due to McDougal's chaotic records, documenting their own losses to the satisfaction of the IRS—much less of the press—would be almost impossible. To try it, he warned, could open "a can of worms you don't want to open." So they didn't. The Clintons took a $1,000 capital gain on their 1993 tax return rather than a loss. "This may be the first time," Joel Achenbach commented in *The Washington Post*, "that a politician's decision not to take a tax write-off is perceived as suspicious." Some Republicans, meanwhile, cite Vince Foster's tax advice to the Clintons as the likely motive for his suicide.

real estate assets to the realtor who was supposed to be its agent. Nor do they see fit to inform readers of McDougal's little $550,950 deal with International Paper—the transaction that the Pillsbury Report notes "did not benefit Whitewater or the Clintons, [but] left Whitewater with a large mortgage but no corresponding asset."

Through the art of selective quotation, McDougal emerges as a businessman flexible enough to expect favors for money but exasperated by the Clintons' unwillingness to meet their obligations. Reports the *Times*, "Newly available documents . . . suggest that the [Clintons] could have had reason to suspect that the venture was failing to pay its bills."

And the evidence? In October 1984, an Arkansas bank sent the Clintons a final payment notice on a Whitewater loan. Hillary had forwarded it to McDougal. "Will you please take care of it, or let me know what I need to do?" she'd asked. McDougal responded within three days. He sent her a check for $4,811 drawn on the Whitewater account and payable to the bank. He enclosed a brief note indicating that everything was perfectly routine.

"Two central questions about the land deal," Gerth and Engelberg state, "are these: Did the Clintons pay their share of the venture's losses? And did Mr. Clinton, as Governor of Arkansas, help his business partner, Mr. McDougal, get any favors from state officials?" The implied answer was that the Clintons were guilty on both counts.

And what corrupt benefits was Bill Clinton suspected of bestowing upon McDougal? Surprisingly, the *Times* passed up a chance to beat up on Arkansas Securities Commissioner Beverly Bassett Schaffer again. Instead, the ace investigative reporters changed the subject to septic tanks. Gerth and Engelberg had plumbed a nugget from footnote #730 on page 132 of the Pillsbury Report. Bill Clinton, it seemed, had arranged an "unusual" meeting in March 1986 between McDougal and state Health Department officials, "who insisted," the *Times* added, "that Mr. McDougal's projects had received no special treatment as a result."

Actually, the *Arkansas Democrat-Gazette* had written about this March 1986 meeting months earlier. Its subject was septic-tank permits at a McDougal subdivision called Maple Creek Farms.

The developer wanted 300; the Health Department would approve only 15. Indeed, the full story was actually quite revealing of Clinton's style. He'd convened the meeting at the state capitol, the governor told aides, because McDougal was "his friend of twenty years who had never asked for a favor."

By all accounts, McDougal went wild. He accused his antagonists of "duplicity and trickery," and described one as "psychotic." A Clinton staffer named Janice Choate thought that McDougal himself appeared seriously disturbed. The governor, however, got furious. Clinton's face reddened, and he raised his voice. He asked McDougal where he got off thinking he could come into the governor's office and bully state employees. Then he apologized for McDougal's tirade and ended the meeting abruptly. The Health Department assigned new inspectors to have another look at the issue. McDougal never got the permits.

Nevertheless, the mighty *New York Times* had spoken. The headline over the Gerth-Engelberg effort said it all: DOCUMENTS SHOW CLINTONS GOT VAST BENEFIT FROM PARTNER. The newspaper's vaunted Washington bureau had succeeded brilliantly in covering its butt with both hands. The general public, in July 1995, was barely paying attention. But as far as the press pack was concerned, the Pillsbury Report was a dead letter. Reporters, in turn, were spared the tedium of reading it. And the shaky premises of the Whitewater "scandal" had been restored. It is not too much of an exaggeration to say that they would never again be seriously questioned.

Ghost Trailing

If you get a witness who says, "Oh, I don't recall," the immediate accusation is "You're being disingenuous." If you have witnesses with conflicting testimony, the allegation is, "Someone's lying." And if you have witnesses that have consistent statements, "It's a conspiracy."

—*Senator Christopher Dodd, November 9, 1995*

◆

B y the time House and Senate hearings on Whitewater began in late summer 1995, the Washington media had turned itself into a wholly owned subsidiary of the Republican Party. The opening of hearings must have come as a great relief to many reporters. No longer would it be necessary to conduct forays into remotest Arkansas; Whitewater had arrived in the nation's capital, where it properly belonged. Furthermore, the unspoken rules of covering such events were understood by all. Once the "scandal" template had been fitted over the keyboard, Whitewater stories would almost write themselves.

On Capitol Hill, GOP staffers would gain the immeasurable advantage of spinning the story by the art of selective leaking. Naughty reporters, it goes without saying, could expect no help from the prosecution. Their editors, in turn, would wonder how come the *Times* and *Post* got all the juicy tidbits while they didn't. Every new fact, almost regardless of where it fit (or didn't) in the grand scheme of things, could be played as a "revelation" that advanced the story.

In terms of news value, particularly on TV, loaded questions asked by celebrity politicians would clearly outweigh answers given by nobodies. As needed, accusations could serve in place of evidence. Flaws in the Whitewater plot line could be dealt with by invoking the story's forbidding complexity. How Whitewater played would become partly a matter of exactly how shameless Republican partisans were willing to be.

And what about the hard-eyed skepticism reporters pride themselves on? Well, Geraldo was already booked, and with the far more significant O. J. Simpson trial taking place simultaneously in Los Angeles, there would be no nightly gatherings of pundits to explain the defense strategy. The all-purpose cover-up charge having been leveled eighteen months earlier, it was simply a given that the White House *had* no strategy. Exculpatory information, much of it *already* suppressed by the might and majesty of *The New York Times* and its assiduous followers, could be safely ignored.

In the event that anybody had forgotten, though, the *Times* weighed in with a stern editorial only two days after Gerth and Engelberg's July 16 article on the Pillsbury Report. President Clinton, "his staff, in the campaign and later at the White House," the *Times* charged, "stonewalled on the details that would have revealed whether he and Mrs. Clinton were telling the truth about their finances. Today's renewed . . . hearings on Whitewater are the bitter fruit of those original evasions."

Even if the media hadn't already committed itself to a prosecution-only version of Whitewater, all the advantages clearly lay with the GOP. And who was calling the shots for the Republicans? Why, our old friends at Citizens United. If James B. Stewart's book *Blood Sport* is to be believed, the mastermind behind the House hearings was none other than David Bossie. Previously, Stewart writes, Bossie "had always deemed Representative [Jim] Leach to be too liberal to be of much use, but after the Iowa congressman spoke out on Whitewater . . . Bossie developed a close relationship with Leach's press secretary, Joe Pinder. . . . An announcement by Leach all but guaranteed press coverage. Pinder would also pass on tips to Bossie that the [House Banking] committee didn't have the resources to pursue. Bossie would do the investigation, then report back to Pinder. Bossie often felt that it was Citizens United that was partly funding the congressional investigation of Whitewater.

"The widely respected Leach proved the perfect cover for disseminating Citizens United research. Still, public recognition that Bossie was working with Leach might have so damaged the congressman's bipartisan credibility that the relationship between Bossie and Pinder was shrouded in secrecy; it isn't clear that Leach himself knew the source of all the information Pinder generated. Pinder charged calls from the office to his home credit card; he borrowed other fax machines. Bossie would hand over documents at obscure restaurants. . . . When someone else answered their phone calls, they always used only their first names and never left messages or phone numbers."

Because Bossie "didn't want to be taken for granted," Stewart continues, he was also funneling information to Senators Lauch Faircloth and Alfonse D'Amato at the same time. Even so, Bossie congratulated himself that the greatest success lay in planting Whitewater stories in the media: not merely at NBC but at *Time, Newsweek,* and *U.S. News & World Report.* Bossie's scrupulous accuracy, Stewart says, won him the grudging respect of reporters vexed by Clinton administration "lies."

Indeed, a "Preliminary Briefing" handed out to reporters by Leach's House Banking Committee is almost indistinguishable from a Citizens United poster. Its heroine was L. Jean Lewis, who had not only "developed evidence of a massive check kiting scheme orchestrated by [Jim] McDougal" but who, the briefing predicted, would testify about "events that suggest an effort by RTC Washington and highly placed political appointees at the Department of Justice to suppress or at least control [her] criminal referrals."

Besides the First Lady, the Leach briefing featured two other villainesses. One was Beverly Bassett Schaffer, the former Arkansas securities commissioner. "Madison needed the State's imprimatur before it could proceed with the issuance of preferred stock," the document explained. "Though preferred stock had never before been issued by an Arkansas thrift . . . Mrs. Schaffer approved the plan just two weeks after its submission." On a "Whitewater's Most

Wanted" poster distributed at about the same time by Citizens United, Bassett Schaffer's caricature appeared with the phrase "AT LARGE" emblazoned in red. "Appointed by Gov. Clinton at the urging of Jim McDougal," read the caption, she "intervened at Hillary's request to keep insolvent Madison Guaranty S&L open."

The third villainess was April Breslaw. Perhaps due to his well-known modesty, Leach didn't see fit to repeat the charges he'd made against Breslaw on the floor of Congress more than a year earlier. "Met with RTC criminal investigator Jean Lewis on February 2, 1994," the briefing noted. The Citizens United "Wanted" poster took a more direct approach. "RTC FLUNKY," read the legend under Breslaw's caricature, "allegedly killed Jean Lewis' investigation of Madison Guaranty Savings & Loan."

The aim of the House Banking Committee hearings, the Leach briefing made clear, would be to dramatize the misdeeds of all three women. They would, however, be accused *in absentia*. No thought seems to have been given to calling the First Lady to testify, and backed by unanimous support of GOP committee members, Leach refused to call Bassett Schaffer or Breslaw. Democrats protested in vain. Also missing from the witness list were any and all RTC officials in Kansas City or Washington who had aroused the ire of Jean Lewis. Nor would the services of the relevant state and federal S&L regulators be required: nobody from the Arkansas Securities Commission, nobody from the Federal Home Loan Bank Board. And certainly not Walter Faulk, the career FHLBB official who had directly presided over Jim McDougal's ouster from Madison Guaranty back in July 1986.

Leach's motives can only be guessed at. Events back home in Iowa may have clouded his judgment. In a state where forty-two of forty-six delegates to the 1992 GOP caucuses had represented Pat Robertson's Christian Coalition, he may have begun to see a reputation for moderation as an impediment to greatness.

Alas, to all but the most perfervid Whitewater believers, the House hearings proved pretty much of a bust. Viewers watching on C-SPAN saw Democrats repeatedly attack what Representative Paul E. Kanjorski of Pennsylvania characterized as a "one-sided political show trial." In his opening statement, Representative Henry Gonzalez of Texas, much criticized for his own handling of inconclusive Whitewater hearings in 1994, put it in terms of simple fairness. "What is even defensible," he asked, "about a hearing that allows only accusers to speak? How do we explain to the people of this country a process so bitterly partisan?" Leach gravely thanked Gonzalez for his remarks, but made no attempt to answer.

Editors of *The New York Times* and *The Washington Post,* meanwhile, so dedicated to the pursuit of civil liberties in far-off lands, apparently didn't find the McCarthyite overtones of the Whitewater hearings worthy of comment. In its news columns, the *Times* hewed closely to the gospel according to Gerth. Indeed, the master himself made what appears to have been his final contribution to the Whitewater saga on August 8, 1995. Gerth's front-page account of the opening day of the House hearings alluded to Democrats' objections to what Representative Bruce Vento of Minnesota called "the timing, the agenda and the witnesses." But it gave no particulars. Readers had to guess what Vento was talking about. Gerth's article rehashed the familiar list of Whitewater suspicions and allegations, including a 1981 letter from Hillary Rodham Clinton to Jim McDougal to the effect that "If Reaganomics works at all, Whitewater could become the Western Hemisphere's Mecca."[1]

Over the weekend, meanwhile, a dent had appeared in Jean Lewis's armor. Knowing that Democrats were planning to question her motives and competence, GOP staffers made a tactical leak of several documents late Friday afternoon, August 5. Among them were an October 16, 1992, letter from Republican U.S. Attorney Charles Banks turning down Lewis's first criminal referral on the grounds of weak evidence and partisan intent; internal FBI cables that also found Lewis's work wanting; and a February 1993 appraisal by Justice Department attorney Mark

---

[1] The likelihood that Mrs. Clinton, a liberal Democrat writing to another liberal Democrat, was being ironic with reference to their end-of-the-road little project in the Ozarks has escaped the notice of every journalist who's quoted it.

MacDougal. "No facts," it said, "can be identified to support the designation of President Bill Clinton [or] Hillary Rodham Clinton . . . as material witnesses to the allegations made in the criminal referral."

An Associated Press story quoting and summarizing the documents ran in many newspapers over the weekend. The *Arkansas Democrat-Gazette,* among others, played up the story prominently. Here, after all, were three knowledgeable, independent appraisals concluding that allegations of criminal wrongdoing by the President of the United States had no merit. Most people would call that news. *The Washington Post* buried the story. *The New York Times,* however, pitched the documents into a memory hole. Jeff Gerth's August 8 account previewed Lewis's testimony as if they simply didn't exist. "Mrs. Lewis," he wrote, "who is scheduled to testify Tuesday, is prepared to say: 'I believe there was a concerted effort to obstruct, hamper and manipulate the results of our investigation of Madison—and the subsequent independent counsel investigation—by individuals at the R.T.C., the Treasury Department, the Justice Department and U.S. Attorney Paula Casey's office in Little Rock.'"

That every professional investigator who examined Jean Lewis's 1992 referral had found it politically motivated and incompetently drawn has *never* been mentioned in the nation's newspaper of record. During the proceedings on Monday, August 8, moreover, Democrats had introduced into the record several documents at odds with Gerth's own Whitewater reporting, including a December 10, 1987, letter from Beverly Bassett Schaffer almost begging the FHLBB to shut Madison Guaranty S&L down.

Even more significantly, Utah Representative Bill Orton had wrung an admission from a federal bank examiner who described the chaos he'd found at Madison in 1986 that there *had not been a single instance anywhere in the United States of a state-chartered, federally insured S&L being shut down by state authorities without the formal cooperation of federal regulators.* To my knowledge, this simple fact, which by itself demolishes the fundamental premise of *The New York Times*'s version of Whitewater, has never been reported anywhere.

By any reasonable standard, Jean Lewis made a terrible witness. In his opening remarks, Representative Leach billed her as the protagonist of "an uplifting and indeed heroic story of middle Americans, public servants in obscure government agencies who refused to be cowed by the power structure." Lewis's testimony, on the other hand, made her appear rash, self-righteous, and eager to draw sweeping conclusions from little or no evidence. She wrapped herself in the flag, praising a military upbringing that had taught her "tenacity, courage, honesty and love of country. . . [and that] under our Constitution, no one is above the law, no matter how powerful."

As predicted, Lewis made sweeping charges of corruption in high places. She had named Beverly Bassett Schaffer in one of her criminal referrals, it seemed, solely on the basis of articles in *The New York Times*. Within the government itself, anybody and everybody who had ever thwarted her will became ipso facto part of a broad conspiracy to obstruct her probe of Madison Guaranty. Asked if she was aware of the felonious overtones of the word "obstruction," Lewis replied that she certainly was. When it came to particulars, however, Lewis fared poorly. Pressed by Democrats for the names and titles of any individuals in the Treasury or Justice departments who had obstructed her probe, she was unable to provide even one. And how long had RTC attorneys "obstructed" her probe with their "unprecedented" legal review? Seven days. How long had Clinton-appointed U.S. Attorney Paula Casey delayed action on Lewis's 1992 referral? She'd acted two weeks after taking the oath of office.

Lewis's allegations against April Breslaw had even less merit. In her prepared testimony, Lewis stated boldly: "It is clear that Ms. Breslaw was there to deliver a message that, quote, 'The people at the top would like to be able to say Whitewater did not cause a loss to Madison,' close quote. Of course, Whitewater did cause a financial loss to Madison, and Madison's failure cost the American people millions of dollars." But Lewis, it turned out, had significantly altered the quote attributed to April Breslaw. (Or maybe the Landmark Legal Foundation lawyer who had helped her prepare it had done so. Any reporter who examined the text of her surreptitious February 2, 1994, tape recording could see that the sentence put in quotes simply doesn't appear there.

After the tape was played aloud to the committee, Representative Maurice Hinchey of New York confronted Lewis. April Breslaw's actual words, he pointed out, were very different from the way Lewis had represented them. The tape also revealed that when Breslaw had pressed Lewis for definitive evidence showing Whitewater helped sink Madison Guaranty, Lewis admitted that she couldn't provide any. But in Lewis's sworn testimony, she had stated categorically that she could. Had she provided any evidence? She had not. Nor, of course, had the Pillsbury Report, which it turned out Lewis hadn't read.

Republicans, for the most part, confined themselves to denunciations of "Arkansas rascality" and praise for Lewis's lonely courage. They compared Democrats who questioned Lewis's veracity to cops badgering a rape victim. But reporters for *The New York Times* and *The Washington Post* owed Jean Lewis, and they protected her. No hint of the weaknesses and contradictions in her testimony appeared in either newspaper.

The *Post*'s coverage was written by Susan Schmidt, the same reporter whom Lewis claimed to have driven empty-handed from her door back in October 1993. RTC INVESTIGATOR SAYS PROBE WAS BLOCKED AT HIGH LEVELS, the headline read. "The federal investigator whose work helped launch the independent counsel's ongoing Whitewater probe," Schmidt wrote, "told a House committee yesterday that there was 'a concerted effort to obstruct, hamper and manipulate' her findings at high levels of the federal government. . . . Jean Lewis gave a detailed description of how an investigation of Madison Guaranty Savings and Loan that began in March 1992 was thwarted by Resolution Trust Corp. and Justice Department officials after Bill Clinton was elected president."

Once again, only *Wall Street Journal* reporters Viveca Novak and Ellen Joan Pollock covered the story evenhandedly. Only the *Journal* conveyed the substance of Democratic protests against the committee's refusal to allow the accused to defend themselves and provided a fair context for Lewis's testimony. "Federal Bureau of Investigation and Justice Department documents," Novak and

Pollock wrote, "contradict Ms. Lewis's claim that there was any attempt to quash her 1992 referral." The article quoted U.S. Attorney Charles Banks's letter, as well as FBI and Justice Department critiques of Lewis's work. In an article a day later, enough of Breslaw's remarks were quoted to convince any sentient adult that all she'd really told Lewis was that her bosses would be relieved to hear that Whitewater hadn't cost the taxpayers any money "because it would rid the RTC of a high profile headache."

In a roundup article a few days later, the *Journal* reporters wrote, "The star witness, Resolution Trust Corp. investigator Jean Lewis, didn't seem wholly credible. . . . Ms. Lewis struck many as ready to draw the most incriminating conclusions from ambiguous circumstances."

On Thursday, August 10, Chairman Leach relented and allowed April Breslaw to testify. Summoned on less than one day's notice, she emphasized her feelings of shock and betrayal—both for Lewis's surreptitious taping of their conversation and for misrepresenting what she'd actually said. Back in February 1994, Breslaw pointed out, Lewis's criminal referrals were already in the hands of the independent counsel. So even if she had intended a cover-up, it was already too late. Besides, she represented the civil side of the RTC. Five days after she and Lewis spoke, her office handed the whole Whitewater mess over to Pillsbury, Madison & Sutro. "It's hard for me to understand," Breslaw said, "how I can be accused of attempting to carry a message or influence someone who has no capacity to be influenced. She had no prospect of ever writing any recommendation to sue or not to sue anyone." Breslaw also voiced her resentment that a U.S. congressman would publicly accuse her of wrongdoing without first asking to hear her side of the story. Leach never would concede that Jean Lewis had acted from anything but the highest motives. But he did, to his credit, apologize to April Breslaw.

The New York Times, however, apologizes to nobody. For whatever reason, Lewis's first day of testimony coincided with Jeff Gerth's last Whitewater story. His replacement, Neil A. Lewis, summarized the day's testimony in one brief sentence: "Ms. Breslaw said she did not mean to deliver such a message and Ms. Lewis had misinterpreted her remarks."

In the U.S. Senate, Alfonse D'Amato's own Whitewater probe had gotten similarly bogged down. After beginning with a theatrical flourish on July 18, as Republican Senator Frank Murkowski of Alaska waved Vincent Foster's empty briefcase before C-SPAN cameras, the hearings settled into a routine that soon became familiar to skeptical onlookers. Amid the glare of TV lights and the clicking of camera shutters, one Republican senator or another would make sweeping charges of corruption, malfeasance, and cover-up reaching all the way to the White House. The media would gravely report each accusation. Subsequent evidence or testimony would then reveal it to be either purely speculative or altogether groundless. Accusers would then either harangue witnesses for lying or quietly drop the charge and proceed to another witness. Sometimes the press would report the collapse; most often it wouldn't. But it never failed to jump on the newest charge, as people say in Arkansas, like a chicken on a June bug.

The New York Times's man at the Senate hearings was Stephen Labaton, who served immediate notice that he was up to the challenge. Among the D'Amato committee's "revelations" on the first day of hearings, according to Labaton's July 19 account, were three noteworthy items:

1. "Handwritten notes by Mr. [Vince] Foster contradict an important conclusion of the report prepared by the former independent counsel in the case, Robert B. Fiske, about the circumstances surrounding Mr. Foster's death. Mr. Fiske concluded in his report that there was no evidence that Mr. Foster or the White House had any concerns about Whitewater during the first half of 1993. But Mr. Foster's notes, which were found in his files, show that he was deeply concerned about how the Clintons would account for their investment on their 1992 tax returns." (In reality, Foster had advised the Clintons *not* to deduct Whitewater losses because Jim McDougal's records were so chaotic. They hadn't.)

2. "Contradicting an account provided by Mr. Hubbell and the Clinton campaign three years ago, Mr. Hubbell today acknowledged that Mrs. Clinton had helped bring Madison as a client to the Rose Law Firm in 1985." (In reality, Hillary Rodham Clinton had herself made this "revelation" in her Whitewater press conference fifteen months earlier. The entire text of that press confer-

ence had been printed in *The New York Times* on April 24, 1994. "I did that," she told reporters of her negotiations with Madison CEO Jim McDougal, "and I arranged that the firm would be paid a $2,000 a month retainer. . . . [It] was really an advance against billing." By the way, keep your eye on this one, because, with the help of Stephen Labaton and columnist William Safire, it would come back with a vengeance some months later.)

3. "Mr. Hubbell also testified that after the 1992 campaign, he took custody of many of the campaign records, including Whitewater and Madison records. He said he kept them in his house and turned them over to the Clintons' lawyers . . . in November 1993." (True, but so what? Where should they have been kept? "The opportunities for destruction or alteration of records," huffed a July 23 *Times* editorial, "have been more extensive than expected.")

Was there no possibility, then, that poor Vincent Foster would be allowed to rest in peace? Absolutely none. Conspiracy nuts refuse to accept what every competent professional who has looked into Foster's death has concluded: that he was clinically depressed and took his own life for irrational reasons having nothing to do with Whitewater or Bill and Hillary Clinton. Yet to appease the nut faction, Republican senators were willing to devote weeks of hearings to the supposition that Clinton aides wrongfully removed incriminating documents from Vince Foster's office. What those documents might reveal—given the fact that duplicates existed in banks, title companies, law offices, accounting firms, county courthouses, and several state and federal agencies—nobody could say. Even the simple fact that there *was* no Whitewater probe at the time of Foster's death in July 1993 outside the mind of L. Jean Lewis deterred the senators not a bit.

But Vince Foster had not only been Hillary's close friend and colleague; he had been a boyhood friend of the President's. He and Bill Clinton had attended kindergarten together in Hope, Arkansas. Another classmate had been David Watkins, the White House official who impulsively asked his assistant, Patsy Thomason, to return to the White House to look for a suicide note in Foster's office on the night of his death. There Thomason encountered Mrs. Clinton's chief of staff, Maggie Williams. Having failed to find a note, the two women later testified, they were sitting together in the office weeping when Foster's boss, White House Counsel Bernard Nussbaum, arrived. Nussbaum, too, was in a state of great distress. To credit the premises of last summer's Senate hearings, it is necessary to believe that the three—none of whom knew the others very well—immediately entered into a conspiracy to strip Foster's office of Whitewater files and later lie about it under oath.

The emotional climate in which subsequent decisions were made over the next two days was described in Senate testimony by former White House Associate Counsel Clifford Sloan. "It was a mood of complete devastation," Sloan said, "of just feeling over-whelmed. Terrible shock, sadness, grief—people just completely dumbstruck. It really seemed like kind of unimaginable pain, the sorrow was so great. And I can remember . . . when the President and [presidentail adviser] Mack McLarty and Bernie Nussbaum addressed the White House staff gathered at around noon of July 21, everybody in that room was . . . just hushed and overwhelmed with grief. In their remarks," Sloan continued, "all three of them really were very choked up. . . . It just stands out in my mind as a time [that was] so stunning, and so sad. To this day when I think back on those days, those are the events and impressions that con-tinue to sear me, and that I continue to remember most vividly."

It was on this very day, if we are to believe the scenario concoct-ed by GOP senators and passed on by eager reporters, that the Whitewater cover-up conspiracy began—orchestrated by the First Lady by telephone from her mother's home in Little Rock and carried out by Maggie Williams, Hillary's friend Susan Thomases, and Bernard Nussbaum.

Furthermore, we know all this, according to a July 23, 1995, front-page article in *The Washington Post,* because White House attorney Steve Neuwirth had tattled on Hillary. LAWYER SAYS HILLARY CLINTON URGED SEARCH LIMIT, read the *Post*'s headline. A next-day column by *The New York Times*'s William Safire alleged that Neuwirth "told congressional investigators that Susan Thomases, Hillary's confidant, told Nussbaum that the Clintons wanted the search [of Vince Foster's office] strictly limited."

Neuwirth opened his Senate testimony August 3 with a prepared statement. He explained that both articles were categorically false. Nussbaum, he said, had never told him anything about what either Susan Thomases or Hillary wanted. He read aloud a Q&A from his deposition, in which he had explicitly rejected the premise of a question implying such knowledge. "I don't know what Mrs. Thomases said," he'd stated.

Neuwirth testified that Nussbaum never told him he'd spoken to Hillary about the search. He had simply assumed that "the First Lady may have been concerned about anyone having unfettered access to Mr. Foster's office" basically because *every lawyer in the White House* was concerned about how to balance the legitimate interests of law enforcement, lawyer-client privilege, and the institution of the presidency itself. They realized that anything they did was apt to set an historical precedent. Indeed, Nussbaum's entire staff as well as Clinton aide Bruce Lindsey—also an attorney—had held a formal meeting about how to deal with the situation on the morning of July 22. All five lawyers who attended testified that the First Lady's opinion had been neither sought nor discussed.

Neuwirth didn't blame the reporters for getting the story backward, he added, because their sources—presumably GOP staffers—had misled them. But was it their sources, one wonders, who prevented Safire and *The Washington Post* from correcting their error? The author of the erroneous article in the *Post* was Jean Lewis's confidant, Susan Schmidt. Do you begin to sense a trend here?

In their own testimony, both Susan Thomases and Maggie Williams denied speaking with Hillary about searching Foster's office. So did Bernard Nussbaum. "I talked to a number of people about this issue as to how the search for a suicide note should be conducted," Nussbaum said. "But I did not speak to the President or the First Lady about this matter. Nor did Susan Thomases or anyone else convey a message to me from either one of them. . . . But I should say that I assumed from the outset of this tragedy that the First Lady—who's a very good lawyer—like any other good lawyer, in or out of the White House, would believe that permitting unfettered access to a lawyer's office is not proper."

Anyhow, why lie about it? Both as client and as president, Bill Clinton had every legitimate reason to concern himself with how the search of Foster's office was handled. So did Hillary.

During his testimony on August 9, Nussbaum made so bold as to challenge the very premises of the Senate hearings. The exact method of searching Foster's office on July 22, 1993, Nussbaum insisted, had never been the issue. "What prompted these hearings," Nussbaum said, "is something different. It is the unfair linkage of two separate, disparate events. The first event involved my transfer, in July 1993, of personal files—including a Whitewater file—to the Clintons' personal attorneys following Vince's death, a transfer which was totally proper and, indeed, known to Justice Department officials. The second separate, disparate event involves the emergence in the fall of 1993 of the Whitewater investigations and the resulting media frenzy. Linking these two events is illogical, unwarranted and unfair. They are totally unrelated."

Nussbaum may as well have stuck his finger in the eye of Howell Raines, *The New York Times* editorial-page editor. It had been Raines's strident editorials that raised the press pack's hackles about the Clintons' files, "presumptuously spirited from the office of the deputy White House counsel, Vincent Foster," to begin with. It was also Raines whose persistent attacks on Nussbaum helped create the climate in which the White House counsel was eventually forced to resign in early March 1994.

Not surprisingly, Nussbaum's remarks went unreported. He was too long-winded. More to the press's liking was Senator Richard Shelby of Alabama, who could always be relied upon to jump in with an accusation of precisely the ten- to fifteen-second duration appropriate for the evening news. He compared the White House counsel's actions to "the fox guarding the henhouse." "You did it your way," Shelby charged, "and the American people will never really know what was in there. . . . You didn't want the people to know, including the Justice Department of the United States of America."

Nussbaum responded by asking whether Shelby would object to police turning his own attorney's office inside out. The senator serenely countered that he had nothing to hide.

Another politician adept at generating sound bites was Senator Lauch Faircloth of North Carolina. In one memorable exchange, he scoffed that Maggie Williams couldn't possibly have forgotten the details of a two-year-old phone conversation with—as Faircloth drawled with wide-eyed incredulity—"the First Lady of the United States of America." As Hillary's chief of staff, of course, Williams talked to her every day.

The accusation Republicans tried to make the most of was that Williams herself had purged Foster's files. After five interviews with the FBI and the independent counsel, a uniformed Secret Service guard named Henry O'Neill thought he recalled seeing Williams carrying something—a stack of files, a hatbox—out of the White House counsel's suite on the night of Foster's death. Williams, crying at times, said that O'Neill was mistaken. She offered the results of two lie detector tests that supported her testimony. Besides differing with everybody else who testified about such basic matters as who was present in the White House that night, O'Neill hadn't recalled seeing Williams carrying anything down the hall to her office until *after* reading a speculative article in *The Washington Times*. The simplest explanation seemed to be that he'd confused the night of July 20 with July 22—when Williams *had* removed a box of Foster's personal effects to be taken to his family.

Senator Faircloth, however, was not to be denied. He was particularly scathing toward Hillary's friend Susan Thomases. In her testimony, Thomases denied that she'd relayed instructions from the First Lady to Nussbaum regarding the search of Foster's office. She and Hillary, she said, hadn't talked about it. Instead, they'd expressed their sorrow and tried to console each other. But Faircloth was having none of it. He read aloud in a mocking tone from a media account stressing Thomases's status as a White House insider: "James Carville says, 'Thomases has the juice.' Another, 'It's not that she has the juice. She *is* the juice. She is the juicer.'" Faircloth paused to allow laughter to subside, then continued. "Finally, the article says, 'She's Hillary's blunt instrument of enforcement. . . .' And then we go back to the calls to Bernie Nussbaum. I mean call, call, call, call, call, call. And you were discussing the weather, his general feelings, politeness, niceness, and all of a sudden you spill the juice, according to you. You no longer had it. Is that right?"

"That's right," Thomases answered after a few more questions in the same vein. "I didn't know the First Lady's opinion."

Amid such badgering, it took no great insight to realize that Thomases and Williams had clearly taken good advice from their lawyers. They testified firmly about what they *hadn't* discussed on the telephone in the two days after Foster's suicide. But they refused to be baited into detailed recountings of imperfectly recalled conversations that could open them to cross-examination of the Shelby-Faircloth variety.

Many in the press pack decided that they were lying. For months afterward, there was loose speculation in media accounts that Thomases and Williams would be charged with perjury. How anybody purported to prove that the women remembered what they said they didn't remember was left to readers' imaginations.

Newsweek columnist Joe Klein had a bit more sense than that. Almost alone in the media, he understood that the Clintons had every right to their own legal files. He also doubted, in the final analysis, that they'd committed any serious crimes. Even so, he put the blame for Maggie Williams's ordeal, not to mention the $140,000 she'd spent on legal fees, squarely on the President and First Lady. "They are the Tom and Daisy Buchanan of the Baby Boom Political Elite," wrote Klein. "The Buchanans, you may recall, were F. Scott Fitzgerald's crystallization of flapper feckless-ness in *The Great Gatsby*. They were 'careless' people. They smashed up lives and didn't know it. . . . From the start, aides pleaded with the Clintons to come clean—to release all relevant documents, answer all questions. They didn't."

But the public wasn't buying. The harder the pack flogged Whitewater during the summer of 1995, the more uninterested people seemed. A Louis Harris poll released on August 13 showed that only one in four adults who were aware of the congressional hearings thought less of President and Mrs. Clinton because of what they'd heard. Only 8 percent of Democrats felt that way, and 35 percent of Republicans. The majority appeared to think

Whitewater amounted to little more than partisan political posturing. But one thing was clear: if those in the press who had staked their career hopes on Whitewater expected to prevail, stronger measures would have to be taken.

No sooner had the Senate hearings closed than independent counsel Kenneth Starr made another timely move. A federal grand jury in Little Rock, his office announced on August 17, had handed down a twenty-one-count fraud and conspiracy indictment involving James B. and Susan McDougal and Arkansas Governor Jim Guy Tucker. A former state prosecutor and U.S. congressman, Tucker had lost two statewide elections to Bill Clinton. The independent counsel's office issued a statement stressing that the indictment "does not charge criminal wrongdoing by President William Jefferson Clinton or First Lady Hillary Rodham Clinton." The new indictments centered around accusations by convicted felon David Hale, the former municipal judge who had accused President Clinton of "pressuring" him to make an improper loan to Susan McDougal in April 1986. In a sworn RTC interrogatory, Clinton had said it never happened. The same allegedly "false and fraudulent" $300,000 loan constituted part of the indictment against both McDougals.

The circumstantial evidence clearly supports the President. The McDougals had used the $300,000, let us recall, partly to pay off personal debts and partly to purchase an 810-acre tract from International Paper. The IP transaction, in turn, had left the Whitewater Development Company stuck with a large debt but no corresponding asset. According to the Pillsbury Report, Jim McDougal had concealed it from the Clintons—just as he had obscured the manner in which the remaining Whitewater lots had been sold. Hence the idea that Clinton had "pressured" Hale to make a loan contrary to his own interests appeared very unlikely. It looked as if Hale, caught in a tight spot and ignorant of the facts, based his story partly on newspaper accounts.

Unlike the Clintons, Jim Guy Tucker had borrowed substantial sums from Madison Guaranty S&L. With the exception of a corporate loan at the heart of the indictment, however, he had also paid it back. Unlike Hillary's law firm, Tucker's had been Madison's principal counsel. When the Madison board of directors was served a "cease and desist" order ousting Jim McDougal by state and federal regulators in July 1986, one of Tucker's partners had been their attorney.

Jim Guy was a scrapper by nature. A Harvard graduate and an amateur pilot, for example, Tucker made his way to Vietnam as a journalist for *Stars and Stripes* after having been mustered out of the Marine Corps for medical reasons. He'd reacted to the indictment with fighting words. No way, Tucker insisted, would he plead guilty. He called Starr's action the "politically driven" product of a "taxpayer-funded invasion of Arkansas." "If you throw enough mud at somebody," Tucker said, "maybe you can make something stick. You file enough indictments against a whole bunch of people, perhaps some who are in fact culpable and include somebody who is not, maybe you'll get one of those to stick. . . . I have not been a part of any conspiracy between their captive witness, David Hale, or anyone else."

But it was the independent counsel's reliance on Hale that generated the most skepticism about the indictment in Little Rock. As a municipal judge who had rarely, if ever, convicted a rich man for DWI, Hale had long been known as a wheeler-dealer. Some of the more than $2 million he'd confessed to scamming from the Small Business Administration had come as a result of setting up thirteen dummy companies with the same mailing address as his own, making them federally guaranteed loans, defaulting, and keeping the cash. Yet everywhere you looked in the independent counsel's indictment of Tucker, it read, "Defendants JAMES B. MCDOUGAL AND JIM GUY TUCKER, and others known to the Grand Jury, including David L. Hale." Supposedly it had been all Jim Guy's idea for Hale to engage in a bunch of real estate flim-flams—none of which Tucker had participated in—in order to cheat the federal government out of $500,000. Then Tucker had borrowed the money from Hale's lending company, Capital Management Services, at interest. And paid it back.

To criminal defense lawyers in Little Rock, the indictment of Tucker made little sense on its face. The advantage of making it a *conspiracy* charge was obvious. By so doing, the prosecution could offer hearsay testimony from the likes of Hale that would otherwise have been excluded. The worst thing the indictment itself proved about Tucker was that he'd done business with Hale. (The Clintons never had.) Concerning the corporate loan Tucker hadn't repaid in full, he'd invested in a sewer company at one of McDougal's real estate developments that failed—taking the utility down with it. He had eventually negotiated repayment terms with the RTC. His lawyers were expected to argue that he had simply made a bad business deal. Take Hale's self-serving testimony out of the mix, and the governor almost looked like his victim, not his co-conspirator. Hale had to find *some* way to launder the cash he'd stolen from the government.

To a remarkable degree, the case seemed to hinge on the veracity of David Hale. If he could be impeached, it seemed to follow that the prosecution case would collapse. There wasn't a defense lawyer in Arkansas who didn't think he or she could tear Hale to pieces on cross-examination. Witnesses galore were available to describe him as a con man and a thief. Hale had been successfully sued by his former mistress for defrauding her grandparents out of the family farm. The judgment had come to $486,496. More recently he'd been accused by the Arkansas insurance commissioner of looting a burial insurance company he'd acquired during the 1980s.

Thereupon hung a revealing little tale. As Tucker's trial approached in early 1996, his lawyers charged that Kenneth Starr's office was hiding evidence favorable to their client. Specifically, they alleged, the independent counsel had intervened to prevent Pulaski County (Little Rock) prosecutor Mark Stodola from receiving evidence against Hale in the alleged looting of the insurance company. The case predated Starr's arrival in Little Rock. Starr's office denied interfering.

But U.S. Judge George Howard compelled the independent counsel's office to turn over a letter from Little Rock Police Chief Louis Caudell to Kenneth Starr. Tucker's lawyers released it to the press. "The investigative portion of this case," Caudell advised, "has been completed for some time; however, at your office's request we have postponed presenting this file for prosecutorial decision. . . . I am now requesting any advice you have in how to proceed in this matter."

Evidently a formidable bureaucratic infighter, Chief Caudell appears to have wanted Starr to know that he had no intention of taking blame if the independent counsel's coddling of Hale became public knowledge. To cover its tracks, Starr's office trotted out Sam Dash, a Washington friend who had served as Democratic counsel during the Watergate hearings twenty-three years ago. Hired as an "ethics consultant" by Starr, he put the best face on things. Dash charged that Stodola had gotten political pressure to press state felony charges against Hale.

Stodola took exception, pointing out that Dash had been flown in by the independent counsel to argue against charging Hale. According to the Little Rock press, Dash then implied that Stodola could be charged with obstructing justice—for performing his constitutional duties. When Stodola announced that he would indeed prosecute David Hale after the McDougal-Tucker trial, *The Washington Post*'s Susan Schmidt produced a story quoting former Attorney General Griffin Bell to that effect. Conservative commentators led by Robert Novak argued that it was all a dastardly plot to terrify poor Hale into going easy on President Clinton. Possibly Griffin Bell was unaware that the state prosecution would *follow* both Hale's federal sentencing and his testimony in federal court. Schmidt's story implied otherwise. Nor did her story make any reference to a letter Stodola sent to Starr as well as to her, noting that he saw "no overlap between Hale's felony state insurance law violation and his crimes against the federal government."

Starr was reported to be angry nevertheless. "It is not logical to presume," Stodola had written to him, "that uncharged, unacknowledged criminal conduct on the part of Mr. Hale will be punished, particularly in light of your plea agreement with Hale which requires that you recommend leniency to the Federal Court in exchange for his cooperation.... The two legal positions are impossibly in conflict with each other." Not to charge Hale, Stodola argued, would be inconsistent with his oath of office. He pointed out that parallel federal and state prosecutions went on in his jurisdiction all the time.

Either way, it hardly seemed to matter to Starr's national political ambitions. By indicting the Arkansas governor, he appeared to have put himself into a win-win position. If he convicted Jim Guy Tucker, he'd be a made man in the Republican Party. If not, his cheerleaders in the press pack could be counted on to blame Arkansas, with its corrupt and incestuous political culture.

As crazy as it may sound, everything went Governor Tucker's way at his 1996 trial except the verdict. The judge dismissed four of eleven felony counts for lack of evidence. As anticipated, David Hale made a terrible witness. Among other absurdities, he even admitted telling falsehoods to the judge who'd accepted his guilty plea. Jurors later said they trusted President Clinton's categorical denial that he'd had any knowledge of Hale's crimes.

But Clinton's videotaped testimony had no direct relevance to Tucker's case. Jim Guy's lawyers may have blundered when they put on no active defense. All but discarding Hale's testimony, the jurors cleared Tucker of five additional charges. But his extensive dealings with Hale and McDougal may have doomed him. McDougal was found guilty on eighteen counts; Susan McDougal, on four. Was Tucker the only virgin in the whorehouse? The jury convicted him on two counts stemming from his sewer-company investment: he'd filed loan applications listing one business purpose, spent the proceeds on another—no major crime, but enough to ruin Tucker and keep the independent counsel in business.

B y late autumn 1995, the revived Senate Whitewater hearings had begun to resemble an absurdist mini-drama. Since the closing of the previous round of hearings, Alfonse D'Amato had begun to take seriously the notion of a conspiracy around Vince Foster's death. Indeed D'Amato's flirtation with the nut right ended up recapitulating the entire Whitewater saga in miniature—including the roguish antics of the two Arkansas state troopers whose tall tales had helped get the whole thing started.

The farcical episode that one is tempted to call "Troopergate 2" began on April 9, 1995, with a story in the London *Sunday Telegraph* by Ambrose Evans-Pritchard. The White House, it alleged, had falsified both the time and place of Vince Foster's death. According to Arkansas state trooper Roger Perry, of "Troopergate 1" fame, a young woman named Helen Dickey had telephoned the

Governor's Mansion in Little Rock at 6:15 P.M. to inform the staff of Foster's death. Perry had been on duty and had taken the call.

At the very least, Evans-Pritchard wrote, that meant somebody in the Clinton administration had known about Foster's death several hours before the Park Police notified the Secret Service at 8:20 P.M. Even more ominously, Foster's body had clearly been moved. Helen Dickey, trooper Perry said, "was kind of hysterical, crying, real upset. She told me that 'Vince got off work, went to his car in the parking lot, and shot himself in the head.'" Furthermore, Perry's story had been confirmed by—you guessed it—trooper Larry Patterson, the other half of the infamous duo who had told the press back around Christmas 1993 that they'd pimped for Governor Bill Clinton. Upon hearing Helen Dickey's tearful story, see, Perry had rung up his old drinking buddy Patterson right away.

"Dickey, a former nanny to Chelsea Clinton," the *Sunday Telegraph* explained, "is a member of the tight-knit 'Arkansas group.' She refused to answer queries about the alleged call to the Governor's Mansion. . . . If the White House received an early warning about Foster's death, why would it have been covered up? One explanation is that a tip-off could have provided a window of time for pre-emptive moves."

Within days, a reprint of Evans-Pritchard's article was published in a full-page ad in *The Washington Times*. The ad was paid for by an outfit called the Western Journalism Center, which urged readers to purchase a videotape entitled "Unanswered: The Death of Vincent Foster," by "award-winning journalist" Christopher Ruddy.[2] On June 15, Ruddy himself weighed in with his own version of "Troopergate 2" in the *Pittsburgh Tribune-Review*, a newspaper of sorts financed by reclusive billionaire Richard Mellon-Scaife. Soon enough, the Internet was buzzing with con-

---

[2] For the farcical nature of Ruddy's "investigation" of Foster's suicide, see *60 Minutes*, October 8, 1995. Didn't fiber evidence on Foster's suit indicate that his body had been rolled in a carpet and moved to Ft. Marcy Park? No, it showed the FBI that Foster's wife, Lisa, had recently installed new carpets in their home. Ruddy also made a great to-do about why the fatal weapon was found in Foster's right hand, since he was left-handed. However, as *60 Minutes* showed, Foster was right-handed. And so on.

spiracy scenarios; letters and faxes began to pour into the offices of senators on the Whitewater committee.

By August, columnist John Crudele of the *New York Post* had taken it upon himself to offer Senator D'Amato a little free advice. "Perry telling his story, followed by Betty Tucker confirming it, followed by Helen Dickey explaining the call would make a great closing act to an otherwise tedious melodrama."

Next, *The Wall Street Journal* editorial page bought into the story. "Troopergate 2" appeared to be inching closer and closer to the respectable press. D'Amato could apparently resist no longer. In a live interview on WCBS radio in New York on September 13, the senator vowed to get to the bottom of the mystery. The Whitewater committee, D'Amato announced, intended to subpoena Helen Dickey. The White House released a sworn affadavit from Miss Dickey to the effect that she had, indeed, phoned the Governor's Mansion and spoken briefly with trooper Perry on the night Vince Foster died—except that the call had been made after 10 P.M. Nor had Dickey said anything about any White House parking lot.

On cue, independent counsel Kenneth Starr sent FBI agents to search Ft. Marcy Park with metal detectors for the third time. According to a *Newsday* account of his WCBS interview, D'Amato insinuated that Foster had been murdered. "It's impossible for that gun to be found in his hand after the discharge," the senator said. "It would have been kicked back and the gun would have jumped out. Yet here it is in his hand by his body. How do you explain that?" Independent counsel Robert Fiske's June 30, 1994, report had already explained it in compelling detail.[3]

---

[3] "After firing," the report concluded, "the trigger of Foster's gun rebounds forward. Based on analysis of scene photographs and an autopsy photograph showing a mark on Foster's right thumb, the Pathologists Panel and FBI ballistic experts concluded that Foster's thumb was 'trapped and compressed' between the trigger and the trigger guard of the gun. This conclusion is corroborated by the statement of Park Police Technician Peter Simonello who removed the gun from Foster's hand. He stated that Foster's knuckle initially prevented him from removing the gun from Foster's hand. As a result, Simonello half cocked the gun causing the trigger to be pulled back. Only then could Simonello remove the gun." One needn't be a ballistics expert, moreover, to know that given a .38 revolver's range and the uncertainties of angle and velocity, chances of recovering the fatal bullet had never been good. Starr was merely grandstanding.

But it wasn't until February 14, 1996, that the sad little farce came to a predictable end when Helen Dickey testified before the Whitewater committee. A White House usher, she said, had told her of Foster's suicide shortly after she'd watched Bill Clinton being interviewed on *Larry King Live* that night.

"Vince Foster was very close to our family," she said. "[We] lived next door to them in Little Rock. It was a very personal thing for me. I immediately began to cry and became hysterical." Dickey phoned her mother and father, then wandered around the White House in a daze. She found the President, who told her the circumstances in which Foster's body had been found. Only then did she think to call the Governor's Mansion. She didn't want Foster's friends there to learn of his death on the news.

After Dickey's testimony, Senator D'Amato was abjectly apologetic. He explained that the young woman had been brought forward only at the request of the Democrats. Thousands of letters and phone calls had come in to the committee about Perry and Patterson's latest revelations. After all, would two sworn law officers actually tell falsehoods about so grave a topic? "Senator Sarbanes," he said, "suggested that we attempt to deal with this in a public way. So I would think that what we've attempted to do is to bring some facts and less of this wild speculation—the kind of thing that, you know, fuels the fire."

And where were troopers Perry and Patterson, the sworn law officers whose manly candor had so impressed *The American Spectator,* the *L.A. Times,* and CNN two years earlier? It turned out that when Senate investigators moved to subpoena their work records and time sheets for the day in question, their attorney told Democratic counsel Richard Ben-Veniste, "Well, maybe the troopers didn't want to testify after all."

Within days, however, Roger Perry was telling the tale to a shocked Reverend Pat Robertson on *The 700 Club.* There is, of course, no such thing as a perjury charge on an evangelical talk show. Former trooper Larry Patterson, meanwhile, was reportedly traveling around Arkansas with our old friend Larry Nichols, conducting a private investigation. They liked people to think it was somehow related to Kenneth Starr's. Remember Nichols? He's the guy who worked for the Nicaraguan Contras when he was supposed to be working for the state of Arkansas. The guy who filed a bogus lawsuit with a bimbo list, then took it all back and apologized. The same guy who narrated "The Clinton Chronicles" tape, which accuses President Clinton of being a drug addict and a murderer.

Now, you may ask yourself why you are reading about this instructive little episode for the first time. Because the London *Sunday Telegraph,* the *Pittsburgh Tribune-Review,* and the *New York Post* weren't about to withdraw the allegation, and the official press never reported it in the first place. So what if Senator D'Amato had called in another false alarm? That was hardly news.

Although the second round of Whitewater hearings, which began in November 1995, had very little more substance than "Troopergate 2," they were endorsed by the establishment press. First, armed with detailed telephone records, Republican senators had yet another go at Maggie Williams and Susan Thomases. Republican staffers produced, and *The New York Times* dutifully reproduced, a list of telephone calls between and among these alleged conspirators that established beyond a reasonable doubt that they had, indeed, spoken with each other several times during the day and a half between the discovery of Foster's body and the search of his office. The sequence of calls—Thomases had paged Nussbaum soon after talking with Hillary Clinton—was alleged to be suspicious.

"It's difficult to believe," said D'Amato, "[that] all of these calls were the result of touching, feeling, holding." Senator Lauch Faircloth denounced Williams's and Thomases's testimony as "an insult to this committee." He demanded that Hillary Clinton be called in and grilled under oath. D'Amato cautiously declined.

The *Times*'s Stephen Labaton, meanwhile, left no doubt which side he was on. "The memory lapses and inconsistencies by Miss Williams and Ms. Thomases," he wrote, "left both women open to repeated attacks from . . . Republicans on the Committee." What Democrats had to say readers would have to guess. Labaton's November 3 story offered no hint. For days, indeed weeks, at a time, no Democrat on the committee asked a question or made an observation worthy of notice in *The New York Times.*

How crazy things had gotten may be inferred from Labaton's account: "Ms. Thomases could not explain with precision a series of telephone calls to the White House and to Mrs. Clinton. The explanations she offered occasionally collided with her earlier testimony. For instance, she testified last summer that she had not decided that she would not attend Mr. Foster's funeral until late on July 22. But today she said she had told Mrs. Clinton she would not be attending the funeral in a call she had received from Mrs. Clinton in Little Rock very early on the 22nd."

Not to be picky about it, but the *Times* account itself collided directly with the hearing transcript. In August, Susan Thomases had explained that the President had offered her a ride to Little Rock on *Air Force One.* But her multiple sclerosis made that a bad idea. Hot weather made her woozy, and she feared the brutal Arkansas sun. After thinking it over, Thomases had phoned Maggie Williams shortly after 5:00 P.M. to decline. "As much as I wanted to be at Vince's funeral . . . ," she'd testified, "I felt it would just be signing up for sickness. It would be just not a sensible, prudent thing for me to do."

During Thomases's November 2 testimony, Senator Robert Bennett of Utah pressed her about a phone conversation she'd had with Hillary Clinton early on the morning of July 22. The GOP hypothesis was that it was then that they'd hatched a plot to thwart the search of Foster's office. But did Thomases testify, as the *Times* reported, that she'd told Hillary that morning that she wouldn't be attending the funeral? She did not. "I don't remember the details of the conversation," she said, "but . . . it was at that point that I believe I first raised with her the *possibility* that I didn't feel well enough to go to Little Rock [my emphasis], and I told her that I would get back to someone before the end of the day and confirm that decision."

Contrary to the *Times,* then, Thomases's November 2 testimony was perfectly consistent with what she'd said in August. In Labaton's defense, it would have been perfectly understandable if he had fallen asleep. Nevertheless, it was now official: Thomases had testified falsely. It would henceforth be incumbent upon reporters to snicker knowingly at the mention of her name.

Within a week, D'Amato's melodrama had descended to its nadir. By the time former Treasury Secretary Lloyd Bentsen appeared on November 7, the committee had embarked upon an investigation of an investigation of an investigation.

Here's the deal: back in 1993, there had been a flurry of contacts between and among White House and Treasury Department officials regarding the RTC's probe of Madison Guaranty. Independent counsel Robert Fiske concluded that no laws had been broken. Even so, Secretary Bentsen ordered an inquiry by the inspectors general of the RTC and Treasury to determine whether any ethical improprieties had taken place. For example: Had information been given to any suspects that would enable them to clean house? Had the White House done anything to discourage the RTC probe? Data gathered was then analyzed by the independent Office of Government Ethics. It, too, concluded that nothing improper had been done. Senate Banking Committee hearings in the summer of 1994 had already aired the matter exhaustively—much to the embarrassment of former Treasury Secretary Roger Altman and two aides who had been forced to resign as a consequence.

Now came the D'Amato committee's charge that the OGE probe of the RTC probe had been flawed because White House counsel Lloyd Cutler had been allowed to use staffers' sworn depositions in the course of his *own* internal probe in July 1994. The idea was that Cutler had conspired with witnesses to tailor their testimony to Congress. D'Amato, of course, professed to find it all "deeply troubling." Both formal investigations were over and done with, however, before Cutler's began. All witnesses had long ago made sworn statements to both the inspector general and independent counsel Fiske. How much tailoring, after all, could be done with two depositions already on the record? The Whitewater committee staff, it emerged during Secretary Bentsen's testimony, had taken thirty *more* depositions without a single allegation that any of the previous investigations had been compromised.

Cutler pointed out that his inquiry was preceded by a joint

press conference with Bentsen on June 30, 1994. "If Secretary Bentsen and I were secret co-conspirators, as has been alleged," he said, "it was certainly inept on our part to tell the world what we were planning to do. . . . The criminal investigation, I remind you, was over, with no criminal charge brought."

Three days and fifteen witnesses later, the Senate investigation of the Treasury Department and White House investigations of the RTC's investigation of the Clintons ended exactly where it had begun: nowhere. The stage was appropriately set for the triumphal return of L. Jean Lewis.

Given her incoherent performance at the House Whitewater hearings, putting Jean Lewis back at the witness table was an act of either pure desperation or sheer folly—or would have been if there had been any chance Lewis's reporter pals at *The New York Times* and *The Washington Post* would fail to cover for her once again. Which, of course, there was not.

To anybody familiar with her House testimony, however, Lewis's opening statement on November 29 was a dazzling piece of effrontery. Seemingly rapt with conviction, Lewis told precisely the same tale of heroic perseverence and patriotic grit: Her investigation of Madison Guaranty had been stifled and harassed at every turn. She accused RTC lawyers of "obstructing" her quest for seven long days. She complained that U.S. Attorney Paula Casey had stalled for two entire weeks, then rejected her 1992 referral—"in direct conflict with information I had received from the Justice Department in Washington and the U.S. Attorney's Office." She charged that April Breslaw had come to her office "to deliver a message that 'the people at the top would like to be able to say Whitewater did not cause a loss to Madison'"—a quote that Lewis had been caught misrepresenting during her House testimony.[4]

Lewis said bluntly that Whitewater had caused a loss to

---

[4] In one of his endearing bursts of candor, Senator D'Amato apologized to Julie Yanda, the RTC attorney whom Lewis accused of obstruction (for, among other things, pointing out the futility of investigating a dead man). Perhaps weary of Republican badgering, April Breslaw chose an odd means of defiance. During her appearance before the Senate committee, she played possum, declaring that she couldn't be sure it was her voice on Jean Lewis's famous tape.

Madison and that the Clintons had profited from it—statements for which she provided no evidence nor ever had. "But if the committee wants to know what the Clintons knew about the corrupt activities resulting in losses to Madison," she ended with a defiant little smirk, "why not invite the Clintons to testify as I am today and have in the past? Why not ask them directly?"

The Clintons, of course, had already answered detailed written interrogatories under oath. The White House had released them to the press back in August. They had also both given sworn testimony to the independent counsel. But who could expect Jean Lewis to know things like that? She evidently didn't read the newspapers, not even newspaper articles about herself. (Although oddly enough, she did cite media accounts as evidence against others.) She supposedly didn't know, for example, that U.S. Attorney Charles Banks had turned her 1992 referral down cold. She had no idea that the Justice Department and FBI had exchanged letters and reports debunking her evidence and motives; months earlier, excerpts had been printed in *The Wall Street Journal* and other newspapers.

When Democrats brought those facts to her attention, Lewis reacted dramatically. But before that happened, Democratic counsel Richard Ben-Veniste had a few nasty political tricks up his sleeve. First he confronted her with an FBI agent's contemporaneous notes to the effect that—contrary to her deposition—she'd begun pestering him about her 1992 referral within days of filing it and had made "very dramatic" pronouncements about altering history. There had been similar testimony from the U.S. Attorney's staff. Evidence showed Lewis had made a minimum of eight attempts to prod the thing along before the 1992 election. In her deposition, she'd sworn she'd made none.

Next, Ben-Veniste produced an aside from a February 1992 personal letter Lewis had written—that is, immediately before she launched her probe of Madison Guaranty. She thought she'd deleted it from a computer disk she'd given the committee, but Democrats retrieved it. A dirty trick? You bet. About on the level of secretly tape-recording colleagues, most people would say. In the missive, Lewis had mocked "the illustrious Governor Bill

Clinton" as a "lying bastard" who'd put his mistress Gennifer Flowers on the state payroll.

Senator Barbara Boxer produced a November 1993 letter from Lewis to an attorney in which Lewis had floated a proposal to market "Presidential BITCH" T-shirts and coffee mugs mocking Hillary Clinton. She had listed her RTC office as her business phone. "Being a woman of basically the same ilk and same type," Lewis countered, "I mean that not as disrespect. . . . I have tremendous admiration for the fact that she is a strong woman." She added that she personally had absolutely no objection to being called a bitch. Ben-Veniste also questioned Lewis about her magical tape recorder. He asked whether it wasn't really the truth that she had bought a brand-new tape recorder specifically for the purpose of sandbagging April Breslaw.

"I purchased that new recorder well after I had that conversation with Ms. Breslaw," Lewis answered. "As I have previously testified, the old one worked sometimes. It didn't sometimes. It was eight years old. . . . I did not deliberately set out, which I believe is your inference, to tape Ms. Breslaw."

But it wasn't until Democrats laid out documents casting doubt on her competence and integrity that Lewis lost it.[5] Senator Paul Sarbanes read to her U.S. Attorney Charles Banks's letter concluding that to act upon her 1992 referral would constitute "prosecutorial misconduct." No sooner had Sarbanes begun to question Lewis about a negative Justice Department appraisal of her work when an amazing thing happened. Lewis shook visibly, tears welled in her eyes, and she collapsed at the witness table. Although she managed to leave the Senate chamber on her feet, Lewis had to be hospitalized overnight and treated for high blood pressure. She never returned. Her Whitewater adventure was over, and not a moment too soon. By any rational standard, her appearance had been an absolute disaster.

SENATE HEARING TOUCHES ON CLINTON'S INTEGRITY, read the headline in *The New York Times*. A LINE OF INQUIRY BACKFIRES ON THE

---

[5] No big surprise. During pre-hearing depositions, she'd vomited when minority staff questioned her.

DEMOCRATS. To Stephen Labaton, the most significant event of the day had been the mention of Gennifer Flowers. As previously, no indications of any weaknesses either in Lewis's work or her testimony were reported. Her "Presidential BITCH" proposal merited no mention. Even Lewis's collapse escaped the *Times*'s notice. "Other Democrats," Labaton wrote, "looked pained by Mr. Ben-Veniste's introduction of the letter and Ms. Flowers into the record. . . . Republicans wasted little time in responding. Referring to the letter's conclusions regarding Mr. Clinton and Ms. Flowers, Senator Richard C. Shelby of Alabama, for instance, said, 'Mr. Chairman, what Ms. Lewis said, I'm sure millions of others believe it.'"

On December 6, the *Times* delivered yet another stinging Whitewater editorial demanding to know "why Mr. McDougal absorbed a hugely disproportionate share of Whitewater's losses." During recent hearings, the newspaper said, "Jean Lewis, a star witness . . . and a government investigator into Madison's practices, repeated her charge that there had been a deliberate effort at both the Justice and Treasury departments to obstruct her inquiry. Ms. Lewis has said flatly that the Clintons knew about and improperly benefited from Madison's freewheeling practices. . . . Why not come forward with the complete story?"

The Clintons, it seemed, were still "acting guilty."

Also on December 6, Richard Ben-Veniste read into the hearings record a status report in the matter of Jean Lewis's magical tape recorder. "Obviously it was important to us," he said, "to learn whether she had purchased the tape recorder prior to the Breslaw meeting, or, as she had contended, whether she purchased it afterwards."

To support her story, Lewis's attorney had sent the committee a receipt dated February 17, 1994—two weeks after the surreptitious recording. A call to her friendly neighborhood Office Depot outlet, however, had shown that the receipt wasn't for a tape recorder. "So yesterday," Ben-Veniste said, "we issued some subpoenas. And we received from Office Depot a receipt which reflects that on January 17, 1994, an Olympus Pearlcorder Model S-924 was purchased by Ms. Lewis. . . . In fact, the new tape recorder was purchased then, in advance of her meeting with Ms. Breslaw. Which would then call into question why—if she had a new tape recorder—would the Breslaw conversation be taped by an old tape recorder?" A less lawyerly mind than Ben-Veniste's might have concluded that Lewis had fabricated the entire tale. *The New York Times* and *The Washington Post*, however, didn't think you needed to know.

B y December, Senate Republicans had backed themselves into a tight spot. For all the help the Whitewater committee was getting from the Washington press, their vaunted probe was getting nowhere, and very slowly. The hearing room was almost devoid of spectators; demand for hearing transcripts was so small that the Federal News Service quit providing continuous coverage.

In the sport of beagling, there exists a phenomenon known as "ghost trailing." Sometimes a hound who gets into faster company than he can handle will ignore the pack and find a rabbit of his own to pursue at a more stately pace. Every once in a while, that rabbit will prove to be imaginary. Other dogs will honor the claim a time or two but, finding no fresh scent line, will henceforth ignore the faker no matter how loudly he bays. In the sport of Whitewater, it didn't appear to matter how much "ghost trailing" Senator D'Amato's committee did, and they had done a great deal of it. During November, there was the so-called mystery call to an unlisted number made by Hillary Rodham Clinton on the night of Vince Foster's death. After weeks of public speculation by GOP sleuths—D'Amato hinted darkly about the CIA—the call turned out to have been made to a White House trunk line no longer in existence. The First Lady had called the office of Mack McLarty, the presidential assistant who'd also attended elementary school with Foster.

When former Clinton lawyer Robert Barnett testified on December 11 about Whitewater files once stored in Webb Hubbell's basement, Republicans called it a "smoking gun" that confirmed a cover-up. But Hubbell had testified about the same files the previous July. *The New York Times* had written an editorial about it. The committee itself had taken possession of the files soon after it came into existence.

Later in December, D'Amato began snuffling and howling over

several pages of notes taken by Clinton aide William Kennedy at a November 5, 1993, meeting. Having learned about Jean Lewis's probe through the newspapers a few days earlier, White House staffers had met with the Clintons' own lawyers to decide what to do. The White House announced that it was willing to hand over the notes, but not without a formal agreement that by so doing the President would not be forfeiting attorney-client privilege.

It was a far from trivial concern. For obvious reasons, judges normally don't let people play with the privilege. Give it up, and it's gone. It's not permissible to show self-serving evidence and hide the rest. The White House didn't want to produce the notes, then find the independent counsel trying to force the Clintons' private attorneys to testify about their conversations. And anybody who thinks Kenneth Starr wouldn't do that hasn't been paying attention. With their customary lack of evidence, Republicans predicted that the notes would show the White House tampering with the investigation. Accompanied by melodramatic babbling in the press about a "constitutional confrontation," Republicans forced the issue to the Senate floor on a straight party-line vote.

Even the *Times*'s Stephen Labaton, a lawyer by training, found it all a bit much. The battle over Kennedy's notes "is a considerable political gamble," he wrote on December 15, "both for the White House and for Senate Republicans. . . . Among some Republicans, who have no idea what is in the material being sought, the fear is that it will produce no bombshells and will thus make the Senators who fought for its release look foolish and unfairly intrusive into the affairs of the Clintons." Labaton added that "the White House's aggressive resistance to releasing the material has also led Republicans to wonder whether the Clinton aides discussed embarrassing facts related to Whitewater that investigators are so far unaware of, although they admit they have no basis for that belief."

Just before Christmas, the White House got its agreement on attorney-client privilege and turned over Kennedy's notes. And what happened next? A sheaf of press clippings released along with the notes demonstrated that the White House lawyers had discussed almost nothing about the probe that hadn't already appeared in the newspapers. What few insights they did have they appeared to have deduced from reporters' questions.

Nevertheless, D'Amato ran straight to the TV cameras to allege that the phrase "Vacuum—Rose Law Firm files" indicated a cover-up. Kennedy gave a statement to the effect that "vacuum" was a descriptive noun, not a transitive verb. Reporters covering Whitewater had to know that, from the Clintons' accountant to L. Jean Lewis, everybody who'd tried to make sense of Jim McDougal's business records had ended up scratching their heads. To my knowledge no media account ever provided proper context.

But nobody really bought D'Amato's scenario anyway. Consider the sheer improbability: six high-dollar Washington lawyers (three from the White House, three from Williams & Connolly) meeting *for the first time* conspiring to hide evidence in a federal investigation of the President of the United States, *writing it down, and keeping the notes*. Indeed, the only useful information to emerge from the entire fiasco was a blow to conspiracy theorists. "VF suicide—David Hale investigation—same day," William Kennedy had written. Some reports questioned whether that didn't show the White House was secretly concerned over a link it had long denied. Kennedy explained that his reference had been to the way conspiracy theories about Vince Foster's death were driving Whitewater coverage. Press clips appended to the notes showed that deep thinkers in the media had already made the connection. But it wouldn't be until William Kennedy testified on January 16, 1996, that the real significance of the passage became clear.

The press, readers may not be astonished to learn, had bungled the story in the first place. *The FBI hadn't searched David Hale's office on the day of Vince Foster's death, but one day later on July 21, 1993.* Did the conspiracy theory tumble?

Don't be foolish. Nobody reported it.

Then D'Amato got real lucky. Thanks to a good guess, a couple of unaccountable White House screw-ups, and one of the most extraordinarily mendacious campaigns of personal vilification in the recent history of American journalism, Whitewater was soon back on the front page.

Unable to pin anything on the President and make it stick, Republican inquisitors went after his wife. Within a matter of weeks, and with the assiduous help of the press, Kenneth Starr hauled the First Lady before the Whitewater grand jury. Stand-up comics began adding her talent for prevarication to Bill Clinton's legendary appetite for bimbos and Big Macs, and her poll ratings sank to record lows. To hype its excerpt from James B. Stewart's book on Whitewater, *Blood Sport, Time* magazine ran a cover photo of Hillary that looked like a poster for INTERVIEW WITH THE VAMPIRE: THE WASHINGTON YEARS.

How it happened is another of those stories within a story that recapitulates the entire Whitewater saga in miniature. Senate Republicans, understand, knew that the RTC was about to release a second, more conclusive volume of the Pillsbury Report in mid-December. It would deal with the Whitewater Development Company and the Clintons' liability for Madison Guaranty losses. The remaining parts of the $3.6 million study, moreover, would quickly follow. With the RTC due to go permanently out of business at the end of 1995, Pillsbury, Madison & Sutro was under a contractual obligation to deliver the report before then.

With the aid of the Clintons' sworn interrogatories, interviews with forty-five other witnesses, and some 200,000 documents, Pillsbury, Madison & Sutro's December 13 report concluded that the President and First Lady had told the truth about Whitewater all along: the Clintons were passive investors who lost money and were kept in the dark about the real status of the project by Jim McDougal. The report failed to challenge their account on a single substantive point, and every last one of Jean Lewis's reckless guesses had been proven false.

"The evidence suggests," the Supplementary Report concluded, "that the McDougals and not the Clintons managed Whitewater. The evidence does not suggest that the Clintons had managerial control over the enterprise, or received annual reports or regular financial summaries. Instead, and as the Clintons suggest, their main contact with Whitewater seems to have consisted of signing loan extensions or renewals."

It wasn't clear that Whitewater had cost the taxpayers a dime.

But if it had, the Clintons weren't liable for it. "There is no basis to assert," the report added, "that the Clintons knew anything of substance about the McDougals' advances to Whitewater, the source of the funds used to make those advances or the source of the funds used to make payments on the bank debt." As for any wrongdoing, "there is no basis to charge the Clintons with any kind of primary liability for fraud or intentional misconduct. This investigation has revealed no evidence to support any such claims. Nor would the record support any claim of secondary or derivative liability for the possible misdeeds of others. . . . There is evidence that the McDougals and others may have engaged in intentional misconduct. There are legal theories by which one can become liable for the conduct of others—e.g. conspiracy and aiding and abetting. On this evidentiary record, however, these theories have no application to the Clintons."

The Wall Street Journal's Novak and Pollock wrote a clear, objective summary of the Supplementary Report's findings on December 18. But what about the other reporters who'd staked their credibility and career hopes on Whitewater? *The Washington Post* stuck a brief mention of the Supplementary Report's existence into the eleventh paragraph of a story devoted to the subpoena battle over William Kennedy's notes.

The New York Times waited until Christmas Eve, then stuck Stephen Labaton's perfunctory summary back on page 12. Judging by the article's dismissive tone, readers could hardly guess that the Pillsbury Report conclusively answered almost every one of the thunderous rhetorical questions *Times* editorial writers had been asking for two years, most recently on December 6. Labaton's story ignored all of the specific passages dealing with the Clintons. "The report noted," Labaton concluded, "that its authors had been unable to interview a number of important witnesses, some of whom have been cooperating with the Whitewater independent counsel. It said its conclusions did not demonstrate that the transactions at issue 'have been proved legitimate or that the evidence exonerates anyone; it simply means that no basis has been found to sue anyone, or in some instances that litigation would be cost-effective.' "

Specifically, neither the McDougals nor David Hale had been interviewed. The disclaimer Labaton quoted occurs on page 3; it refers to transactions that the report concludes the Clintons had no knowledge of and in which they played no part. The *Times* version had approximately the intellectual honesty of a *Pravda* article on the Hitler-Stalin pact.

The demonization of Hillary Rodham Clinton, meanwhile, had already begun. It had started in a front-page story in *The New York Times* on December 19, 1995. Written by Labaton, it centered on time sheets detailing the First Lady's legal work for Madison Guaranty. Mentioned in notes taken by Susan Thomases during the 1992 Clinton campaign, the time sheets had been mislaid. Since the *Times* had already done its bit to turn Thomases into a suspect character, focusing on her role was natural.

In the real world, Hillary's time sheets were of dubious importance. The great majority of the data they contained was readily available through other sources. Indeed, their contents, when they finally materialized, only served to buttress Pillsbury, Madison & Sutro's ultimate conclusion that her legal representation of Madison S&L had involved no improprieties. The RTC investigators issued one final report on February 25, 1996, making that unequivocally clear. But the pattern of Whitewater accusations had grown as predictable as the tides. Like medieval cartographers populating unknown oceans with sea serpents and dragons, GOP inquisitors invariably predicted, and the press rarely doubted, that just over the horizon lay the damning evidence that would bring the Clintons down. A little creativity with mere facts, therefore, only served a higher cause.

But what clearly had persuaded *Times* editors to put the latest accusations on the front page wasn't that they involved the First Lady. It was their gravity. In no uncertain terms, Labaton's story laid out a case for two felonies: perjury and obstruction of justice. Not only had somebody gotten rid of the time sheets but Hillary had lied under oath to Whitewater investigators.

Labaton recounted once again Jim McDougal's foolish tale that Bill Clinton had jogged by Madison's office to solicit legal business for Hillary because the couple needed the cash. Other

Madison officials, the story claimed, had affirmed it. (Purely by double hearsay about what McDougal said Clinton had said a year after the fact, the paper neglected to add.) But the real force of the accusation against Hillary concerned her former colleague Rick Massey. "Mrs. Clinton said in a sworn statement this year," Labaton wrote, "that Mr. Massey, then a first year associate at the Rose firm, had been contacted by a friend at Madison, John Latham, with a request for legal help. . . . Mr. Massey, who is now a partner at the Rose firm, told Federal investigators he 'does not know how or why Madison selected the Rose Law Firm,' according to a summary of his October 1994 interview with the Federal Deposit Insurance Corporation."

As always, the *Times* story set the parameters. But a really astounding bit of journalistic malpractice occurred on *Nightline* that same night. In introducing Whitewater as a topic, host Ted Koppel dutifully cited "the reluctance of the Clinton White House to be as forthcoming with documents as it promised to be" and the "appalling memory lapses" of Susan Thomases. Then he turned to reporter Jeff Greenfield, who posed a rhetorical question and answered it. "Hillary Clinton did some legal work for Madison Guaranty at the Rose Law Firm, at a time when her husband was governor of Arkansas," he said. "How much work? Not much at all, she has said."

On the screen came file footage of the First Lady from her April 22, 1994, Whitewater press conference. "The young attorney, the young bank officer, did all the work," she said. "It was not an area that I practiced in. It was not an area that I know anything, to speak of, about." The camera cut to a close-up of Thomases's handwritten notes, blown up onscreen. "She did all the billing," they read. Greenfield treated it as a damning revelation. No wonder, he concluded, that "the White House was so worried about what was in Vince Foster's office when he killed himself."

What viewers didn't know, however, was that the *Nightline* story had been greatly enhanced by the magic of computerized editing. Greenfield had seamlessly removed exactly thirty-nine words from what the First Lady had actually said. The transcript of her April 1994 press conference reads as follows: "The young attorney

[and] the young bank officer did all the work, *and the letter was sent. But because I was what we called the billing attorney—in other words, I had to send the bill to get the payment sent—my name was put on the bottom of the letter.* It was not an area that I practiced in." [My emphasis]

The simple fact is that Hillary Clinton hadn't been asked how much work she'd done for Madison. Her answer referred to a specific incident—the S&L's unsuccessful May 1995 proposal to issue preferred stock. She'd answered in copious detail, but Greenfield had yanked a video clip out of context, tampered with its meaning, stuck a different question in front of it, and used it to portray the First Lady as a prevaricating harpy. Even by Whitewater standards, it was a shameless act.

Within days, the doctored quote was everywhere. ABC News used the clip on its evening news broadcast. So did CNN. The *Times* editorial page found it useful, as did Maureen Dowd. Dowd's colleague William Safire used a slightly different version in an accusatory column. "When you're a lawyer who needs a cover story to conceal close connections to a crooked client," he began, "you find some kid in your office willing to say he brought in the business and handled the client all by himself." The column went downhill from there.

There can be no doubt that what made the story take off, however, was White House aide Carolyn Huber's belated discovery of the missing Rose Law Firm billing records. Huber found the time sheets in a box in her office on January 4, 1996. She promptly called the Clintons' lawyer, David Kendall, who immediately conveyed them to Kenneth Starr and Senator Alfonse D'Amato. Starr hauled the First Lady before a grand jury in record time. Nobody seems to know how the time sheets came to be where Huber found them. Mrs. Huber, who supervised the Clintons' personal correspondence, had formerly been the Rose Law Firm's office manager. In subsequent Senate testimony, she was unequivocal. She'd originally happened upon the time sheets in the Books Room on the third floor of the White House in August 1995. She'd absently stuck them in a box and taken them to her office for later filing. Then in January 1996, she'd opened the box.

For two reasons, few questioned Huber's account. A Clinton loyalist, she appeared painfully sincere. Second, and far more important, her version gave all the Hillary-haters in the press the opportunity they'd been waiting for: here at last was a simple, dramatic Whitewater event that even the dullest voter could grasp. "Logic suggests," wrote the irrepressible Safire, "the avidly sought billing records were not put there to be found and filed, but were parked there temporarily. . . . Can you imagine the sinking feeling of the 'Someone' when he or she came back to the room and found the records gone?"

Safire, having had ample experience of skullduggery as a Nixon aide during Watergate—as he playfully pointed out—constructed an imaginary scenario in which "Someone" secretly needing to destroy bulky records couldn't think of a way to do it inside the White House. "You cannot put them in a wastebasket; the trash will be brought back by the Secret Service. . . . Asking for a shredder would arouse suspicion. You cannot put them in a burn bag for fear it will be examined.

Nor can you light a fire in August." But you could stick them in a briefcase, carry them to Outer Mongolia, and feed them to yaks. Inasmuch as it matters, which is very little, the problem with Huber's account is obvious: if, indeed, she'd never looked at the folded-over sheets in August—and there's no reason to doubt her—how then had she recognized them as the same documents in January? Ordinary common sense would say that when you find lost papers you never knew you had, it's hard to be sure where you got them. Indeed, when the Clintons' attorney, David Kendall, later testified about the matter on February 8, he said that Huber had been highly uncertain at first. "She said a number of different things that were inconsistent," he said. "She was flustered. She was upset. Her hands were shaking. She said that she had brought the documents over from the residence at some earlier point. She said she thought it was maybe three months ago. A little while later in the conversation she referred to bringing them over ten months ago. She was very confused about the timing. . . . She was unclear about where she had found them. I had the impression from the various things she said that they were on top of something—not inside a drawer or a box. But she was unclear whether she found them on a table or a shelf . . . Her stories were extremely vague." Co-counsel Jane Sherburne seconded Kendall's account. They'd decided not to press Huber on the issue because they didn't want to be accused of trying to influence her memory.

Again, the simplest explanation that fits the facts would seem to be that the billing records lay undiscovered in Huber's office in the Old Executive Office Building all the while the Clintons' lawyers searched the White House in an effort to comply with subpoenas. Why, after all, would anybody conceal documents that confirmed one's memory in exhaustive detail? In her sworn testimony to RTC investigators, Hillary Clinton had recalled one phone conversation with Beverly Bassett Schaffer. Her time sheets showed exactly one—on April 29, 1985. Asked if she'd done any work on a Jim McDougal real estate development called Castle Grande, she'd answered no. Republicans charged that an unused 1985 real estate option she'd prepared for Webb Hubbell's father-in-law contradicted her. But the billing records, like all internal Rose Law Firm documents, referred to the transaction in question as "the IDC matter." Once again, the First Lady stood accused of failing to answer a question she'd never been asked. Everything she said the records would show they did show.[6]

Ghost trail or not, *Newsweek* and *Time,* as usual, jumped in with both feet. Having been red hot on the topic all along, *Newsweek*'s Michael Isikoff seemed to relish the chance to exhume poor Vince Foster yet again. "The printouts," he wrote, "were covered with the late Vince Foster's handwriting: it is Foster's suicide that lends Whitewater its aura of menace."

If anything at all, what Foster's handwriting implies is an inno-

---

[6] IDC stood for Industrial Development Corporation, from which the property had been bought. The Castle Grande deal had been comprehensively studied in the Pillsbury Report's December 28, 1995, volume dealing with the Rose Law Firm's representation of Madison Guaranty. If there were any improprieties in Castle Grande, the report concluded, they were McDougal's and nobody else's. "The option," it pointed out, "was created many months after the [dubious] transaction closed. . . . While Mrs. Clinton seems to have some role in drafting the May 1, 1986, option, nothing proves that she did so knowing it to be wrong, and the theories that tie this option to wrongdoing . . . are strained at best." After studying Hillary Clinton's billing records, Pillsbury, Madison & Sutro came back with an even stronger statement.

cent explanation. Why? Because the White House lawyer died, let us recall once again, months before there *was* a Whitewater probe. The records Carolyn Huber found weren't originals; they were xeroxed copies of computer printouts run in February 1992. Hence it's likely that they hadn't seen the light of day since the 1992 campaign. Nor could anybody who wanted to hide them have had any way of knowing how many more copies might be floating around. Storing the 1992 campaign records and putting them in order was one of Mrs. Huber's secondary tasks at the White House.

But exculpatory evidence had been ruled entirely out of order. *Time*'s Richard Stengel made the obligatory observation that "Hillary Rodham Clinton now faces a crisis that even the most artful public relations may not be able to fix." Then he made a prediction: "Mrs. Clinton has stated that the lion's share of the work on Madison was done by a 'bright young associate' named Richard Massey. Mrs. Clinton also implied in a sworn statement to the RTC in May 1995 that Massey brought Madison's business to the firm. Committee sources tell *Time* that Massey will testify this week that he did not bring Madison in as a client and that he assumed Mrs. Clinton was involved."[7] The stage was set for high drama at the Whitewater hearings. At long last, D'Amato and Faircloth had found their "smoking gun." When Rick Massey testified against his former law partner, the pack predicted, the First Lady would go down. William Safire advised the President that it was time to hire himself a separate criminal defense attorney.

Meanwhile, a few words about "Travelgate" and the David Watkins memo that opened a second front in the media's 1995–96 "winter offensive" against the First Lady. Few would argue that the 1993 firings of the White House office staff had been the Clinton administration's finest hour. The questions are: Did Hillary order the firings? And then did she lie about it?

First, a few words about the circumstances, as aptly summarized by Joe Conason in the *Columbia Journalism Review:* "A federal office is discovered handing out lucrative, no-bid deals to private contractors over

[7] Not quite. Mrs. Clinton said Massey had done the lion's share of work on the 1985 preferred stock issue.

a period of many years, without so much as a written contract. Auditors from a major accounting firm find that the office did not keep adequate records for many of its transactions, which ran into millions of dollars annually. Eventually, it comes out that the director of the office has secretly funneled more than $50,000 into his personal checking account. Later still, it is revealed that when an anonymous staff whistleblower wrote a letter to the General Accounting Office years earlier, alleging favors from contractors and other improprieties, his complaint was brushed aside by the White House counsel—even though the office director admitted accepting contractor gifts, which legal experts say may have been a violation of federal law."

What we learned from [head of administration] David Watkins's now famous memo to [presidential adviser] Mack McLarty—which he never sent—was whom he was afraid of. "You explained," he wrote, "that [the Travel Office] was on the First Lady's 'radar screen.' . . . We both knew that there would be hell to pay if . . . we failed to take swift and decisive action in conformity with the First Lady's wishes."

"Travelgate" was reported even more dishonestly than Whitewater. Michael Isikoff's version in *Newsweek* was typical: "Watkins' memo suggests," he wrote, "that White House staffers were less than accurate when they told Congress Mrs. Clinton played 'no role' in Travelgate. . . . *Newsweek* has learned that Watkins told the FBI in 1993 about a phone call concerning the Travel Office in which Mrs. Clinton said 'action needed to be taken immediately to be certain that those not friendly to the administration were removed and replaced with trustworthy individuals.'"

Newsweek's scoop was roughly two years late. A March 18, 1994, Justice Department report on the Travel Office flap gives detailed accounts of Hillary's talks with both Watkins and Vince Foster. Watkins, it says, "understood from Foster that the matter was 'on her radar screen.'" The 1994 report gave the following account of a conversation whose existence Isikoff breathlessly reported twenty-two months later: "According to Watkins, he telephoned Mrs. Clinton. He relayed the information he had received . . . about sloppy and near non-existent record-keeping procedures by the Travel Office. [He] also told her that the auditors had found petty cash unaccounted for. In short, he informed her that things in the Travel Office were worse than they had originally thought. . . . According to Watkins, Mrs. Clinton said that she had talked with [Clinton pal] Harry Thomason and that he believed that Watkins could have a new travel operation in place very quickly. She also said that she had received advice from several others that 'we've made a mistake by not getting our people into jobs sooner.'"

In May 1994, only twenty months before the *Newsweek* revelation, the General Accounting Office had released its report. "Mr. Watkins," it said, "talked with the First Lady and told her that [the accounting firm] KPMG had found sloppy management in the Travel Office. He said that she urged that action be taken to get 'our people' into the Travel Office to help achieve the twenty-five percent White House staff cut. According to Mr. Watkins, the First Lady also mentioned, in the context of the Travel Office, that the administration had been criticized for being slow in making appointments."

When asked, Hillary had denied giving anybody a direct order to fire the Travel Office staff. Nobody in the White House has ever contradicted her. In short, the Travelgate aspect of the press's Hillary's-a-liar campaign was another put-up job.

Would Hillary's soft-spoken, balding former partner, Rick Massey, deliver the final blow to her credibility, as predicted? Would he contradict the account she'd given of how the Rose Law Firm came to represent Madison Guaranty S&L? Would the First Lady, having told almost precisely the same story to RTC investigators under oath, find herself facing perjury charges? Would the President be forced to hire a separate criminal defense attorney?

Well, don't you think you'd have heard by now? On the other hand, the press had gone too far to turn back. The only way ordinary citizens were going to get a halfway objective account of Massey's January 11 testimony was to watch on C-SPAN or order a transcript from the Federal Document Clearing House. They weren't about to get it from the press. Before it was over, Massey's day at the Whitewater hearings degenerated into a kind of mad quibble-fest. Actually, it began that way.

In his usual brilliantly malicious fashion, GOP counsel Michael Chertoff did his best to prevent Massey from simply telling his story. In his own lawyerly way, Massey went out of his way to help him. "Now, I see here that you have [Madison executive] John Latham—comma—Hillary Rodham Clinton," Chertoff observed. "Was it your custom when you did your bills, if you had multiple people in a single conference to have commas between them, but if you had separate events to have a semicolon between them?"

"I wish my practice were that precise," Massey answered. "I can't say that."

But when all was said and done, not only had Rick Massey failed to contradict Hillary but any tighter fit between their stories would have been suspicious. Nor had he been contacted about his testimony by the White House. What Massey didn't remember, eleven years later, was whether he had first approached Mrs. Clinton about talking to Jim McDougal about representing Madison Guaranty or she had approached him—a chicken and egg question of absolutely no consequence.

What he did recall, however, was that as a twenty-six-year-old associate at the Rose firm in 1985, he'd taught a class in securities law at the University of Arkansas–Little Rock. In that class was John Latham, an officer at Madison Guaranty. The two had known each other in college. During the semester, Latham began staying after class to ask Massey pointed questions about possible capital-raising mechanisms for Madison.

Massey gave out free advice for a couple of weeks. "I should say for the record," he testified, "that I asked [Latham] to lunch one day and I pitched the business, asked for their work. They were a growing S&L. We liked working for companies like that, so I pitched the work. . . . I think the pitch was basically, 'Gee, you're asking me all these questions. Why don't you hire us and put us to work on some of these things?' "

Nobody at Rose had asked Massey to approach Latham; he'd taken it upon himself. When the work came in a few weeks later—one day after Hillary Rodham Clinton had met with Jim McDougal at his office on April 23, 1985, as she'd specified to the RTC—it came directly to his desk. He didn't have to ask for it.

Furthermore, Massey had also known that some in the firm thought McDougal was a deadbeat and objected to taking

Madison on as a client without a prepaid retainer—also exactly as Hillary had said. But what he didn't remember was talking to her first. "I do not remember," he testified, bringing "a proposal in hand to her and discussing with her that there were partners in the firm that were dissatisfied with McDougal and 'Here's a proposal and let's work it out . . . It's *possible* that I had a conversation with her about 'Gee, I think we might be able to get these folks' work. You know McDougal. Maybe you would go talk to him.'"

But it's clear Massey had that talk with *somebody* at the Rose firm, and that somebody told Hillary. Unless, that is, the woman is clairvoyant. After hours of back-and-forth, Massey agreed with Democratic counsel Richard Ben-Veniste that landing the client had been a "team effort." As to whether he'd done all the work, as Hillary Clinton had said during her April 1994 press conference, Massey put it this way in response to Republican Senator Connie Mack of Florida: "I will tell you my impression, which is not varied by the time sheets, was that these were primarily one-man jobs, and that I did primarily all of the research, writing, drafting, and so forth. Mrs. Clinton had a role in these matters. I view it as a supervisory role. In terms of who was in the trenches and doing the work, Senator, it was me."

Indeed, Hillary had never attended any meetings or participated in conference calls with state or federal regulators. Her sole contact had come in a five-minute phone conversation with Beverly Bassett Schaffer before the first letter went out. As for the legality of the preferred stock deal itself, the highly suspicious transaction *The New York Times* had placed at the heart of the whirlwind? Legally speaking, Massey testified, it was a no-brainer, a piece of cake. As Beverly Bassett Schaffer had told Jeff Gerth four years ago, it was all the Federal Home Loan Bank Board's idea to begin with. "Sir, there is no better form of capital than cash," he said, "and we were trying to raise cash for the institution."

Is it even necessary, at this point, to document that the media's version of Massey's testimony bore scant relationship to reality? AT WHITEWATER SESSION, A STRUGGLE TO RECALL, read the headline over Stephen Labaton's account in the *Times*. "In five hours of testimony before the Senate Whitewater committee, a lawyer for Hillary

Rodham Clinton's law firm said today that he could not remember events of 11 years ago clearly enough to support the First Lady's account of how the firm came to represent a troubled Arkansas savings and loan association. Under Republican questioning, the lawyer, Richard Massey, appeared to contradict significant aspects of Mrs. Clinton's account. But under Democratic questioning, he offered support for some of what she has said." Which parts, Labaton left to the reader's imagination. He did mention Massey's pitch to Latham, but concluded by pointing the finger of suspicion back toward an implicitly corrupt bargain between Jim McDougal and Governor Bill Clinton. If the reporter bore any ill will toward Republican staffers who'd clearly leaked him an absurdly inaccurate version of Massey's previous statements, he managed to conceal it.

Fellow Whitewater careerist Susan Schmidt spun the story precisely the same way in *The Washington Post.* Massey, she wrote, testified "that he does not believe he was responsible for signing up Madison as a client, as [Hillary] has asserted. . . . She has said that Massey came to her with a proposal for a stock plan to help Madison raise capital after meeting with Madison president John Latham. She said he asked her to work as the firm's billing partner and work with James B. McDougal, the S&L's owner, to resolve a past billing dispute Rose had had with him. 'I don't believe it happened that way,' Massey said."

When investigators for Pillsbury, Madison & Sutro looked into the matter in their final report, issued February 25, 1996, they concluded what any sensible observer with no stake in the outcome *would* decide: that the whole topic was much ado about very damn little. "The recollections of Mrs. Clinton and Massey are consistent in broad outline, although discrepancies emerge in the detail. The purported recollections of Jim McDougal are inconsistent with those of the others and upon analysis make little sense."

Contrary to McDougal's oft-cited account in *The Los Angeles Times,* the Pillsbury Report concluded, the Rose Firm had clearly been hired for the specific purpose of working on the preferred stock proposal. "Most significantly," it said, "the alleged economic motivation makes no sense. . . . There is no evidence that the Clintons ever received anything like $2,000 a month from this engagement, and every reason to believe that they never received more than a trivial sum of money. . . . Even if all the retainer had been earned in fees, Mrs. Clinton's share would have been less than $20 a month."[8] But you didn't read it in the newspaper.

Some important people, though, must have watched Massey's testimony on C-SPAN. Either that or the White House had done some uncharacteristically effective hell-raising behind the scenes. For that evening's *Nightline* aired key parts of Massey's testimony that bolstered Hillary Clinton's version of events. The program pointed out that few, if any, of Senator D'Amato's dire predictions had proved accurate. Jeff Greenfield was nowhere in sight. D'Amato got so flustered in a live interview that he kept calling Ted Koppel "David"—even after being corrected twice.

Even Stephen Labaton came in for a share of embarrassment. On Saturday, January 13, *The New York Times* ran in its page-two "Corrections" slot an "Editor's Note" stipulating that Labaton's article on Massey's testimony "should also have included testimony that seemed to support" the First Lady—and listing several particulars. A stingy retraction, but a retraction all the same—the first after years of wildly inaccurate, patently biased coverage.

On Monday, January 15, came a similarly overdue but penetrating column by Anthony Lewis. Never uncritical of the Clinton administration, Lewis was the first important voice at *The New York Times* to break ranks on Whitewater. "From the moment Bill Clinton took office as president," Lewis wrote, "Republicans set out to destroy his legitimacy. Their method was to attack his honor, principally through charges about the long-ago deal known as Whitewater.

"Three years and innumerable investigations later, Mr. Clinton has not been shown to have done anything wrong in Whitewater. One charge after another has evaporated.

"But the Whitewater accusation machine grinds on. Senator Alfonse D'Amato, the New York Republican who chairs a committee on the subject, announces that a document will show some-

---

[8] When it dropped its representation of Madison in July 1986, the Rose firm had returned close to $9,000 to the savings and loan as unearned advance billings.

thing terrible. The press breathlessly reports that—and fails to point out that the document, when produced, is not what Senator D'Amato said it was.

"The D'Amato performance is right out of the Joe McCarthy book: Promise horrors and prove nothing. But there is a big difference. The press cottoned on to Senator McCarthy and checked out what he said. On Whitewater, the press too often seems an eager accomplice of the accusers.

"The performance of the press is especially troubling. Some of the coverage of Whitewater reads as if the reporters or editors were committed to finding something wrong—as if they had an investment in the story."

Everybody who read it knew exactly who Lewis was talking about; his indictment was all the more powerful for its lack of specificity.

Two days later, Frank Rich wrote a very funny piece about D'Amato's incoherence in the face of Ted Koppel's pointed questions on *Nightline.* "Part of Mr. D'Amato's hesitancy derives from the fact that he doesn't have his act together," Rich wrote. "However evasive or lawyerly the First Lady's answers to her own TV and radio interlocutors may sound on the book-tour trail, they still are more specific than the broad innuendo and dubious Watergate analogies spewed by Mr. D'Amato . . ."

U.S. News & World Report editor Mortimer B. Zuckerman wrote a stinging editorial in the January 29, 1996, issue drawing parallels between Senator Alfonse D'Amato's handling of Whitewater and Senator Joseph McCarthy's 1954 "investigation" of communism in the U.S. Army. Without pointing to *The New York Times* and *The Washington Post* editorial pages, where they first appeared, he drew up a list of Whitewater allegations against the Clintons and refuted each one by directly quoting the Pillsbury Report.

But elsewhere, the ritual drumbeat went on. On the same day Frank Rich's column appeared, a *New York Times* "news" story about the First Lady's book tour by Todd S. Purdum trotted out the familiar list of topics she had supposedly dissembled about. He took sharp issue with Hillary's attempts to focus attention on the

Pillsbury Report's finding that the Clintons lost money on Whitewater and "that we never, ever took any kind of money whatsoever from Madison Savings and Loan."

"In fact," Purdum countered, "the report, which states that it was not meant to exonerate or charge anyone, concluded that it was impossible to determine whether money from Madison had gone to support Whitewater because a number of records were missing."

In fact, as any alert sixth-grader can see, what Jim McDougal may or may not have done is a completely different question. But I'd bet that Purdum had never, ever read the report in question. He was merely parroting the company line.

Maybe your humble, obedient servant here ought to have been gratified, having predicted that it would all come down to a National Bitch Hunt almost two years earlier. A subsequent careful reading of the April 1995 Pillsbury Report and the Clintons' RTC interrogatories, however, made it clear why they'd opted for a professional investigation rather than entrust their Whitewater records to the tender mercies of the Washington press. Even so, the White House's relative passivity in the face of D'Amato's latterday opportunism remained a bit of a puzzle. For once the public seemed to be paying attention to Whitewater, making it a time of political peril but also of great opportunity. Chatty TV interviews and written interrogatories weren't going to cut it. Why not force the issue? Why not insist on appearing before D'Amato's Whitewater committee? If it was a bitch they wanted, maybe Hillary needed to show them one.

But then as political strategists, the Clintons have always been their own best advisers. After the 1994 congressional elections, the Washington press had all but written Bill Clinton's political obituary. Nobody's doing that in 1996.

Beverly Bassett Schaffer finally got her chance to set the record straight on January 25, 1996. Ever since she'd made the mistake of cooperating with Jeff Gerth four years earlier, Whitewater had taken over her life. In a series of increasingly accusatory articles, *The New York Times* had portrayed her as a corrupt hack—the linchpin of an implied conspiracy among Jim McDougal, Governor Bill

Clinton, and big-shot lawyer Hillary Rodham Clinton to keep Madison Guaranty open despite insolvency and regardless of the cost to taxpayers. To reach this conclusion, Gerth had ignored not only the richly documented history of Madison itself but reams of state and federal laws regarding S&L regulation. And history, too. Not one bankrupt S&L, nationwide, had been closed by state regulators without the aid of the Federal Savings and Loan Insurance Corporation.

There had been a personal betrayal, too. Concerned, after hours of interviews, that *Times* reporter Jeff Gerth had a shaky grasp of the facts but no end of opinions, Bassett Schaffer had written him a series of detailed memos—twenty pages in all—to educate him about the S&L debacle. Among her virtues, candor and forthrightness among them, she also writes far better than Jeff Gerth.

Gerth's thank-you was to portray her as suspiciously forgetful. "Mrs. Schaffer," he wrote, "said she did not remember the Federal examination of Madison. . . . In 1985, Mrs. Clinton and her Little Rock law firm . . . twice applied to the Securities Commission on behalf of Madison, asking that the savings and loan be allowed to try two novel plans to raise money.

"Mrs. Schaffer wrote to Mrs. Clinton and another lawyer at the firm, approving the ideas. 'I never gave anybody special treatment,' she said."

Never mind that the so-called novel plan to raise capital by selling preferred stock had been suggested by the Feds to begin with. Never mind that Bassett Schaffer never approved the scheme but had merely ruled it *legal*. (It's common practice today.) Never mind that she imposed strict financial conditions that prevented the S&L from even filing a formal application. Never mind that she'd helped engineer a cease-and-desist order in 1986 that ousted McDougal from Madison. Never mind that she wrote strenuously urging the FHLBB and FSLIC to shut Madison down fourteen months before they did so.

If Whitewater had a malefactor, it was supposed to be Beverly Bassett Schaffer. Hadn't the mighty *New York Times* said as much? Didn't the lordly *Washington Post* pick up the cry? In December 1993, she'd found herself chased through Fayetteville by an NBC-

TV crew guided by GOP "dirty tricks" operative David Bossie—by 1996, incidentally, an aide to Senator Lauch Faircloth.

Republican congressional inquisitors, however, had been ducking her for the better part of two years. At the August 1995 hearings chaired by Representative Jim Leach, she'd heard herself accused of suspect behavior by witnesses she'd never met. L. Jean Lewis had named her in a criminal referral. Her name and caricature appeared on "Wanted" posters circulated by Citizens United. Despite Democrats' protests, however, Leach refused to let her testify.

Between the never-ending media crush and the emotional stress, Bassett Schaffer had given up her law practice. In the interim, she had been vindicated professionally. The Pillsbury Report concluded that she and her staff had done nothing wrong. "If anything," the RTC investigators wrote, "Arkansas regulators took a more aggressive position toward Madison Guaranty than did the FHLBB. . . . On December 10, 1987, Beverly Bassett wrote a letter to Stewart Root, Director, Federal Savings and Loan Insurance Corporation, stating that Madison Guaranty (and two other Arkansas thrifts) are 'unquestionably insolvent and have been so for a long time. . . . We must request that these associations be transferred immediately to the FSLIC.' That did not happen for reasons that had nothing to do with Bassett."

But Senate Democrats had publicly badgered the Whitewater committee chairman until he decided to risk letting Bassett Schaffer testify. Republicans apparently figured they'd finally come up with a way to make her look bad. It seems that back in July 1986, she'd sent Clinton aide Sam Bratton a note notifying him that Madison and Jim McDougal were in deep trouble—exactly as she'd notified Clinton in 1985 when S&Ls in Conway and Harrison, Arkansas, failed. She'd thought it her duty. She was the head of a state agency; the governor was her direct superior. By then, the Madison board of directors had been summoned to Dallas for a mandatory meeting with state and federal regulators. Rumors were all over Little Rock; reporters were sniffing around. She also thought McDougal might look to Bill Clinton for help, and she wanted to warn the governor to bar the door.

Hoping to trap her in a lie, Senate investigators refused to depose her in advance. In his cleverly insinuating fashion, Republican counsel Michael Chertoff led off by asking if she'd "felt a need to let Mr. Clinton know that Mr. McDougal would be removed from the savings and loan?"

But Bassett Schaffer never thought about lying. When she'd written the note to Clinton, she said, she hadn't *known* exactly what was going to happen to Jim McDougal, only that it wasn't going to be good. Besides her duty to notify the governor of an impending event likely to bring both press inquiries and worried calls from Madison Guaranty depositors, she wanted to be sure McDougal had no wriggle room whatsoever. "My impression was," she said, "that Jim McDougal was the kind of person who would call up the governor's office and very likely, or possibly, go over there and try to involve the governor's office. It could happen.... I didn't want him [Bill Clinton] to have anything to do with him."

"But why did you put in [the note]," Chertoff asked, "'because of Bill's relationship with McDougal, we probably ought to talk about it?'"

"Because of their relationship. Because of Mr. McDougal's history of bragging about his relationship with Bill Clinton. Because of his having told people over the years that he was friends with Bill Clinton, you know, bragging about the relationship. . . . I believe that Jim McDougal abused his relationship with Bill Clinton, and might again."

"And he abused it in order to get influence?" Chertoff asked. "Is that what you're saying?"

"Well, he didn't get any," she snapped. "But he certainly tried."

For seven exasperating hours, Bassett Schaffer took on every question the committee could throw at her. With the truth on her side, she whipped them, as people in Arkansas say, like a rented mule. Even the normally shameless D'Amato appeared taken aback a time or two when Bassett Schaffer fixed him with a glare and let him know how absurdly transparent were his elaborate pretenses to misunderstand what was patently clear.

From the perspective of people back home, Bassett Schaffer's finest moment may have come when Senator Paul Simon asked her why she found the whole Whitewater fiasco so distressing. "It's personal," she said. "I don't think it's been fair to me—actually, to the entire state of Arkansas. It's really been very personal, very vicious. It's been an effort to vicariously destroy Bill Clinton piece by piece by ruining the people that he trusted, that worked for him—good people—who didn't do anything wrong. The job's been done very well. And a lot of people have been hurt unnecessarily for purposes of winning an election. And I just think there's something wrong with that."

Even *The New York Times* quoted that, virtually the first answer elicited by a Democrat to be cited in the newspaper since the Senate Whitewater hearings began. But the *Times* lead *did* stress that Bassett Schaffer had "tipped off Governor Bill Clinton's office that Federal officials were about to force the removal of his business partner from an ailing savings association." Of course, she'd never known a thing about the Whitewater investment, and had so testified. Nor had she known McDougal would be forced out; if she'd gotten her way, Madison would have been shut down. But *The New York Times* could print anything it liked. As far as Beverly Bassett Schaffer was concerned, she'd gotten her say. They could take it or leave it. By that time, the opinions of the people back home were the only opinions she cared about.

Epilogue

> It is first agreed and settled among them what suspected persons shall be accused of a plot: then effectual care is taken to secure all their letters and other papers, and put the owners in chains. These papers are delivered to a set of artists, very dexterous in finding out the mysterious meanings of words, syllables, and letters. . . .
>
> —*Jonathan Swift,* Gulliver's Travels

✦

And then came *Blood Sport,* the definitive Whitewater book, everybody said, from Pulitzer Prize–winning journalist James B. Stewart. The book debuted in a lengthy excerpt in the March 18, 1996, issue of *Time.* Billed as "The Truth About Whitewater," it was illustrated by a cover photo of the First Lady, eyes averted, unsmiling and lit in such a manner as to make her look as pale as if she'd had her blood drained. Photo editors must have sorted through bins of contact sheets to find one that made the poor woman look that damn guilty.

Two years of supposedly diligent spadework, and what had James B. Stewart come up with? "As the legal process unfolds, the question of whether specific laws were broken," he wrote in *Time,* "should not obscure the broader issues that make Whitewater an important story." (I love that phrase "specific laws." It adds an air of solemnity to what's otherwise a tacit admission that, like everybody else who has dug into the thing, he's found no scandal.)

But that wouldn't sell any books, so Stewart dragged up our old friends "character and integrity." How the Clintons have dealt with Whitewater tells us that theirs are pretty bad. "Much of what appears here," he told *Time* readers with grave solemnity, "will seem at odds with statements made by the President and First Lady, some of them under oath.... That the Clintons had virtually nothing to do with Whitewater and were simply 'passive' investors; that the McDougals didn't really absorb significantly more losses than the Clintons; that Hillary wasn't responsible for Madison Guaranty's becoming a client of the Rose firm; that she wasn't familiar with a real estate development called Castle Grande and didn't work on it."

If by now it's necessary to critique the near-crazed indifference to truth in that paragraph, then truly this book has failed. Need it be added that there's nary a word in *Blood Sport* that would cause a moment's discomfort to any influential member of the press? Indeed, Stewart's book consists largely of recycled press clippings together with some amazingly self-serving downhome bunkum and balderdash. Suffice it to say that if James B. Stewart had encountered Jim and Susan McDougal and David Hale back in 1978 or thereabouts, he would now be the proud owner of half the federally protected wetlands between Little Rock and the Mississippi.

And did the press love it? Oh lordy, does an ape like looking in a mirror? Here and there, an occasional reviewer was made uneasy by Stewart's methods. The best book reviewer in the United States, Michiko Kakutani of the *Times*, wrote that Stewart had "created a novelistic narrative filled with colorful scenes.... We are not only given explicit dialogue from 15 years ago, but also access to people's private thoughts. The problem is that this technique sacrifices verifiability for verisimilitude, and substitutes color for hard analysis. Scenes that Mr. Stewart could never have observed firsthand are recounted from an omniscient viewpoint. Mr. Stewart rarely identifies the sources for such scenes; nor does he take into account the subjectivity and often self-serving nature of memory. The reader never knows whether the quotes Mr. Stewart has put in the mouth of an individual (whom in some cases he has not even interviewed) are from a first or secondhand source." She also noticed that everybody who served as a source for Stewart comes off well, while others get trashed. But verifiability? Hell, why start now? Kakutani had no real defense against the book's methods.

Nor had far less gifted reviewers, like Thomas Powers in *The New York Times Book Review,* who described *Blood Sport* as "one of the best books on American politics in recent years." Thomas Powers, you see, is a fellow long-troubled by "dark suspicions aroused when it was learned that one of [Vince] Foster's jobs had been to prepare tax returns for the Whitewater project and, more ominous still, that the Whitewater files in Foster's office at the time of his death had been turned over to the Clintons." But shouldn't a fellow who just read the definitive Whitewater book know that Foster prepared the Clintons' *personal* taxes? Is it necessary to say all over again that *the files belong to the client*? But if critics can't defend themselves, what are *Blood Sport*'s swindled readers to do?[1]

Let's talk about character and integrity for a moment—James Stewart's. *Blood Sport* is a book in which troopers Roger Perry and Larry Patterson are he-man patriots who chafed at delivering Bill Clinton to Gennifer Flowers's door and who say she called the Governor's Mansion constantly when Hillary wasn't around.[2] *Blood Sport* is also a book in which an intrepid Jeff Gerth dealt honorably and forthrightly with Beverly Bassett Schaffer; in which what "floored" her about his March 8, 1992, article wasn't his depiction of her as a corrupt hack—not a syllable about that—but learning for the first time about Whitewater; in which, nevertheless, after thinking it over, she asks her husband, "Archie, what's so bad about this?" This, incidentally, on the very day she bitterly

---

[1] In fairness, *Blood Sport* doesn't appear to have contributed to Powers's worry about the files.

[2] In his gentlemanly fashion, Stewart discredits rumors about an affair between Hillary and Vince Foster. So how does he square his belief in Perry and Patterson with the scenes they described to *The American Spectator*'s David Brock about the pair making out at stoplights in Little Rock? Or the one in which Foster supposedly cupped Hillary's breasts in front of Carolyn Huber while Hillary squirmed and cooed, "Oh, Vince"? He doesn't. Stewart simply censors these grotesque lies out of existence because they don't suit his purposes.

wrote Gerth threatening a libel suit against *The New York Times*—
information that she gave Stewart.[3]

Blood Sport is a book in which L. Jean Lewis is depicted as a
crackerjack investigator of unimpeachable integrity, which omits
altogether the saga of her magical tape recorder ("unbeknownst
to Breslaw, Lewis had a tape recorder running") and credits her
tales of "unprecedented" RTC stalling without mentioning that
the delay was only seven days. Stewart feigns, and clumsily, that he
hasn't a clue as to who leaked half the RTC documents in Kansas
City to Gerth and Susan Schmidt.

Blood Sport is a book in which, contrary to Hillary Rodham
Clinton, "Richard Massey denies that he had anything to do with
securing the [Madison Guaranty] business," and knew nothing
whatever about it until it was dumped in his lap after Hillary's
April 1985 meeting with Jim McDougal. "It defies common sense,
Stewart thinks, "that Hillary would have shown up at
[McDougal's] office purely by coincidence." Stewart returns over
and over to McDougal's silly story about the "jogging incident."

Blood Sport is a book in which Judge David Hale was appointed by
Governor Bill Clinton rather than Governor Frank White, as history records; in which two separate and conflicting tales are told
about Hale's now-famous $300,000 loan to Susan McDougal; in
which Hale is described as "a figure of some note in Little Rock. . . .
Hale was a devout Baptist whose father had been a poor farmer."
Stewart makes no mention of the thirteen dummy companies or
the $2.04 million Hale pled guilty to scamming from the Small
Business Administration. Hale's loans to the "Democratic 'political
family,'" we are led to believe, were what got him in trouble.

Because Stewart was in such an all-fired hurry to get his book
out, he couldn't possibly have known that virtually every *prosecution*
witness at Governor Jim Guy Tucker and the McDougals' fraud
and conspiracy trial in Little Rock described Hale as a liar. Nor
that Hale himself confessed to numerous whoppers on cross-exam-

---

[3] Stewart writes in passing that my own cavils against Gerth's articles "involve issues best
evaluated by confirmed Whitewater enthusiasts." But not, apparently, enthusiasts writing 460-
page books about the topic. He mentions one: whether or not it's "unfair and misleading" to
call Jim McDougal an S&L operator, since he didn't own one when Whitewater began.

ination. But he began telling the truth, we're to believe, the moment he started talking to "Justice Jim" Johnson, David Bossie, Floyd Brown, Susan Schmidt, and Jeff Gerth back in September 1993.

Well, okay, except for Hale's guilty plea before U.S. District Judge Stephen Reasoner in 1994. On cross-examination, our devout Baptist friend, who hasn't got a scrap of paper to prove his charges against President Clinton—and who couldn't narrow down the date that he and the President supposedly met to hatch their crooked loan scheme to closer than six weeks—was forced to admit that he'd actually fibbed to the judge too. Tucker's lawyers proved he'd stolen even more than he'd admitted. He'd been nervous, Hale said. He'd forgotten a couple of fraudulent loans to a couple of dummy companies. Kenneth Starr's intrepid prosecutors, who were supposed to know the score, stood quietly by.

Blood Sport also is a book in which a Pulitzer Prize–winning financial journalist—one who crucified junk bond genius Michael Milken in his last book—pretends he can't grasp that there's anything fishy about the way Jim McDougal handled Whitewater. Until *Blood Sport* came out, the big scandal about the Clintons' ill-fated investment was supposed to be that they'd done business with what Senator D'Amato calls a "criminal enterprise" run by McDougal. But now the McDougals are the victims. The way Stewart tells it, Hillary's a greedy bitch because she refused to give up her equity in a worthless company. "All these years of our paying for them," Stewart quotes McDougal as saying. "We paid the bills. Bill blasted us over the property taxes [i.e., Clinton's name was published on the delinquent list when McDougal was supposed to be paying them], and now Hillary is annoyed with me? . . . Well, fuck them."

And fuck them he did. But what doesn't make sense is why Hillary or anybody would hang on to stock in a worthless company. Well, how about if they didn't know it was worthless? How about if their esteemed partners had peddled the company's assets for pennies on the dollar but somehow neglected to say so? Might that possibly explain Hillary Rodham Clinton's seemingly irrational behavior?

Of course, that's precisely what did happen, and judging by the detailed account Stewart gives of the transactions, he has read enough of the April 1985 Pillsbury Report to cleverly tell half the story. The McDougals' self-serving half, to be precise. And he cites the Clintons' RTC interrogatories here and there, so we know he's read them too. But he leaves out the key documents and letters that show what actually happened.

But then came Stewart's big book tour. For a while you couldn't turn on a TV talk show without seeing Mr. Pulitzer Prize. *Nightline, Washington Week in Review, Charlie Rose,* National Public Radio—the man was everywhere. And just about everywhere he went, Stewart made the same pitch. *Blood Sport* uncovered no big crimes in Whitewater, just a lot of deceit, bad character, and political opportunism. But surely, Ted Koppel urged during Stewart's March 11, 1996, *Nightline* appearance, there was something. "What is it you would say," Koppel asked, "if you were obliged, in fifteen or thirty seconds, to summarize what is troublesome about Whitewater and what will still come back to haunt the Clintons?"

No murder, no perjury, no obstruction of justice, no bank fraud—none of that. No, Stewart opined, what Whitewater came down to in the end was the Clintons' refusal "to abide by financial requirements in obtaining mortgage loans." Huh?

Gravely, *Blood Sport's* author went on to stipulate that in filling out a personal financial statement for a 1987 Whitewater loan renewal, Hillary Rodham Clinton had "vastly inflated" the value of the property. This to the bank that owned the loan and appraised the land, which makes it a head-scratcher to start with. Boy, talk about your nickel-and-dime accusations. And there was more. "It is a crime to submit a false loan document," Stewart told the *Nightline* audience. In his cautious, thoughtful way, however, he added that determining the guilt of the President and First Lady was "a question for a prosecutor and a jury to decide."

But you can put a hold on the handcuffs and the one-piece his-'n-her orange jumpsuits with the presidential seal. Because Joe Conason at *The New York Observer* was pondering this allegedly felonious document, thoughtfully reproduced in the Appendix to *Blood Sport,* when he noticed something funny. Down at the bottom of the page, above the suspects' famous signatures, was this funny little notice: *"(BOTH SIDES OF THIS STATEMENT MUST BE COMPLETED.)"*

Conason wondered about that. Surely not. It couldn't possibly be. Curious, however, he made it his business to check it out. He put his hands on a copy of the original statement. And guess what? All the information Stewart accused Hillary Clinton of fudging was right there, in the First Lady's quite legible hand. Mr. Stewart had simply neglected to check the second page.

Appendix

✦

The following four articles are reprinted by permission of
The New York Times.

CLINTONS JOINED S.& L. OPERATOR IN AN OZARK REAL-ESTATE VENTURE

By JEFF GERTH

March 8, 1992 Special to *The New York Times*

WASHINGTON, March 7 — Bill Clinton and his wife were business partners with the owner of a failing savings and loan association that was subject to state regulation early in his tenure as Governor of Arkansas, records show.

The partnership, a real estate joint venture that was developing land in the Ozarks, involved the Clintons and James B. McDougal, a former Clinton aide turned developer. It started in 1978, and at times money from Mr. McDougal's savings and loan was used to subsidize it. The corporation continues to this day, but does not appear to be active.

Mr. McDougal gave a detailed account of his relationship in several interviews in the last two weeks. This account, along with an examination of related local, state and Federal records and interviews with dozens of others in Arkansas, found the following:

• Available records covering the most active period of the real estate corporation, called Whitewater Development, appear to show that Mr. McDougal heavily subsidized it, insuring that the Clintons were under little financial risk in what turned out to be an unsuccessful enterprise. The corporation bought 200 acres of Ozark Mountain vacation property and planned to sell it in lots. During this period, the Clintons appear to have invested little money, so stood to lose little if the venture failed, but might have cashed in on their 50 percent interest if it had done well.

• The Clintons and Mr. McDougal disagree about what happened to Whitewater's records. Mr. McDougal says that at Mr. Clinton's request they were delivered to the Governor's mansion. The Clintons say many of them have disappeared. Many questions about the enterprise cannot be fully answered without the records.

• After Federal regulators found that Mr. McDougal's savings institution, Madison Guaranty, was insolvent, meaning it faced possible closure by the state, Mr. Clinton appointed a new state securities commissioner, who had been a lawyer in a firm that represented the savings and loan. Mr. Clinton and the commissioner deny giving any preferential treatment. The new commissioner approved two novel proposals to help the savings and loan that were offered by Hillary Clinton, Governor Clinton's wife and a lawyer. She and her firm had been retained to represent the association.

• The Clintons improperly deducted at least $5,000 on their personal tax returns in 1984 and 1985 for interest paid on a portion of at least $30,000 in bank loan payments that Whitewater made for them. The deductions saved them about $1,000 in taxes, but since the error was more than three years ago, Internal Revenue Service regulations do not require the Clintons to pay.

The complicated relationship between Mr. McDougal and the Clintons came to light in an investigation by The New York Times of the Clintons' tax records and business relationships. It raises questions of whether a governor should be involved in a business deal with the owner of a business regulated by the state and whether, having done so, the governor's wife through her law firm should be receiving legal fees for work done for the business.

Confusion Is Cited

Asked about these matters, the Clintons retained two lawyers to answer questions. The lawyers said the improper tax deductions were honest errors, made because there was confusion over who really owned a certain piece of Whitewater property and who was responsible for the loan taken out to buy it, Whitewater or the Clintons.

The deed for the land and the loan papers are all in the Clintons' names.

The lawyers said they were not in a position to answer questions about where the money that went into Whitewater came from. But generally, they said they thought neither the Clintons nor Mr. McDougal had profited from the venture. They also said the Clintons were once liable for about $100,000 in bank loans that financed Whitewater's original purchase of land. But the lawyers have only been able to find original documents showing $5,000 that the Clintons paid.

Some questions about the relationship and the Clintons' role in it may be difficult to resolve because of differing accounts and the missing records.

The two lawyers representing the Clintons are Susan P. Thomases, a long-time friend, and Loretta Lynch, a campaign aide, who participated in several hours of interviews at Ms. Thomases' Manhattan offices Thursday and Friday.

Payments on Debt

The records that are available, and Mrs. Thomases' account, show that Whitewater made payments between 1982 and 1985 on Mrs. Clinton's $30,000 real estate debt, reducing the debt by about $16,000 while also paying at least $14,000 in interest. At least one of those checks was signed by Mr. McDougal.

Mrs. Clinton originally borrowed the $30,000 from a bank also controlled by Mr. McDougal, Bank of Kingston, but "Hillary took the loan on behalf of the corporation," Ms. Thomases said. That, she explained, is why Whitewater made the payments.

The Clintons' 1984 and 1985 tax returns show that they took deductions for interest payments of $2,811 and $2,322 that Whitewater had made.

"It clearly is an error," Ms. Thomases said. She noted that the tax returns for those years were prepared by accountants in Arkansas.

The Clintons' gross income in 1984, as reported on their tax returns, was about $111,000 and they paid $22,280 in Federal taxes. In 1985, their reported income was about $102,000, and they paid $18,791 in Federal taxes.

Longtime Friendship

Mr. Clinton and Mr. McDougal had been friends since the 1960's. When Mr. Clinton became the nation's youngest Governor at 32 years old, he took Mr. McDougal into his administration as an aide for economic development. It was at about this time that the men formed Whitewater.

A few years later Mr. McDougal, having left government in 1979, bought control of a small savings and loan association, Madison Guaranty, and built it into one of the largest state-chartered associations in Arkansas.

But over time, the savings and loan got in trouble, like many others around the country. Finally Federal regulators took the savings and loan away from Mr. McDougal, and a Federal grand jury charged him with fraud, though he was acquitted. The Clintons were not involved in those proceedings.

Mr. McDougal began having personal problems, too. He was found to be suffering from manic-depressive illness, though he was judged competent to stand trial. In the interviews, Mr. McDougal appeared stable, careful and calm.

A year after the Clintons and McDougals bought the Ozark Mountain property and founded Whitewater Development in 1979, the corporation bought a modular house for about $22,000 and placed it on one of its lots. That lot was then conveyed to Mrs. Clinton, and the deed indicates that she paid nothing for it. Ms. Thomases says this was an error by Whitewater. The deed, she said, should have shown the price and said that Mrs. Clinton paid.

But the house was carried on the books as a Whitewater corporate asset and used as a model house to attract other buyers, according to Whitewater records produced by Ms. Thomases. Because the records are incomplete, it is unclear exactly what happened. But about the same time, Mrs. Clinton personally borrowed $30,000 from Mr. McDougal's bank to pay for the house and the lot.

Ms. Thomases said Mrs. Clinton and the corporation regarded this as a corporate debt, though it was in Mrs. Clinton's name. The corporation included no one but the Clintons and the McDougals. It was this debt that Whitewater made payments on until the end of 1985.

One year after acquiring the property, Mrs. Clinton sold it for $27,500, with payments to be made over time, records show. It is not clear who received the buyer's down payment of $3,000. But Ms. Thomases said it was the corporation that took the loss on its books. A few years later, the buyer went bankrupt and stopped making payments, and then he died.

In 1988 Mrs. Clinton bought back the house from the estate of the buyer. Records show that she paid $8,000 and then resold the property a short time later for about $23,000, after closing costs. The Clintons reported a capital gain that year of $1,640.

Ms. Thomases explained that the capital gain was small because, as part of that transaction, Mrs. Clinton had to pay off Whitewater's remaining $13,000 debt on the property, originally incurred by Mrs. Clinton. The payments the previous owner had been making to Whitewater before he went bankrupt had been used to help pay off that debt.

Account Overdrawn

It was during the period when Whitewater was making the Clintons' loan payments that Madison Guaranty was putting money into Whitewater.

For example, Whitewater's check ledger shows that Whitewater's account at Madison was overdrawn in 1984, when the corporation was making payments on the Clintons' loan. Money was deposited to make up the shortage from Madison Marketing, an affiliate of the savings and loan that derived its revenues from the institution, records also show.

It was also in 1984 that Madison started getting into trouble. Federal examiners studied its books that year, found that it was violating Arkansas regulations and determined that correcting the books to adjust improperly inflated profits would "result in an insolvent position," records of the 1984 examination show.

Arkansas regulators received the Federal report later that year, and under state law the securities commissioner was supposed to close any insolvent institution.

As the Governor is free to do at any time, Mr. Clinton appointed a new securities commissioner in January 1985. He chose Beverly Bassett Schaffer, a lawyer in one of the firms that had been representing Madison.

Fund-Raising Ideas

Ms. Thomases, after talking to Mr. Clinton this week, said the Governor chose her because they were friends, and because he wanted to appoint a well-qualified woman to an important post.

In interviews, Mrs. Schaffer, now a Fayetteville lawyer, said she did not remember the Federal examination of Madison but added that in her view, the findings were not "definitive proof of insolvency."

In 1985, Mrs. Clinton and her Little Rock law firm, the Rose firm, twice applied to the Securities Commission on behalf of Madison, asking that the savings and loan be allowed to try two novel plans to raise money.

Mrs. Schaffer wrote to Mrs. Clinton and another lawyer at the firm approving the ideas. "I never gave anybody special treatment," she said.

Madison was not able to raise additional capital. And by 1986 Federal regulators, who insured Madison's deposits, took control of the institution and ousted Mr. McDougal. Mrs. Schaffer supported the action.

U.S. Investigating Clinton's Links to Arkansas S.& L.

By JEFF GERTH with STEPHEN ENGELBERG

November 2, 1993 Special to *The New York Times*

WASHINGTON, Nov. 1 — Federal investigators are raising questions about ties between President Clinton and an Arkansas businessman, a political patron of Mr. Clinton in the 1980's whose failed savings and loan is now under investigation.

Government officials and lawyers familiar with the case said the President was neither the subject nor a target of the investigation, which is still in its early stages.

But the inquiry focuses on questionable financial dealings involving the savings and loan, Madison Guaranty, from which Mr. Clinton benefited both personally and politically. The savings and loan's owner, James McDougal, was one of Mr. Clinton's closest associates in Arkansas and was, at various times, his business partner, political fund-raiser, family banker and senior aide when Mr. Clinton was Governor of Arkansas.

Advantageous Relationship

Mr. Clinton's banking commissioner advised him in 1983 that Mr. McDougal was engaged in questionable banking practices. But the two men nevertheless maintained a business and political relationship throughout the 1980's that helped both men. When Mr. Clinton needed someone to raise $35,000 to retire debts from his 1984 re-election campaign, he turned to Mr. McDougal.

Mr. McDougal denies any wrongdoing. His lawyer, Sam Heuer, said his client was under investigation by the United States Attorney in Little Rock, Ark. Last month the Federal agency that disposes of failed savings and loans, the Resolution Trust Corporation, asked the United States Attorney in Little Rock to examine several possible violations of law in the operations of the savings and loan, including transactions that may have helped Mr. Clinton pay his campaign debts.

According to Federal officials, court documents and lawyers familiar with the case, the two Federal agencies have been trying to find out whether more than $250,000 in business loans was improperly diverted from Madison in April 1985 to several sources, including Governor Clinton's re-election campaign.

The officials said the campaign received $12,000 in cashier's checks from Madison, some of which appeared to have been paid for by the business loans. The former Clinton aide who deposited the money said neither she nor Mr. Clinton was aware of any irregularities about its source.

Investigators have asked prosecutors to see whether the campaign contributions were linked to efforts by Madison to win state approval for an unusual plan to raise new capital by issuing stock, the officials said.

Finally, prosecutors are studying a $300,000 loan from a federally sponsored lending company to Mr. McDougal's wife, Susan. The man who made the loan,

David Hale, was indicted in September on unrelated charges.

In an effort to win leniency from prosecutors on the eve of his indictment, Mr. Hale offered prosecutors information about Mr. Clinton and other Arkansas politicians, but was unable to reach a plea agreement. Mr. Hale asserted in interviews with reporters that Mr. Clinton had personally pressed him to make the $300,000 loan.

A White House spokesman said Mr. Clinton had no recollection of any such conversation. Mr. Hale said Mr. McDougal told him the money would help conceal earlier favors for the Governor.

New Prosecutor

The criminal investigations of Madison and Mr. Hale's lending activities are being directed by the new United States Attorney in Little Rock, Paula J. Casey. On Sunday, The Washington Post disclosed the Resolution Trust Corporation's request to Ms. Casey, and The Wall Street Journal reported on the inquiry today.

Mr. Hale's lawyer has questioned Ms. Casey's independence. She was a volunteer in Mr. Clinton's campaigns for governor and was his student at the University of Arkansas law school. Ms. Casey would not discuss the case but told Mr. Hale's lawyer that she was not afraid to prosecute anyone.

Mr. McDougal, who is at the heart of the inquiry into the savings and loan's affairs, continues to blame regulators and prosecutors for his downfall, calling them overzealous. He was acquitted of Federal bank fraud charges involving Madison in 1980.

Mr. McDougal met Mr. Clinton in the late 1960's, when both men worked on the staff of Senator J. William Fulbright, the Arkansas Democrat and longtime chairman of the Senate Foreign Relations Committee.

Ozarks Real Estate Deal

In 1978, the McDougals brought Mr. Clinton and his wife, Hillary, into a real estate deal, buying 200 acres of the Ozarks in northern Arksansas. Later, the property was transferred to their company, Whitewater Development, with both couples sharing the liabilities and potential profits.

When Mr. Clinton first took office as Governor in 1979, Mr. McDougal joined him as an economic development aide. But he soon returned to business, buying a bank in northern Arkansas and a savings and loan in a small town about 75 miles from Little Rock.

By 1983, Mr. McDougal's bank was in trouble with Arkansas regulators. The state's banking commissioner, Marlin S. Jackson, ordered the bank to stop making imprudent loans. Mr. Jackson, a Clinton appointee, said in an interview last year that he told Mr. Clinton at the time of Mr. McDougal's questionable practices.

Meanwhile, the savings and loan continued to grow, from $6 million in assets to more than $100 million by 1985. It opened a branch in Little Rock near the

Statehouse and began making loans to prominent Democrats, including Mr. Fulbright and Jim Guy Tucker, a Little Rock lawyer who is now Governor of Arkansas.

Records also indicate that Madison was helping Whitewater, the real estate business owned by the Clintons and McDougals. In 1984 and 1985, as the company continued to post losses, check ledgers show that the company had frequent, sizable overdrafts on its account at Madison.

Also in 1985, Madison Marketing, a McDougal family business that derived all of its revenue from the savings and loan, provided the funds for Whitewater to make a $7,322 payment on a loan taken out by Mr. Clinton from another bank, according to bank records.

The Clinton Presidential campaign said last year that the McDougals had contributed a disproportionate share of Whitewater's money, $92,000 against $68,000 by the Clintons.

In interviews last year, Mr. McDougal seemed to view his relationship with Mr. Clinton as unbalanced. On the one hand, he said, "Bill never turned me down on something I asked for, and I only asked for it occasionally."

But on the other hand, Mr. McDougal said, he helped the Clintons in numerous ways, from agreeing to hire Mrs. Clinton to do additional legal work at Madison, to paying on Mr. Clinton's behalf part of the loans on the Ozark property.

Favors on Both Sides

Mr. McDougal said in the same interviews that 1985 was a year of favors on both sides. In early 1985, he said, Mr. Clinton asked him to raise enough money to retire about $35,000 in debts left from his 1984 campaign.

Betsey Wright, who ran the 1984 campaign, confirmed that Mr. Clinton had made the request and said it led Mr. McDougal to be the host for a small fund-raising event in 1985 at the savings and loan. Mr. Clinton attended that event.

As for the source of the donations, Ms. Wright said: "I'm sure we would have no idea. Any hint of a problem and we would not have accepted."

At least $12,000 worth of cashier's checks issued by Madison wound up in the campaign's coffers in April 1985, Federal officials said. Some came from a business loan that Madison made to a McDougal associate and was never repaid. The rest was from Mr. McDougal's personal and corporate accounts, the officials said.

Days before Mr. McDougal held his fund-raising event for Mr. Clinton, Madison learned that it faced a serious problem. Federal regulators were concerned by the savings and loan's rapid growth and the failure to have on hand enough capital to meet Federal requirements.

State Approval Needed

Madison's proposal was to raise money to meet the capital requirement by selling a form of stock never issued before in Arkansas by a savings and loan. Because it was a state-chartered institution, Madison needed the approval of Arkansas regulators.

The savings and loan did not rely on its usual outside counsel for this issue, turning instead to the Rose law firm of Little Rock, where Mrs. Clinton was a senior partner. In written answers to questions last year, she said she met with Mr. McDougal once in April 1985 to discuss working for Madison. She declined to elaborate.

In the documents forwarded to prosecutors, investigators for the Resolution Trust Corporation have questioned whether the campaign contributions were connected to Madison's effort to get state regulators to approve its stock plan, Federal officials say. By May, Arkansas regulators had concurred that the stock plan was legal, but it was never carried out.

James M. Lyons, a Denver lawyer who reviewed Mr. Clinton's dealings with Mr. McDougal for the Clinton Presidential campaign last year, said today that there was no connection between the contributions and the effort before the state regulators.

Mr. McDougal, in interviews, denied any impropriety in connection with the campaign contributions or the attempt to win approval for the stock plan.

At the end of 1985, Mr. McDougal said last year, Mr. Clinton did do him another favor, helping set up a state revenue office in a Little Rock building owned by a subsidiary of Madison.

By the fall of 1985, Mr. McDougal faced mounting pressure, some of which came from the prospect of a Federal audit scheduled for early 1986.

David Hale, a Democratic municipal judge in Little Rock who operated a federally sponsored lending company, said he was approached by Mr. McDougal in late 1985 to make loans that would help the "political family" of Arkansas Democrats.

Mr. Hale's company was part of a Small Business Administration program intended to provide capital for businesses owned by "socially or economically disadvantaged" people. Mr. Hale was recently indicted on charges of misleading the Government about the condition of his lending company. He has since resigned as a judge and is contesting the charges.

In interviews before his indictment, Mr. Hale said Madison financed a land deal in February 1986 in which he was paid hundreds of thousands of dollars more than the property was worth. Court records show that this loan was never repaid, resulting in a loss of $672,000 to taxpayers.

Questionable Transactions

With profits from that deal in hand, Mr. Hale said he had been able to fulfill Mr. McDougal's request for a $300,000 loan to his wife.

Mr. Hale said in an interview that Mr. McDougal told him the $300,000 would not be used by the designated borrower. Instead, he said, it would conceal questionable transactions by Madison, including indirect help for the Clintons.

Mr. Hale asserts that Mr. Clinton twice pressed him to make this loan. Mark D. Gearan, the White House communications director, said the President had "no recollection" of any such conversation and did not believe it took place.

Mr. McDougal denied any wrongdoing in his dealings with Mr. Hale, saying he thinks the $300,000 wound up in his real estate ventures.

Federal officials are now trying to trace where the $300,000 lent by Mr. Hale ultimately went.

HEAD OF FAILING S.& L. HELPED CLINTON PAY A
$50,000 PERSONAL DEBT IN 1985

By JEFF GERTH with STEPHEN ENGELBERG

December 15, 1993 Special to *The New York Times*

WASHINGTON, Dec. 14 — The owner of a failing Arkansas savings and loan association raised money for Gov. Bill Clinton in 1985 to help relieve the Clinton family of a $50,000 personal debt that the Clintons would otherwise have had trouble repaying, newly discovered documents show.

The disclosure that the money covered a heavy private debt, rather than a less personally onerous campaign obligation, shows that the savings and loan executive, James McDougal, performed a more valuable favor for Mr. Clinton than has been previously known.

Federal investigators and Congressional officials are looking into the costly collapse of Mr. McDougal's savings and loan, and one aspect of the inquiries is whether his friendship with the Governor influenced the state regulatory treatment he received.

The Government took over the institution, Madison Guaranty Savings and Loan, in 1989 at a cost to taxpayers of more than $60 million. That was five years after Federal regulators first found numerous violations at Madison and three years after they acted to remove Mr. McDougal.

Three months before Mr. McDougal helped Mr. Clinton cover his debt, the Governor had appointed as the new state regulator in charge of savings and loans a Little Rock lawyer who had previously represented Mr. McDougal's troubled institution.

Over the next 18 months, up to the point where Federal officials removed Mr. McDougal, the new regulator took no significant action against Madison, even as she was moving vigorously against another failing institution with similar problems.

Bruce Lindsey, a senior Presidential adviser chosen by the White House to respond to questions about Mr. McDougal, said today that the relationship between the Clintons and the savings and loan owner had been entirely proper.

But Mr. Lindsey said he was unable to answer specific questions about the $50,000 debt or its repayment. As for the appointment of the regulator, Beverly Bassett Schaffer, he said, "The President felt she was a respected securities attorney and turned out to be a respected securities commissioner."

$50,000 Loan From Aide's Bank

A Federal investigation uncovered evidence some time ago that Mr. McDougal had diverted money from his institution to help repay debts left over from Mr. Clinton's 1984 re-election campaign.

But the newly discovered documents, and interviews with onetime political aides to Mr. Clinton, show for the first time that the campaign's only debt was to Mr. Clinton, who had contributed $50,000 to help finance his own candidacy. Mr. Clinton borrowed the money from the tiny Bank of Cherry Valley, which was owned and run by a senior aide to the Governor.

By borrowing the money and giving it to his campaign, Mr. Clinton was incurring a liability that his financial records suggest he barely could have met without help.

Just a few weeks after Mr. McDougal raised the money for him, Madison Guaranty won approval from Mrs. Schaffer, Mr. Clinton's new financial regulator, for a novel plan to sell stock. And Federal investigators have learned that Mrs. Schaffer previously served for a short time as one of Madison's lawyers.

In her legal work, the investigators say, she gained inside knowledge of some of Madison's wrongdoing. Yet when she became a regulator, she never told her subordinates that she had worked for Madison, present and former state officials say. And she continued to make decisions about the institution despite state ethics guidelines that, according to leading ethics experts in Arkansas and nationally, suggest she should have stepped aside.

Mrs. Schaffer, now a lawyer in Arkansas, denied in an interview that Madison had received preferential treatment and said her predecessor in the post had allowed Madison to pursue risky investments. She said Mr. Clinton had not intervened on behalf of Madison, adding of her own role: "I didn't try to protect anyone. And I didn't try to hurt anyone."

In an interview last year, Mr. McDougal said the appointment of Mrs. Schaffer and his role in retiring the campaign debt were part of a relationship in which he and Mr. Clinton had done favors for each other. Mrs. Schaffer was his preferred candidate for the post of regulator, he said.

By 1985, however, he had come to resent Mr. Clinton's requests for help on such matters as the campaign debt, Mr. McDougal said.

"I was beginning to feel I was getting used," he said. "I would have gotten Bassett anyways," he said of Mrs. Schaffer.

Rapid Growth, 'Willful' Violations

Mr. McDougal's relationship with Mr. Clinton dates from the 1960's, when they met while working as aides to Senator J. W. Fulbright, Democrat of Arkansas.

Mr. McDougal later served for a year as Governor Clinton's economic development aide, then left government and in 1982 bought a savings and loan in Augusta, Ark., a sleepy rural town. The institution, Madison Guaranty, quickly got caught up in the go-go ethos of the early 1980's. Its growth was exponential, from assets of $3 million to more than $120 million by 1985.

Federal auditors took a dim view of Mr. McDougal's activities. A 1984 review found "unsafe and unsound lending practices" and concluded that "the viability of the institution is jeopardized."

Mr. McDougal promised to make amends, and state and Federal regulators eventually allowed him to go forward, provided he made adjustments to his books and obtained required state approval for several large real estate projects.

One of those was a project to sell land on a foggy Canadian island off the coast of Maine. In violation of Federal land law, Madison had sold scores of lots without making disclosure of risks to purchasers and had failed to register any such disclosure statement with the Department of Housing and Urban Development, according to state and Federal records and former Madison officials.

Madison's lawyers learned of these omissions in 1984. Mrs. Schaffer, then at the Little Rock firm of Mitchell, Williams, Selig, Jackson & Tucker, wrote a memo describing the failure to comply with land law as "willful," Federal officials say.

Madison registered with HUD in February 1985 and began providing buyers the federally required disclosure on the project's considerable risks. One year later, roughly half the buyers of Canadian lots had canceled their purchases, increasing Madison's losses and pushing it to the brink of insolvency, according to a 1986 Federal examination of the institution.

As Mr. McDougal faced questions from Federal regulators, Mr. Clinton was gearing up for his 1984 re-election campaign for governor. By the fall of 1984, he had raised hundreds of thousands of dollars for the drive, and polls showed him comfortably ahead.

Still, in the final week Mr. Clinton put himself at significant personal financial risk to inject an additional $50,000 into the coffers. He and his wife, Hillary, applied for a loan from the Bank of Cherry Valley, a tiny institution in northeast Arkansas then run by W. Maurice Smith, who was also a senior aide to the Governor.

Mr. Smith said in an interview that the loan had been unsecured, meaning that the Clintons had not been required to pledge any collateral and would repay the loan on the basis of their joint income. According to the Clintons' tax returns, their combined income in 1984 and 1985 was about $100,000 a year.

Further, they had only modest personal assets. They did not own a home, and they had substantial debts. Records released by the Clinton Presidential campaign in 1992 show that in 1984, the couple owed more than $75,000 in bank loans stemming from their investment in Whitewater Development, an unsuccessful real estate company that they owned jointly with Mr. McDougal and his wife.

Asked whether he was aware of the Clintons' debts when he approved the loan, Mr. Smith said that "if it was in their financial statement" that they filed with the bank as a requirement for the loan, then "I knew about it."

A Spring Evening Worth $35,000

In January 1985, Mr. Clinton named Mrs. Schaffer as head of the State Securities Department, the Arkansas agency that shared with Federal regulators the responsibility for overseeing state-chartered savings and loan associations.

Separately, his political aides began raising tens of thousands of dollars for his 1986 re-election bid. At the same time, according to Mr. McDougal and

Betsey Wright, who had managed the 1984 campaign, Mr. Clinton asked Mr. McDougal to take care of the debt still left over from 1984.

"He asked me to knock out the deficit," Mr. McDougal recalled.

In the spring of 1985, Mr. McDougal held an early-evening fund-raising event at Madison's office in Little Rock, near the governor's mansion. There, he says, he delivered about $35,000 in checks to Ms. Wright.

The records reflecting the contributions from the fund-raiser are missing from campaign documents on file with the Pulaski County clerk in Little Rock. But among the documents that are on file there are those listing Mr. Clinton's $50,000 contribution to his own campaign.

Investigators reviewing Madison's records in the wake of its collapse found evidence that led them to suspect that some of the campaign donations assembled by Mr. McDougal had been improperly diverted from the savings and loan, Federal officials have said.

The investigators traced checks totaling $12,000 from Madison to the Clinton campaign's account at the Bank of Cherry Valley. Those checks were issued on April 4.

The day before, senior Madison officials met in Dallas with Federal regulators who wanted to know how the savings and loan intended to meet minimum requirements for capital. Madison said it planned to raise the money by selling stock, according to a Federal memo describing the meeting. The institution planned to issue preferred stock, the sale of which had rarely, if ever, been attempted by an Arkansas savings and loan.

The search for new capital took Madison to the offices of Mrs. Schaffer, who had the ultimate authority to approve any such stock sale. One of the lawyers employed by Madison to argue its case before the state regulators was Mrs. Clinton.

Within weeks, Mrs. Schaffer wrote a letter to Mrs. Clinton giving preliminary approval to Madison's stock plan.

The sale never went forward. But this fall the Resolution Trust Corporation, the Federal agency that disposes of failed savings and loans, asked the Justice Department to examine a number of Madison's transactions, and Federal officials say the state's approval of the stock plan was among the matters raised by investigators.

The R.T.C. noted that Mrs. Schaffer's approval of the stock sale had come in the face of her own, prior knowledge that Madison had failed to comply with Federal land-sale laws.

Mrs. Schaffer says that even in not stepping aside in matters involving Madison, she acted properly. Citing lawyer-client confidentiality, she declines to discuss what she learned when she represented Madison. Whatever she learned, she now says, did not seem important later, when she became a state regulator.

2 Institutions, 2 Approaches

Mr. McDougal, who was acquitted of Federal bank fraud charges in 1990, maintains he did nothing wrong. He blames overzealous regulators for his problems.

But a blistering Federal report in 1986, three years before Madison was seized, found that records were missing or inaccurate, that the institution was probably insolvent and that millions of dollars had been improperly diverted to Mr. McDougal, his friends and his family.

State records show that from 1984 to 1986, as Madison hurtled toward collapse, Arkansas regulators imposed no special requirements on it. The state's only action against Madison was to concur when Federal regulators removed Mr. McDougal in the summer of 1986.

But Arkansas regulators were not hesitant to move against another failing institution.

Mrs. Schaffer said she had urged Federal regulators to shut down Guaranty Savings and Loan, a $450 million institution based in northern Arkansas that was closed in December 1985. She said the problems at Guaranty had been growth that was too rapid, bad loans outside of Arkansas and reliance on large deposits brokered by other financial institutions—virtually the same problems that regulators found at Madison.

Mrs. Schaffer said she had moved against Madison as soon as legally possible, relying on her own staff and acting in conjunction with Federal regulators. Even looking back now, she said, "I don't see what I could have done differently."

TOP ARKANSAS LAWYER HELPED HILLARY CLINTON TURN BIG PROFIT
Commodities Trading in 70's Yielded $100,000

The following article is based on reporting by Dean Baquet, Jeff Gerth and Stephen Labaton and was written by Mr. Gerth.

March 18, 1994 Special to *The New York Times*

WASHINGTON, March 17 — Starting just before Bill Clinton was elected Governor of Arkansas, Hillary Rodham Clinton made about $100,000 in one year in the commodities market with the help and advice of a friend who was the top lawyer for one of the state's most powerful and heavily regulated companies.

The investments, made in a commodities trading account that was opened three weeks before Mr. Clinton was elected Governor in 1978, substantially altered the finances of the Clintons. At the time, Mr. Clinton was Attorney General. He and his wife were rising stars in Little Rock whose salaries were modest by the standards of their peers.

The proceeds helped them to buy a home, to invest in securities and real estate and eventually to provide a nest egg for their young daughter, according to the couple's associates and a review of the family's financial records.

Tyson's Fortunes

But the trades, which came to light during a two-month examination of the Clintons' finances by The New York Times, also left them in the position of having relied significantly on the help of one of the state's premier powerbrokers, James B. Blair, a Clinton confidant who at the time was the primary outside lawyer for Tyson Foods Inc., of Springdale, Ark., the nation's biggest poultry company.

During Mr. Clinton's tenure in Arkansas, Tyson benefited from a variety of state actions, including $9 million in government loans, the placement of company executives on important state boards and favorable decisions on environmental issues. Even today, critics in Congress and elsewhere have complained that the Clinton Administration is too close to Tyson and the poultry industry it dominates, sparing it from some of the tougher Federal inspection guidelines enacted against the meat industry.

Her Money, Her Risk

In a written statement, the Clintons' personal lawyer, David Kendall, said today that Mrs. Clinton had traded in commodities futures "with her own funds and assumed the full risk of loss."

"She did so through two different trading accounts in her own name in Little Rock and Springdale, Ark.," he said. "Mrs. Clinton reported gains and losses on her tax returns as appropriate."

Mr. Blair, in telephone interviews on Wednesday and today, confirmed that he had encouraged Mrs. Clinton to invest in the normally risky commodity markets and to open an account at a Springdale brokerage, and that he then used his investing skills to help guide her through a series of lucrative trades.

Mr. Blair and Administration officials designated to discuss the matter — but who would speak only on condition of anonymity — said Mrs. Clinton had put up the stake with which she began trading. The officials would not say how much money Mrs. Clinton had put at risk.

Lisa Caputo, Mrs. Clinton's press secretary, said in a statement tonight: "Mrs. Clinton consulted with numerous people, and she did her own research. This was her own risk; the commodity investments were her own responsibility."

The Administration officials said that Mrs. Clinton also studied financial data, including some in The Wall Street Journal.

John Podesta, a White House spokesman, said tonight: "Hillary and Jim were friends. He gave her advice. There was no impropriety. The only appearance is being created by The New York Times."

Mr. Blair, who himself made several million dollars trading commodities, said he saw no conflict of interest; he said he had helped Mrs. Clinton as a close friend, not because of the position held by her husband.

Speaking of the Clintons, he said: "Do they have to go weed their friends out and say they can only have friends who are sweeping the streets? They have friends who are high-powered lawyers. They have friends who write books, who write poetry."

Mr. Blair and the Administration officials estimated Mrs. Clinton's profits at $100,000. The officials said she opened her trading account in mid-October 1978, three weeks before Mr. Clinton was elected with 63 percent of the vote. She got out of the market on Oct. 17, 1979, just as the rising market in cattle futures from which she had profited was collapsing.

Protecting State Jobs

As Governor and as a candidate for President in 1992, Mr. Clinton was forthright in defending the assistance that the state government gave to Tyson, which is among Arkansas's largest employers, saying that it was good for the state's economy.

Archie Schaffer, director of media, public and government affairs for Tyson, denied that Mr. Clinton had done any special favors for the company or the Arkansas poultry industry.

"I can tell you that I disagree totally with any suggestion that the Clinton gubernatorial administration gave the poultry industry or Tyson any breaks," he said. "That's just nonsense." Mr. Schaffer said he knew nothing of the commodity trading.

The history of the commodities trades casts a new light on the Clintons' personal finances and on their relationship to the poultry industry and to Mr. Blair, who remains a powerful figure where politics and business intersect in Arkansas.

Source of Down Payment

The trades have never been publicly disclosed. During the 1992 Presidential campaign, the Clintons and their aides gave conflicting accounts when asked to explain where the couple got the money to make a $60,000 down payment on a house in 1980. During the campaign, aides declined to release the Clintons' tax returns for the late 1970's and did so again today.

When the question of the down payment first arose, the campaign said it had come from an investment by Mrs. Clinton, one that the officials declined to describe. At another point, the officials released a statement in Mrs. Clinton's name that said the money had come from "our savings and a gift from my parents."

Today, the Administration officials said that the down payment had come from savings, including the proceeds of the successful commodities trade.

The Clintons and Blair
Low-Paid Stars, Longtime Power

Bill Clinton came from a family of modest means, and for all his political prominence, neither he nor his wife, Hillary Rodham, had ever made much money.

Mr. Clinton was elected State Attorney General in 1976, at the age of 30. His annual salary then was $26,500. Two years later, on becoming the nation's youngest governor, his salary rose to $35,000, leaving him one of the nation's lowest-paid governors.

Mrs. Clinton, like her husband a Yale Law School graduate, had joined him in teaching law at the University of Arkansas in Fayetteville in the mid-1970's. For the nine-month 1975-76 school year, each was paid $18,090, a university spokeswoman said. When Mr. Clinton's election as Attorney General took them to Little Rock in 1977, she joined the Rose Law Firm there as an associate. Her starting salary is not public, but within a year after making partner in 1980 it was $46,000.

Mr. Blair, 11 years older than Mr. Clinton, was already established in the world of business and politics in Arkansas. By the late 1970's, he had become one of the state's most successful trial lawyers.

His firm, Crouch, Blair, Cypert & Waters, was in Springdale, the center of Arkansas's booming poultry industry. In addition to advising some of the state's biggest poultry companies, it represented big trucking companies and the local utility. Mr. Blair was also a force in statewide political circles. In 1974, he ran the final, doomed re-election campaign of Senator J. William Fulbright, Mr. Clinton's political mentor.

While a partner at Crouch, Blair, Mr. Blair became general counsel to Tyson, which was founded in 1936, when John Tyson began hauling live chickens from Arkansas to Chicago. Mr. Blair eventually left the law firm and went to work directly for the founder's son, Donald J. Tyson, now chairman and chief executive. Over the years Mr. Blair has served as a director of more than 20 Tyson-controlled companies across the country.

The Trades
Exquisite Timing in a Risky Game

Mr. Blair said in the interview that he first ventured into the stock market in 1956, when he was 20 years old. Through the 50's and 60's, he said, he made more money in stocks than he did practicing law. In the 1970's, he began trading commodity futures.

Mr. Blair's timing was impeccable. In the tiny Springdale office of Refco Inc., a trading firm based in Chicago, a rag-tag group of brokers, some of whom had been small-town liquor salesmen and clerks, was making millions of dollars, capitalizing on a stunning boom in futures contracts prices. The office's founder, a professional poker player named Robert Bone, was a 13-year Tyson executive who had turned a knack for gauging odds into a small fortune.

Mr. Blair said Mrs. Clinton had got into the commodities market at his suggestion.

"I recommended to her that she open an account at the Refco office," he said. "I was on a streak, on a streak that I thought was very successful, and I wanted to share this with my close friends, as I did with my fiancée, as I did with my law firm, as I did with my children, as I did with my fiancée's children and as I did with the person who was the best person at my marriage, which was Hillary, a tennis partner and friend."

Mr. Blair advised Mrs. Clinton to get into the cattle futures market because, he said, "I specifically was trading the cattle futures, and thought I knew what I was doing." He added, "I'm damn good at it."

On Blair's Advice

Mr. Blair, a close friend and lawyer for Mr. Bone, who was known as Red, said Mrs. Clinton had started with a small stake. Mr. Kendall declined to say today how much money she had put up.

According to trading records examined by The New York Times and people familiar with the trades, she opened her account in the Refco office, using Mr. Bone as her broker. The account was opened in mid-October 1978, when Mr. Clinton was described in Arkansas newspapers as the favorite in the governor's race.

Mr. Blair said he had helped guide Mrs. Clinton's trades. "We discussed whether she ought to be long or short" in her trades, Mr. Blair recalled, referring to betting whether prices would rise or fall. "It was done in consultation," he said. "I gave her my best advice."

Mr. Blair said that while he would make specific trading recommendations, Mrs. Clinton "determined the size of the trade."

Around the time of Mr. Clinton's 1978 election, Mrs. Clinton opened another commodity trading account, this one with Stephens Inc., a large brokerage firm in Little Rock, Administration officials said. But they said that the bulk of her trading profits had come from the Refco account.

Mr. Blair said he had nothing to do with the decision to trade from the Stephens account.

People familiar with Mrs. Clinton's trading said she had profited from most but not all of the trades.

In commodities trading, a speculator essentially bets on the future value of a commodity, like cattle or pork. Trading in such futures contracts is among the riskiest and most volatile of investments. By some estimates, more than three-quarters of all investors lose money. But a sophisticated trader, or one with special knowledge of a market, can turn a small stake into millions of dollars.

According to records and people familiar with the trades, Mrs. Clinton made most of the $100,000 in proceeds trading in cattle futures.

But after several go-go years, the cattle futures market collapsed in the fall of 1979, shattering the Refco office, leading to huge losses and lengthy litigation and sending some of the traders, including Mr. Bone, into bankruptcy.

The Administration officials said Mrs. Clinton closed her Refco account in mid-October 1979 and her Stephens account in early 1980.

Administration officials said she had got out of the market because after she became pregnant with her daughter, Chelsea, she did not have the time to keep up with developments and found the investments too nerve-wracking.

Mr. Bone does not recall how much money Mr. Blair made during the boom or lost during the bust. But he remembers that when Mr. Blair departed from the markets, "He left happy."

The Benefits
Proceeds Gave Clintons Nest Egg

Other than a brief reference to $449 in commodities trading losses on their 1980 tax return, there is no evidence that the Clintons ever returned to the highly volatile commodities markets.

But their brief involvement substantially improved their fortunes. Based on the tax returns they have released, the commodity trades were by far their most successful investment.

In mid-1978, in seeking a loan from a bank in Flippin, Ark., that financed the real estate venture called Whitewater, the Clintons reported having few assets, executives of the bank have said. The main reason they got the loan, the bankers added, was the creditworthiness of the Clintons' partner in Whitewater, James B. McDougal, who at the time was a developer.

But in November 1979, shortly after Mrs. Clinton closed her Refco account, the Clintons were able to acquire $55,463 in bonds, according to their 1980 tax return. And in December 1980, after Mr. Clinton was voted out of the governor's office, the Clintons were able to make the house down payment.

Mr. McDougal has also said that in 1980, Mrs. Clinton approached him for advice about putting money in tax shelters. Mr. McDougal, who made his remarks in a 1992 interview with the Times, recalled Mrs. Clinton saying that she needed to shelter large profits that Mr. Blair had helped her make in the commodities market.

The personal ties between Mr. Blair and the Clintons have remained strong. On some visits to Arkansas, the Clintons stay at the waterfront vacation home of Mr. Blair and his wife, Diane. The Wall Street Journal has reported that on the President's inauguration night, the Blairs spent the night at the White House.

During the 1980's, Mr. Blair was appointed to the board of the University of Arkansas, where he served as chairman. Mrs. Blair, a political science professor at the university, was appointed last year to the board of the Corporation for Public Broadcasting, which helps channel Federal funds to the nation's public broadcast stations.

Mr. Blair has also remained a behind-the-scenes adviser to Mr. Clinton since his first days in public office. For example, during the 1992 campaign—and after the election — Mr. Blair helped devise strategies for blunting criticism about the Clintons' involvement with Mr. McDougal and Whitewater, said Mr. McDougal and Susan Thomases, a campaign aide.

The Growth of Tyson
Company Thrived in Clinton Years

The ties between Mr. Clinton and Mr. Blair's client remained strong as well. Mr. Clinton's record of support for the poultry industry and Tyson in particular has been a subject of debate for years in Little Rock, and it became an issue during the 1992 Presidential campaign. Even today, critics in Congress and others have accused the Clinton Administration of not being tough enough on the industry, particularly in inspecting chickens. Today, a spokeswoman for the Agriculture Department defended its record and said the department was moving to tighten inspections after years of neglect.

The criticism of Tyson's connection to the White House goes beyond its poultry interests. The company owns Arctic Alaska Fisheries, a large fish-trawling business based in Seattle. Last April, small fishing outfits in the Northwest complained that Tyson's relationship with the Clinton Administration was one reason the Government reversed course and instituted rules that would allow Arctic Alaska and other big trawlers to dominate the nation's $100 million whiting catch. The Commerce Department, which wrote the rules, denies the accusation.

Mr. Podesta, the White House spokesman, said: "The President and Jim Blair have never discussed Blair's clients' business with the Federal Government. During the Clinton Administration, we know of no instance of his ever lobbying a Clinton White House official or discussing matters of concern between his client and the Federal Government."

Throughout the 1970's and 1980's, Governor Clinton and his administration made several significant decisions that helped Tyson become one of the world's biggest poultry companies. In campaigns for Governor and President, when questioned about his support of the company, Mr. Clinton said he had fought for the industry because it was one of the biggest employers in a depressed state.

As Attorney General in 1978, Mr. Clinton intervened in a lawsuit that eventually loosened Federal regulations so that Tyson and other Arkansas poultry processors could vastly increase their productivity.

As Governor, Mr. Clinton reappointed a Tyson veterinarian to the Livestock and Poultry Commission, a regulatory body often criticized as being too close to the industry.

'Clinton Understands'

Mr. Tyson, in turn, has been a major fund raiser for Mr. Clinton and has praised him for creating a friendly environment for the growth of the poultry industry.

Last year, three days after Mr. Clinton's inauguration, Mr. Tyson was asked what influence he hoped to have with the new President.

"I would be irresponsible to my company and my industry if I didn't have any input," Mr. Tyson said after a speech in Anchorage. "Clinton understands the needs of business. There were several times in our company's growth that we could have taken opportunities outside of the state, but we chose to stay in Arkansas because he understands the balance between economic development and environmental issues."

Mr. Schaffer, the Tyson spokesman, said the company received no special treatment on environmental questions. The company has spent "tens, if not hundreds of millions of dollars" upgrading its plants to avoid pollution problems, he said.

But environmentalists and many Arkansas residents have complained that the balance was often tilted toward industry. The instance they cite most frequently was a long legal battle that followed the discovery that a Tyson plant in Green Forest, a town of 1,600 in northwest Arkansas, had been leaking waste into Dry Creek.

After Delay, Disaster

In 1977, the state pollution control agency reissued the license for Tyson's Green Forest plant on the condition that the company meet with city officials to work out a plan for treating its wastes. But the state never enforced the order, and in May 1983 the waste from the plant seeped into the town's drinking water. Residents became ill, and 15 months later Governor Clinton declared the town a disaster area.

In a lawsuit in 1989, some residents contended that the company was responsible for a pattern of pollution around the state, abetted by a state government that refused to do anything about it.

"The various regulatory authorities legally charged with protecting the water, land and people of Arkansas from this well-known pollution have failed to take any meaningful enforcement action," the Green Forest residents said in their lawsuit. The lawsuit produced evidence that Mr. Clinton was personally briefed on the pollution problems at Green Forest, and it contended that his administration had failed to take significant action. State officials and the company denied any wrongdoing.

As one example, the residents cited the state Pollution Control and Ecology Commission, which levied an $11,000 fine when Tyson's was found to have dumped waste from its plant in nearby Berryville onto private property. Mr. Blair took part in negotiating that settlement, according to court papers.

The lawsuit also revealed one instance in which Mr. Blair threatened to go to the Governor's office when the state's top health officials tried in 1987 to get the company to stop dumping sludge into Green Forest's drinking water supply.

On May 19, 1987, in response to a letter from Dr. Ben N. Saltzman, director of the state Department of Health, Mr. Blair wrote that the Pollution Commission had given the company permission to dump sludge. Tyson, he wrote, was caught in a turf battle between warring agencies.

"It seems to me it is time to have a major meeting in the Governor's office with the Governor's staff and get the turf problems ironed out," he wrote.

The meeting never took place.

The Green Forest case was recently settled out of court. The terms were sealed.

The following four memoranda are reprinted by permission
of Beverly Bassett Schaffer.

TO: Jeff Girth [*sic*], New York Times
FROM: Beverly Bassett Schaffer
RE: Madison Guaranty Savings and Loan
DATE: February 25, 1992

On February 14, 1992, I spoke with you by telephone concerning the above
referenced Arkansas savings and loan that was closed during my tenure as
Arkansas Securities Commissioner and Savings and Loan Supervisor. We discussed a number of items during our telephone conversation, many of which I
was unable to fully address at that time due to my lack of specific recollection of
matters that occurred as much as seven years ago.

Since then I have reviewed my personal and work calendars from 1985 and
1986, reviewed certain documents pertaining to Madison Guaranty and spoken
with Charles Handley at the Securities Department, who participated in each
and every decision concerning savings and loan matters during my tenure. I
believe it is important that I give you the benefit of my personal knowledge concerning these matters.

In 1984, I was a practicing attorney with expertise in securities law. I was a
member of the Mitchell Law Firm in Little Rock which I had joined in 1978 as a
law clerk and later became an associate and partner. In 1977, while I was a law
student, I worked full time for a year for Bill Clinton when he was serving as
Attorney General. I had first met Bill Clinton in 1974 when I worked as a volunteer in his first campaign for elective office as a congressman (he lost). My
brother, Woody Bassett, who is also a practicing attorney in Fayetteville, is a
long time close friend and supporter of Bill Clinton's and has been active in
Democratic party matters for years.

Sometime in mid-1984, I learned that Lee Thalheimer, a friend of mine and
law school classmate of my brother's, planned to leave his post as Securities
Commissioner. I discussed with my brother my interest in seeking the job
because I wanted to build my expertise as a securities lawyer and, for a variety of
reasons, I was not happy at the law firm. I know that my brother discussed this
with Bill Clinton and his then Chief of Staff, Betsey Wright, several times in
1984 and I did as well.

In early January, 1985, I met with Governor Clinton at the Governor's Mansion to discuss in general the kinds of issues facing the securities industry at the time. It was a lengthy meeting and I do not recall any mention at all of savings and loans. A few days later, the Governor called me at home to tell me he planned to appoint me as Securities Commissioner. He asked that I not say anything about it until he had had a chance to call the other persons who had asked for the job to personally tell them of his decision. Later that same week, on Friday, January 18, 1985, Joan Roberts, who was the Governor's press secretary, called me at my law office to tell me that the Governor planned to announce my appointment that day and asked me to get a resume and picture to the Governor's office right away. Members of my law firm often asked me about the appointment and I declined to share with them my conversations with Bill Clinton. On the day it was announced, however, I told the members of my law firm, including John Selig, of the Governor's decision. I believe this is how John Selig learned of my appointment. I do not believe he learned about it from Jim McDougal and I am certain I knew of the appointment long before John Selig.

I do not believe Jim McDougal, a man I have never met, had anything to do with my appointment. If he ever claimed he did, I believe he was blowing the usual hot air that pollutes the environment in the state capitol. I would have paid no attention to John Selig or any other member of my law firm who claimed to know anything about my appointment. I did not seek and in fact discouraged involvement by the law firm in my appointment. There are many reasons why I felt that way but suffice it to say that I sought the appointment for myself, not for the law firm. I did not return to the firm when I left the Securities Department in 1991.

During 1984, when apparently Jim McDougal was claiming he influenced my appointment (or at least someone is now saying he did), he was deeply involved in a business transaction with Sheffield Nelson. It involved Madison Guaranty Savings and Loan. I believe Charles Handley is aware of the transaction and there may be a public file at the Securities Department. I mention this only so that you know why I believe that Sheffield Nelson was and is in a position to advance, with some degree of specificity and believability, a distorted and <u>malicious</u> version of the events and circumstances surrounding my appointment.

I do not wish to enhance my credibility by dumping on someone else. But I must tell you that the relationship between Sheffield Nelson, Jim McDougal and Madison Guaranty in 1984 — not mine — is the one that warrants scrutiny. My predecessor, who was a Republican appointee, was serving as Securities Commissioner at the time. He approved a risky, speculative real estate development project at a time when the savings and loan was in dire need of capital to support such a project. The savings and loan was not required to first increase its capital base and take steps to meet its minimum net worth requirements before receiving approval to proceed with the development project. Without the necessary capital base, the savings and loan would be unable to absorb potential losses from its direct investment in the venture. I believe that the ven-

ture may have been approved, at least in part, based upon the personal financial strength of the outside investors, rather than the institution. I believe that
the venture later proved to be a significant financial drain on the institution.

Throughout 1984, both state and federal savings and loan regulators were
pressuring savings and loans to raise capital. Many, including Madison Guaranty,
were not meeting their minimum regulatory net worth requirements. Indeed,
Madison Guaranty was operating under a Supervisory Agreement with the
FHLBB which required them to take steps to bring the association into compliance with those requirements. When our Department was approached by the
Rose Law Firm in 1985 about a plan for Madison to issue preferred stock, I
believe that Charles and I both felt that the savings and loan was making an
effort to address their obvious lack of adequate capital, but we had some concerns about whether the savings and loan laws authorized the issuance of preferred stock. Charles Handley is not an attorney and although I relied heavily on
his advice on savings and loan matters, I believed this matter was a very narrow
legal issue that had to be treated as such. I am confident after looking at the
statutes again this week, that our interpretation of the law was absolutely correct.
Assistant Commissioner Nancy Jones agreed with the Rose Law Firm's position
and I believe there are hand written notes of hers (N.J.) in the file to this effect.
Although we officially agreed that state law authorized the issuance of preferred
stock, we cautioned the savings and loan that it should seek the assurance of the
Federal Home Loan Bank Board (FHLBB) of Dallas that the preferred stock, if
issued, would be considered "permanent capital stock" for regulatory net worth
purposes. Under RAP accounting, the FHLBB had certain rules that differed
from GAAP. There are notes in the file from Nany [sic] Jones (who is a C.P.A.)
to me indicating she believed the preferred stock Madison Guaranty intended to
issue would be "permanent capital stock" for FHLBB purposes.

With regard to the brokerage services subsidiary, I specifically recall that
Charles and I agreed that we would not consider approving the activity unless
the savings and loan first raised the capital to bring the savings and loan into
compliance with its net worth requirements. Charles wanted to use their
request for approval to engage in brokerage services as leverage to insure that
they would proceed forthwith to raise the badly needed capital. Although we
were not persuaded that a private market for savings and loan securities of this
sort existed at the time, we could not be certain. If Madison Guaranty was able
to raise the capital, many of our concerns about the safety and soundness of the
institution would be alleviated. As such, we decided to condition our approval
of an application for a service corporation to engage in brokerage activities on
the savings and loan first raising the capital to bring them into regulatory compliance. [A "wild card" provision was added to the state savings and loan laws by
the legislature in 1969. It is this provision that clearly allowed state chartered
savings and loans to engage in any business practice or activity authorized for a
federally chartered savings and loan. In the mid-1980's, federal savings and
loans were allowed to engage in securities brokerage activities. Assistant
Commissioner Nancy Jones believed that the savings and loan could engage in

this activity without our prior approval. Charles Handley and I took the position, however, that it was not a preapproved activity and that the savings and loan could not do it without our prior approval. Thus, we gained the necessary leverage to insist on an immediate infusion of additional capital.]

Madison Guaranty apparently abandoned the effort to issue the preferred stock shortly thereafter, although I do not specifically recall being told the reasons. Before the savings and loan could have offered or sold the preferred stock it was required by the state securities laws to file a disclosure document with the securities registration division of our office. The transaction would have been subject to our review and approval as to the adequacy of disclosure to potential investors of the preferred stock. No filing was ever made. Since we had given the savings and loan only until December 31, 1985 (a matter of months) to raise the capital and they were not able to do so, the savings and loan never engaged in brokerage activities.

I fail to see how our handling of these matters placed depositors at risk or furthered the demise of Madison Guaranty in any way. Obviously, if the savings and loan had been able to raise the capital, both state and federal regulators would have been relieved of a major source of concern. If not, the savings and loan would not engage in brokerage services for even a day. In fact, it did not.

I do not believe that the involvement of the Rose Law Firm in these matters influenced the Department's decisions in any way. My staff was involved deeply in the decision making process and each decision had a statutory basis. Our Department acted neither favorably toward the savings and loan, nor arbitrarily or capriciously. We acted reasonably.

In the spring of 1986, we had numerous conversations with the FHLBB of Dallas about Madison Guaranty. We were all quite concerned about matters that had surfaced during the most recent examination of the institution. Its net worth was further eroding. Far worse, however, were the findings of self-dealing and insider abuse. The Board of Directors of the institution appeared to be completely dominated by Jim McDougal. The service corporations (none of which were approved during my tenure) were draining the institution. It was during this time that the FHLBB sought our advice and approval as to the proper regulatory course of action. We all agreed that it was critical to remove Jim McDougal from the institution. It was decided to seek the voluntary ousting of McDougal first by means of a Consent Cease and Desist Order. Absent consent, the FHLBB would seek a formal removal order, with the State's full agreement and consent.

On July 11, 1986, Charles Handley and I flew to Dallas to meet with the FHLBB and the Board of Directors of Madison Guaranty (the meeting was originally scheduled for July 24, 1986). Walter Faulk was the Principal Supervisory Agent in charge of the meeting and Karen Bruton attended the meeting on behalf of the Enforcement Division of FSLIC in Washington, D.C. The Madison Guaranty Board had been summoned to Dallas to discuss the findings of the examination. Jim McDougal did not attend. John Selig and Breck Speed attended the meeting on behalf of the Madison Board. [In June, 1986, John Selig had asked our Department for forbearance on certain concerns we had raised with the association about its direct investments in its service corporations. The savings and loan had earlier promised to address the matter by April, 1986. We did not respond to the June, 1986 request because we knew then that by July, 1986, McDougal would be gone and the issue would be moot.]

At the meeting, we jointly confronted the Board with the findings of self-dealing and insider abuse (there are handwritten notes of mine in the file from the July 11, 1986 meeting). The Board was presented with a Cease and Desist Order that, among other things, called for the Board to fire Jim McDougal and other family members. (A copy of the Order is in the files of the Arkansas Securities Department.) It was a long and confrontational meeting. The Madison Guaranty Board members and their lawyers appeared stunned. One of them, Steve Cuffman, an attorney, acted very responsibly and soberly. He indicated the Board would likely consent to the entry of the Cease and Desist Order. John Selig indicated that the Board would cooperate but would like a few days to review the order and work on minor revisions. I believe the order was entered the last week in July, 1986. At the same time, the savings and loan was placed under another Supervisory Agreement that required approval from Dallas of every subsequent decision of any significance.

For a few months, Steve Cuffman essentially ran the institution. Later, Tommy Trantham was hired by a new Board of Madison Guaranty and approved by the Dallas bank to babysit the institution until FSLIC found some money to pay off depositors. In 1987, we received an annual audit for calendar year 1986 reflecting that Madison Guaranty was insolvent. Shortly thereafter, we asked that the institution be transferred to the FSLIC on the grounds of its insolvency. There can't be anyone left in America who doesn't know by now that FSLIC was dead broke in 1986. Madison Guaranty was the least of their problems. Further, since Jim McDougal had been removed from the institution, there was little harm done in letting it sit, as did hundreds of others, while new management searched for ways to salvage its worthless assets.

I believe that my office did everything possible during my tenure to deal with the savings and loan disaster in general and with Madison Guaranty in particular. State law requires that an institution that is insolvent or operating in an unsafe or unsound manner be placed in receivership and that the FSLIC be appointed the receiver. If FSLIC refused (which we were told it would on several occasions), we could have asked the court to appoint another receiver. However, there would be no depositor payoff and we were obviously worried about triggering panic around the state among depositors of both state and federal savings and loans. State law does not provide for the removal of officers and directors of savings institutions. Federal law does, however, and we depended heavily on the cooperation of the FHLBB of Dallas to exercise this authority. I believe we worked well with the FHLBB in the case of Madison Guaranty and moved quickly to remove the source of the problem.

In the case of other state chartered savings and loans, we fought bitterly over the timing and manner of their disposition. We repeatedly asked the FHLBB to transfer insolvent institutions to the FSLIC. Indeed, the files at the Securities Department reflect a letter in 1987 from me to the Director of FSLIC in Washington, D.C. pleading with the FSLIC to place three institutions, including Madison Guaranty, in receivership. However, I believe that ultimately federal regulators had the absolute final say-so on these matters since all of the institutions were federally insured. Federal law granted the federal regulators absolute authority to seize a state chartered association without prior approval of the state regulator. In 1985, at our urging, the FHLBB seized state-chartered Guaranty Savings and Loan in Harrison, Arkansas. The institution sued the State, the FHLBB and FSLIC claiming that FSLIC could not take over the institution unless the state regulator first went to state court to appoint a receiver. The Eighth Circuit Court of Appeals upheld our actions, and found that federal law pre-empted state law on these matters in the case of any conflict. The ruling in this case influenced our later decisions not to proceed with a receivership without the concurrence of the FHLBB and FSLIC.

I think all of us who had responsibility for savings and loans during the 1980's felt overwhelmed at times and lacking in the necessary power, authority or resources to act as effectively or decisively as we might have under ordinary circumstances. While I never find it hard to defend the decisions we made at the time or the actions we took, I often find them hard to explain.

I hope my thoughts have been helpful in clarifying our earlier conversation. Please let me know if I can be of further assistance.

BBS:sa
D: BBS0083.097

TO: Jeff Girth [*sic*], New York Times
FROM: Beverly Bassett Schaffer
RE: Madison Guaranty Savings and Loan
DATE: February 28, 1992

This is a follow-up to our telephone conversation Wednesday. We talked about three or four issues not clearly addressed in my first memorandum.

First, it is true that in our letter to the Rose Law Firm, we addressed a very narrow legal issue regarding the savings and loan laws and the Arkansas Business Corporation Code. Our letter did not address federal law or applicable federal regulations. The savings and loan was required to seek approval from the FSLIC, not our office, as to the form of the security prior to its issuance. We had no reason to think the FSLIC would approve preferred stock that could not be included in the association's net worth. There would be no point in pursuing such an offering.

Nevertheless, I am certain that Charles Handley discussed with Rick Massey his concerns about federal regulatory treatment of the preferred stock. It is my understanding from Charles that Mr. Massey subsequently provided Charles with a FHLBB bulletin or regulation regarding the issuance of preferred stock and assured Charles that the preferred stock would be structured in accordance with existing federal regulations so that it would in fact be deemed permanent capital stock for net worth purposes. (I believe there are copies of those regulations or bulletins in the file.)

Second, I am certain that our Department had no definitive proof of insolvency of Madison Guaranty until calendar year 1987. The FHLBB documents to which you referred Wednesday in no way constituted a full and final examination report admissible in state court as evidentiary proof of insolvency. During this time, Madison Guaranty had been told to obtain new appraisals of its real estate properties in order to determine the value of the real estate investments of the savings and loan. Those appraisals were not formally ordered until McDougal was fired in July, 1986. Indeed, the difficulty in obtaining definitive real estate appraisals delayed the completion of the audit for 1986 performed by the new auditors hired after McDougal was gone. We did not receive it until the summer of 1987.

State law required that proof of insolvency be submitted in connection with a petition for a receivership or shortly thereafter. The audit for the association reflected no such insolvency and the examination reports of the FHLBB were inconclusive.

Further, the 1985 preliminary examination report which was the subject of our meeting in Dallas in July, 1986, did not contain a definitive finding of insolvency either. The comments in that report all refer to the net worth deficiency of the savings and loan, rather than insolvency.

Even if we had had proof of insolvency in 1985, I cannot say our actions would have been different. State law requires that when the savings and loan supervisor determines that a savings and loan is insolvent, the state must notify the savings and loan of such insolvency. The savings and loan then must present a plan to the supervisor as to how the solvency will be restored within a reasonable time. A plan to issue $3,000,000 of preferred stock within 90 to 120 days might well have been sufficient to satisfy delaying any receivership until at least the expiration of the offering period.

Third, we intended that our approval of the brokerage subsidiary be conditioned on the association first raising the capital before it began operations. You maintain our letter could be read to say that the savings and loan subsidiary could begin operating as long as the capital was in place by December 31, 1985. Perhaps the wording of the letter is ambiguous, but we firmly believed that our agreement was as I have stated.

In the file, there is a handwritten memo to me from Charles in December, 1985, concerning a telephone conversation he had had that day with John Latham. In that conversation, he asked Mr. Latham if the savings and loan had completed its application with our securities broker-dealer registration division. He said "no" and that there were additional items he had to file before the application could be passed on. Charles then reminded Mr. Latham of our agreement that the broker-dealer could not begin operating until the capital was in place. From Charles' notes, it appears that Mr. Latham said that that was not his understanding of our agreement but that the savings and loan would abide by those terms anyway. I do not believe the savings and loan ever completed the broker-dealer application.

Finally, it may be important for you to know that state law grants the savings and loan supervisor no emergency acquisition authority similar to that of the FHLBB and FSLIC. The appointment of a receiver or conservator under state law requires advance notice to the savings and loan and the filing of a petition in state chancery court, which is a public proceeding. Both we and the FHLBB agreed that the lack of ability under state law to seize the institution without notice, remove management and immediately take control of the institution from hostile, uncooperative management rendered our receivership provisions essentially useless under the circumstances in which we found ourselves in 1985. The FSLIC did not want management tipped off as to the timing of a seizure and the mere filing of a public petition at that time might well have created panic among depositors and a run on the institution between the time the petition was filed and the actual appointment of a receiver. Certainly, it was critical to maintaining public confidence in the insurance fund that FSLIC be prepared to accept the receivership. We all agreed that any receivership should be handled under federal law and, of course, that meant that the FHLBB and FSLIC controlled the timing.

D:BBS0085.097

TO: Jeff Gerth, <u>New York Times</u>
FROM: Beverly Bassett Schaffer
DATE: March 13, 1992
RE: Madison Guaranty Savings and Loan

It is my understanding that the <u>New York Times</u> may publish another story concerning Madison Guaranty Savings and Loan.

This is to inform you that I am in the process of retaining counsel to sue your newspaper for libel based on the false statements in the March 8, 1992 article concerning the circumstances of my appointment in 1985 as Arkansas Securities Commissioner. Any further reference to my appointment in like manner will be considered a separate cause of action.

As you know, in advance of the publication of your story, I provided you with a detailed account in writing of the facts relating to my appointment and the actions taken by the Arkansas Securities Department during my tenure. This information was ignored and, instead, you based your story on the word of a mentally ill man I have never met and documents which you admitted to me on the telephone on February 26, 1992 were incomplete.

Of course, Mr. McDougal, who you described in your article as "stable, careful and calm," has since repudiated virtually every statement attributed to him in your story. In addition, the document you relied on to support the asserted fact that federal examiners had determined that the savings and loan was insolvent in 1984 was an internal FHLBB memorandum, not an examination report. That memorandum merely discusses the potential effect that certain adjustments <u>might</u> have <u>if</u> they were made. They were not made. In fact, the 1984 federal examination report in the files of the Arkansas Securities Department contains a finding that, not only was the savings and loan not insolvent at the end of 1984, it was meeting the minimum net worth requirements of the FHLBB. I warned you that you were wrong about the 1984 examination report and that subsequent documents would prove I was right. You ignored this warning. In addition, you ignored the fact that our office had an independent audit in our possession that refuted any "finding" of insolvency.

Again, the <u>New York Times</u> defamed me in its March 8, 1992 story concerning this matter and any further reference to me of the kind previously published in your newspaper will be further evidence of malice.

D: BBS0089.097

TO: Jeff Gerth, <u>The New York Times</u>
FROM: Beverly Bassett Schaffer
RE: Madison Guaranty Savings & Loan
DATE: November 19, 1993

I understand that recently you suggested that my previous limited participation in a single matter concerning Madison Guaranty when I was in private law practice created a conflict of interest during my service as Securities Commissioner.

My sole involvement in matters concerning the S & L consisted of limited ministerial support and minor drafting tasks delegated to me by a partner in the law firm in which I was an associate. Those assignments related only to the Campobello Island matter. (I believe I am the person who last year brought that project to your attention.) At no time was I ever included in other aspects of the representation of the S & L. Madison Guaranty was not my client and, in fact, I am not even aware of the extent or the nature of the representation undertaken by the firm or carried on after my departure. I was never included in any internal discussions with other members of the law firm as to any sensitive financial or regulatory matters. Nor did I participate in any meetings or conversations that might have taken place with the McDougals. As I told you last year, I have never met either one of them.

The rules of professional conduct of attorneys in Arkansas concerning successive private and public service provide that a lawyer serving as a public officer may not participate in a matter in which the lawyer participated personally and substantially while in private practice, unless no one is, by lawful delegation, authorized to act in the lawyer's place.

The level of participation necessary to present a conflict of interest must be <u>both</u> personal and substantial. The only matter in which I ever had any personal participation was Campobello and it was not substantial. Furthermore, the conflict arises only when the subsequent service requires the attorney to participate in the <u>same</u> "matter" in which he previously had a substantial involvement. The decisions in which I participated, with the advice and guidance of my staff, did not involve Campobello.

As to whether there was any satisfactory way to eliminate the appearance of a conflict, my answer is "no". State law allows the Securities Commissioner to delegate his duties as savings and loan supervisor only to an assistant securities commissioner. There was only one assistant commissioner on the small staff of 23 when I came to the Department. There had been a second one in earlier years assigned to the savings and loan division, but that position was eliminated during a previous administration. The existing assistant commissioner was the only CPA on the staff and the only staff member with experience in broker-dealer examinations. We had considerable problems in the local securities firms at that time, which consumed virtually all of her time. Had I reassigned her to the S & L supervisory duties, then it would have left us badly understaffed on the securities side, which was and is the primary function of that Department.

As to any claim made by federal regulators that they looked to the states to take the lead in the disposition of <u>any</u> state chartered S & L, I must express disgust and disbelief. They turned the train loose, and now they say they expected me to throw my body on the tracks to stop it. Someone is telling you lies. Or maybe they're just telling you what you want to hear. All I know is that there are lots of people we worked with at the FHLBB in Dallas who know better.

D:BBS0206.097

UNDER THE SURFACE OF WHITEWATER

Editor's note: "Fool for Scandal: How the New York Times *Got Whitewater Wrong"*
(October 1994), by Gene Lyons, prompted a spirited response by readers and became the
basis of a forum held at the National Press Club in Washington, D.C., and broadcast on
C-SPAN. The Times *declined to attend. The following letter was sent by Joseph Lelyveld,*
the executive editor of The New York Times, *to a* Times *reader, who then sent a copy to*
the editors of Harper's Magazine. *It was reprinted in the February 1995 issue of*
Harper's *with the permission of* The New York Times.

We too have read the Gene Lyons story in *Harper's Magazine* and seen the
forum on C-Span, and I have to tell you that our faith in Jeff Gerth, our
reporter, and our coverage of the Whitewater affair has not been shaken in the
least. The Lyons article is full of egregious misrepresentations of our coverage,
not to mention our intent. It is wild and shoddy journalism, and I am sorry you
appear to be persuaded by it.

Let me go back to the basic facts of our coverage. It did not turn on a suggestion that the Clintons did something illegal. It turned on two facts: that the
Clintons put up much less than half the initial investment in Whitewater but
nevertheless got half the ownership; and that the then governor's partner subsequently managed a failing savings and loan institution that was subject to state
supervision by a banking commissioner the governor appointed. Nothing in
Lyons's article undercuts either of those statements. We also noted that Mrs.
Clinton did legal work for the bank while her husband was governor, also a fact
that Lyons doesn't challenge. The central question we raised about this state of
affairs was whether it was appropriate for a governor to be involved in a business deal with the owner of a business regulated by the state.

On Mrs. Clinton's amazingly successful investment in cattle futures, we
again never suggested that she did something illegal. We simply reported the
existence of the deal, something the Clintons had never disclosed, and we
reported that Mrs. Clinton was guided in her investment by the chief lawyer for
the biggest agribusiness company in the state.

There you have the gist of the two major stories we broke. We have no great
passion for these old Arkansas tales. We did not think they should shake the
foundations of the republic. And, of course, we would much rather devote our
reporting efforts to current issues confronting the country. But it was clear to us
that they were stories that had to be reported and then not suppressed. They

had to be reported, we felt, because these were highly unusual investments that the Clintons had never disclosed and, indeed, had gone to considerable lengths to conceal. For me as an editor the basic test of fairness was this: Would we have printed these stories if the name had been Phil Gramm or Ed Meese rather than Bill Clinton? It was clear to me that we would have felt obliged to do so.

Lyons gets a lot very wrong in his article:

He says the banking commissioner, Ms. Schaffer, could not have acted under state law. He should read the law; he is wrong. It was her obligation to act.

He says that a report by federal bank examiners on Madison in 1984 was no evidence that the bank was insolvent because it was not formally an audit but only prepared for supervisory purposes. He apparently doesn't know what bank examiners do. What they do is supervise, and what they concluded in this case was that Madison was in trouble.

He says that our reporter relied on a man named Sheffield Nelson. He refers to a transcript of a conversation with Jim McDougal [the owner of Madison Guaranty Savings and Loan] that Nelson released to the press as evidence to back up that assertion. In fact, the transcript was released after our [initial] Whitewater article appeared, not before, and mainly had to do with the article. So it could not have been the basis for the article. I know the reporting effort that we made on this story and what we got and didn't get from Nelson. What we got, basically, was McDougal's phone number. No one, I can assure you, handed the *Times* this story.

Lyons challenges a statement in our article that Madison was one of the largest state-chartered savings and loan institutions in Arkansas, but to do so, he relies on a list of banking institutions that included federally chartered savings and loan institutions. Again, he apparently does not know the difference.

Lyons criticizes an article we published last year for relying on allegations made by David Hale. In fact, although we knew about Hale's allegations and although we had interviewed him, we deliberately withheld publication of his allegations because we knew he was an unreliable character who was plea-bargaining with the U.S. attorney on another case. We never wrote an article about his allegations, and mentioned them only in passing after they had been reported in detail in other papers.

I could go on, but my drift is clear. I am arguing that Lyons's article was in no sense a careful rebuttal but a scattershot, sloppy polemical assault on the integrity of our reporters and of this newspaper. In lambasting our news reports, he makes much of our editorials. Neither I nor the reporters who worked on these stories had anything to do with our editorials or any other expression of opinion in this paper. We practice a policy of strict separation between the news department and the editorial page. It was never violated in this case, I can assure you.

It may be, when the Whitewater affair has finally played itself out, that the country will conclude it didn't amount to much. That will be fine with us. But the basic facts we reported will still remain true—the fact that the Clintons had a partnership with the head of a failing savings and loan while Mr. Clinton was governor and the S&L was under state supervision, and the fact that Mrs. Clinton made all that money in futures. The President, as a candidate, had claimed to have made substantial financial disclosures, but he did not report these facts. We did. Having ascertained them, I still don't see how we could have done otherwise.

I am sorry to have gone on at this length. I hope I haven't tried your patience, but, as you will understand, I cannot take lightly attacks on the integrity of this paper. I'm grateful that you took the trouble to let us know your concerns.

Joseph Lelyveld
Executive Editor, *New York Times*
New York City

Gene Lyons responds:

Joseph Lelyveld's letter is extraordinarily revealing. It's in essence a political document, having less to do with the ruck and moil of the Whitewater controversy than with positioning the *New York Times* as it wishes to be seen: lordly, disinterested, and magisterial.

Hence Lelyveld feels free to ignore the substance of what I actually wrote and said. He gallantly defends aspects of the Whitewater story that nobody disputes. He denies what everyone from Senator Alfonse D'Amato to the *Times*'s own editorial writers has understood to be the meaning and import of Jeff Gerth's reporting, and disregards aspects of the newspaper's coverage he now finds inconvenient.

Much like Gerth's original reporting, Lelyveld's letter is filled with factual errors, all running in a prosecutorial direction. Also as in Gerth's work, fact, fiction, and insinuation are so closely woven into one fabric that untangling them requires careful explication.

Now then, let's get down to cases: It's simply not true that "the Clintons put up much less than half the initial investment in Whitewater but nevertheless got half the ownership." Gerth failed to examine public records in the Marion County courthouse. Had he looked, he would have discovered that the $20,000 the Clintons borrowed for the $203,000 investment was not the sum total of their contribution but only the down payment. Along with the McDougals, the Clintons were also jointly and individually responsible for a $183,000 mortgage note.

Whether or not it's "highly unusual" for two young couples to enter a real estate partnership (or, for that matter, to profit from commodities trading tips made by a good friend) I leave to *Harper's Magazine* readers to determine. But it's also demonstrably false that the Clintons "had never disclosed and, indeed, had gone to considerable lengths to conceal" their Whitewater investment. The first Whitewater story in the Little Rock press appeared in the *Arkansas Democrat* on October 24, 1979, during Clinton's first term as governor, and made occasional appearances on the business pages in later years.

One reason Arkansas reporters made little of Whitewater during Jim McDougal's 1990 bank-fraud trial in U.S. District Court (he was acquitted) was that the story had so clearly failed to develop. What's more, Jeff Gerth told the *American Journalism Review* that he became curious when he found an entry labeled "Whitewater" in one of the Clintons' state financial disclosure forms. They had released records dating as far back as Bill Clinton's first term as governor and Hillary's employment with the Rose Law Firm—substantially more than required by law.

Maybe failure to publicize Hillary's 1978–79 commodity trades indicates a wish to keep them under wraps, but the Clintons did nothing to conceal them. Because her cattle-futures mentor, Jim Blair, gave similar help to about a dozen people—many of whom, like Blair himself, lost money when they stayed in the game a few months longer than Hillary—the trades were fairly common knowledge in Fayetteville.

Jeff Gerth also told the *American Journalism Review* that his first move on the Whitewater story was to call one of two Arkansans he knew: Sheffield Nelson. If Nelson gave Gerth nothing more than Jim McDougal's phone number, he acted very much out of character. During his 1990 gubernatorial campaign, Nelson made an issue of Clinton's ties to McDougal, and he's done his best to flog the issue ever since.

Yet another of Gerth's sources, according to Trudy Lieberman in the *Columbia Journalism Review,* was Citizens United, the well-funded, right-wing Republican organization led by Floyd Brown. The publisher of the organization's newsletter, *Clinton Watch,* told *CJR* that "we have worked closer with the *New York Times* than the *Washington Times.*" Gerth responded, "If Citizens United has some document that's relevant, I take it. I check it out like anything else." (Had Gerth done any checking at all, he might have spared himself the embarrassment of falsely reporting that the state of Arkansas under Bill Clinton had loaned Tyson Foods $9 million.)

As to my own allegedly "wild" and "shoddy" misrepresentations, let me answer by dissecting the following sentence from Jeff Gerth's original March 8, 1992, Whitewater story: "After Federal regulators found that McDougal's savings institution, Madison Guaranty, was insolvent, meaning it faced possible closure by the state, Clinton appointed a new state securities commissioner, who had been a lawyer in a firm that represented the savings and loan."

First, federal regulators did not, in fact, determine that Madison Guaranty was insolvent between 1984 and 1986, the years Gerth's stories covered. The S&L took issue with the 1984 Federal Home Loan Bank Board's preliminary report, prevailed on the issues, entered into a formal supervisory agreement with the FHLB, then hired the bank examiner herself to carry out agreed-upon reforms. Unlike Gerth, I've confirmed these facts with both Walter Faulk, then director of supervision at the FHLBB, and Sarah Worsham Hawkins, the examiner who wrote the report from which Gerth selectively quoted.

Second, Arkansas regulators had no choice except to defer to the federal agencies that held the real regulatory power—the Federal Savings and Loan Insurance Corporation (FSLIC) and the FHLBB. Indeed, the Eighth Circuit Court of Appeals in St. Louis had ruled in the 1985 case of another Arkansas S&L that when state and federal law conflicted, federal law took precedence. (Hence Lelyveld's complaint about the relative size of state-chartered vs. federally chartered S&Ls is a cavil. Standard reference sources list them together because the distinction is basically historical.)

Third, what I still find shocking is that Jeff Gerth was notified of these facts in writing by former Arkansas Securities Commissioner Beverly Bassett Schaffer long before his original March 1992 Whitewater article. "It may be important for you to know," she wrote Gerth in February 1992, "that state law grants the savings and loan supervisor no emergency acquisition authority similar to that of the FHLBB and FSLIC."

Bassett Schaffer's certified letter all but begging the FSLIC to move on Madison was dated December 10, 1987; she got no answer. (Federal regulators finally closed Madison's doors in February 1989.) Altogether, her detailed, persuasive account of her dealings with Madison Guaranty came to twenty typed pages. Interestingly, the memos fail to mention Whitewater. Bassett Schaffer says this is because she was unaware of the Clinton-McDougal partnership and because Gerth never mentioned it. Her account squares not only with the documentary record but with the record of every knowledgeable source—state, federal, and private—that I could find.

Rather than exploring or rebutting these complexities, Gerth simply shoved Bassett Schaffer's memos out of sight. His March 8, 1992, story portrayed her as suspiciously forgetful. Bassett Schaffer, Gerth wrote, "said she did not remember the Federal examination of Madison." Subsequent articles—like Gerth's December 15, 1993, Whitewater article in the *Times*—made her the very linchpin of an implied conspiracy to keep Madison Guaranty open for Jim McDougal's benefit. Frankly, I doubt *Times* editors knew the memos existed. Had *I* concealed such evidence from *Harper's Magazine*, I suspect that my byline would never appear in this magazine again.

Edited transcription of the forum sponsored by *Harper's Magazine*
held at the National Press Club, October 25, 1994

Participants

Lewis H. Lapham (Moderator): *Harper's Magazine*
Gene Lyons: *Arkansas Democrat-Gazette*
Jeff Birnbaum: *The Wall Street Journal*
Trudy Lieberman: *Columbia Journalism Review*
Stan Crock: *Business Week*
Brian Duffy: *U.S. News & World Report*
Tom Hamburger: Minneapolis *Star-Tribune*
John Camp: CNN

LEWIS LAPHAM: Thank you very much for coming to the conversation this
afternoon. It proceeds from an article in this month's *Harper's Magazine* entitled
"Fool for Scandal: How the *New York Times* Got Whitewater Wrong." The contention of the article and of its author, Gene Lyons, who is here among the panelists, is that the Whitewater scandal is based almost entirely on rumor, gossip,
hearsay, and flat-out fabrication—and that there is no scandal there. It's like
hunting the snark. The article is an anatomy of how a scandal is made out of
whole cloth. The evidence so far seems to support the argument made by
Lyons.
   The story begins, as far as I know, in March of 1992 with a piece in *The New
York Times* by a reporter named Jeff Gerth. Then, over the course of the next
two years, a great deal of money is spent, a great many column inches are printed, there's a lot of television coverage, there are two congressional hearings,
there are two independent prosecutors. The presidency is daily said to rise or
fall on what will be the next revelation. The conversation gets into not only
fraud, bribery, and financial chicanery but also, in its more remote reaches, into
possible murder, drug dealing, crooked relations with Indonesian dictators, and
so forth. It becomes a very spectacular melodrama, and at the moment there is
still an investigation: there is still an independent prosecutor at large who is
presumably gathering evidence. What we are going to talk about this afternoon
is how such things come to pass. The *Times* was invited as well as Gerth and his
editors, but they have chosen not to come.

I am going to start with Gene Lyons, who will speak for about five minutes, and then go back and forth among my panelists. Then the discussion will be open to questions from everybody else in the room.

GENE LYONS: Thanks, Lewis. I might say before I say anything else that I am very grateful to *Harper's* for having run this piece, and for the great editing and fact-checking it got, and for the magazine's support in putting on this press conference.

Now, I don't expect to be greeted with hosannas of praise and joy for having done this piece. This is a tough story for the press, because the press, and the media generally, it seems to me, has gone off whooping down a false trail. There's no scent under our noses any longer, and we've got to turn back and try to find out where we went wrong. I am certain that some of you will mind me saying so, but if you want to find the scandal in Whitewater you'd better get up search teams and hunt Washington for eight-year-old heroin addicts.

I'm obviously making reference to the case of Janet Cooke, a reporter for *The Washington Post,* who invented an eight-year-old heroin addict, received a Pulitzer Prize for her story about him, and was ultimately forced to recant the story and leave journalism. The story was shocking and horrifying but not altogether unlikely. In the case of Jeff Gerth and *The New York Times,* the story wasn't quite invented from whole cloth. But in my view that makes it worse, because when you simply invent a fictive character, nobody gets hurt; when you use real characters and make up a fictive story, real people get hurt.

There was a Whitewater real estate development deal. There was a Madison Guaranty Savings and Loan. There is a Jim McDougal, who ran the savings and loan into bankruptcy. You can find him now in a mobile home in the fair town of Arkadelphia, living on Social Security disability payments, since he's disabled and mentally ill. There is even a Judge David Hale. He is a known figure, although he wasn't appointed by Bill Clinton, as has been reported many times. He was appointed by Clinton's predecessor, the Republican Frank White, and has been re-elected every two years since then.

Therefore, at the start you had what I've heard referred to as a smoking quid pro quo. You have the governor of Arkansas involved in a real estate deal with a savings and loan operator who later went bankrupt. Did Clinton do anything to help his pal out when his pal got in trouble or did he not, and if so, what did he do? These are good questions to pursue. My contention is simply that the reporting of Jeff Gerth is not much better than the reporting of Janet Cooke.

What happened was that Gerth got about halfway down the trail to this story and—I'm guessing now, this is not a fact—began to sense that he was running out of material, all of which had been fed to him by Sheffield Nelson, Clinton's 1990 gubernatorial opponent and a legendary dirty political fighter in Arkansas, and by Jim McDougal, who at this point was outraged with Clinton for what he perceived to be Clinton's abandonment of him. So I think what happened was that at some point the trail began to run out, and the decision was made to print what Gerth had. Which I think is essentially a hoax. Not a conspiracy, a hoax. The only complaint that has been made to me specifically from *The New York Times* is that I didn't talk to any editors or senior people at the *Times*. That is absolutely true. I was not interested in the inside-baseball aspect of the story: who edited what, how it got in the paper, whether or not it was fact-checked. My contention is that the story couldn't have been fact-checked.

The whole story started on March 8, 1992, when Jeff Gerth's initial report appeared, a report that has been praised in the *American Journalism Review* for containing 80 to 90 percent of what we now know about Whitewater. I hope that after you've read my article you'll be persuaded that 80 or 90 percent of what you think you know about Whitewater is, in fact, provably and demonstrably false based on hard evidence that was simply suppressed or ignored in the writing of the story. At this point in March, it was after the New Hampshire primary, before Super Tuesday, and before the New York primary, which was going to be contested. If a story on Clinton's finances was going to have any impact on the nomination process, it was going to have to happen soon. My guess is that most people at the *Times* figured what most people in the country figured on March 8, 1992: Clinton ain't gonna get the nomination, and if he gets it he sure ain't gonna win. And so I think it was seen as a little throwaway story.

The situation got out of hand once Clinton became president. The RTC in Kansas City, which was given all the information on Jim McDougal and Madison Guaranty back in 1986 and didn't do anything with it because they had billion-dollar failures to deal with and didn't have any serious evidence of wrongdoing, now picks up the ball and runs with it. Then they leak information to Jeff Gerth and reporters at *The Washington Post* and other places, and the reporters begin to call people in the Treasury Department and the White House, and everybody goes into full-scale panic mode because my guess is the people at the Treasury Department believed what they read in *The New York Times*. Most of us normally do. They don't know the details of this story. They don't know if the boss is guilty as charged or innocent. This now is a full-blown Washington scandal. The whole thing has gone crazy since then.

I thought I would go back to the March 8, 1992, story and look at a couple of key points and then discuss them. Let me read the headline and the lead sentence from Gerth's original article and tell you what I think is wrong with them: "CLINTONS JOINED S.&L. OPERATOR IN AN OZARK REAL-ESTATE VENTURE. Bill Clinton and his wife were business partners with the owner of a failing savings and loan association that was subject to state regulation early in his tenure as Governor of Arkansas, records show."

What's the problem with this? Well, the time sequence is crazy. When Bill and Hillary Clinton made their original Whitewater investment, in 1978, Jim McDougal wasn't involved in banking or in a savings and loan association. That came three and five years later. Nor was Clinton governor in 1978; he was Arkansas attorney general. So the headline and opening paragraph were at best misleading. Determining the actual sequence of events from Gerth's original story is almost impossible.

Now let me get to what I think to be the classic Jeff Gerth sentence in that March 8 story: "After Federal regulators found that Mr. McDougal's savings institution, Madison Guaranty, was insolvent, meaning it faced possible closure by the state, Mr. Clinton appointed a new state securities commissioner, who had been a lawyer in a firm that represented the savings and loan."

It's a classic sentence. The first clause, "After Federal regulators found that McDougal's savings institution . . . was insolvent," is provably false. Federal regulators did not find that Madison Savings and Loan was insolvent either in 1984 or in 1985, or even in 1986. The documents are in the Arkansas Securities Department and at the Federal Home Loan Bank Board for anybody who wants to look at them. You can call the federal officials who were involved with the case, and they will tell you what happened. Nobody at *The New York Times* evidently talked to the federal officials at the Federal Home Loan Bank Board who were involved in this decision; at least the officials I talked to said they never talked to anybody at *The New York Times*.

The second clause, "meaning it faced possible closure by the state," is also false. In practical fact, the power of the state to close down bankrupt savings and loans is purely theoretical. For one thing, Arkansas law makes no provision for repaying depositors of failed financial institutions. Second, as Jeff Gerth was informed in writing by the Arkansas securities commissioner, the Eighth Circuit Court in St. Louis had previously ruled that in cases where federal law and state law conflicted, federal law took precedence. So that the state couldn't have closed down Madison Guaranty even if it was insolvent, which in 1984 through 1986 it wasn't.

The third clause is maybe the most misleading and in some ways the most unfair, because it singled out an individual who actually performed a very difficult job under very difficult circumstances. Gerth basically took this woman, Beverly Bassett Schaffer, who cooperated with him at every stage of the game, and basically made her into a crook and a liar. At which point, unfortunately, she refused to talk to reporters at all, and that hasn't helped her a bit. But Gerth's piece insinuates throughout that Clinton, faced with a crisis in which his buddy needed help, went out and appointed a hack who would do his bidding.

Bassett Schaffer told Jeff Gerth when he called her, and told him in writing in great detail, that "Jim McDougal did not get me my job, I have never met Jim McDougal, I have never spoken to Jim McDougal on the phone, I do not know his wife. I have never heard Bill Clinton mention has name." If you read her memos, you'll see there is no mention of Whitewater. Why? She says it's because she never heard of Whitewater and Gerth never said anything to her about it. This is how cops and prosecuting attorneys operate. Every error that was made in this story, every omission, every misleading paragraph and clause, ran in the self-same prosecutorial direction.

In fact, Beverly Bassett Schaffer's appointment as Arkansas securities commissioner in January 1985 had absolutely nothing to do with Jim McDougal's problems. The incumbent, whose name is Lee Thalheimer, had resigned his position. He was appointed by the Republican Governor Frank White. He stayed on for two years under Clinton and decided to quit to re-enter private practice. I told Gerth this, and Beverly Bassett Schaffer told me she told Gerth this.

Well, I could beat this thing to death and probably will before the day is up. But it seems to me the same is true for the commodities-trading story. You've got Hillary Clinton's commodities trades over here, you've got Tyson Foods and the state government over here. I don't know any state anywhere in the United States where a large private employer and the fastest-growing industry would be treated with great hostility by the government. Everything good that happens to Tyson Foods over a period of six or eight years is portrayed as the result of some kind of skullduggery. You've got the same kind of spin, you've got the same kind of omission of basic facts that alter the whole picture. You've got a lawsuit in which you imply that one person who isn't party to the suit is the defendant, you omit another defendant, and you write the story in such a way as to make it appear that there's a conspiracy where a fair accounting says there's a damn mess.

LAPHAM: Next, we are going to hear Jeff Birnbaum from *The Wall Street Journal.*

JEFF BIRNBAUM: I cannot comment about *The New York Times* because, basically, I don't work for them. But it's too bad they're not here, because it makes this whole endeavor sort of empty and it would be a much more interesting conversation.

First, I should explain that I write for the news pages of *The Wall Street Journal* and not the editorial page. We are completely separate entities, so anything good or ill you might have to say about *The Wall Street Journal*'s editorial page, you should address to them.

There is one part of Mr. Lyons's piece that I think is worth pulling out and examining: there might be pressure, he suggests, for news organizations to print articles about subjects to which they devote a large amount of resources. I agree that this is a danger we should all be aware of, and I can happily report that *The Wall Street Journal* news pages were aware of it and were very careful to act on it. After it was learned that [White House counsel] Bernie Nussbaum removed some Whitewater files from the office of Vince Foster, we were curious about that—and probably for some reason. Several *Wall Street Journal* reporters were assigned to the subject. In other words, we devoted considerable resources to the Whitewater issue. We ran a series of articles over a long period, and almost all of them ran at the lower portion of our back page, depending on the story. We had one front-page story on the subject, but it dealt primarily with the Hillary Clinton commodities trade.

And so we, at least consciously, tried to base our stories on the facts that our considerable resources gathered rather than on the considerable resources that we devoted to the subject. We did not make the case of quid pro quo but rather laid out the facts as we found them.

LAPHAM: I, too, regret the absence of the *Times,* but on the other hand a great deal of the press, as well as the rest of the country, tends to follow the *Times.* I expect that one or more of our panelists will address that follow-on effect. I'm not sure whether she is going to talk about that side of it or not, but Trudy Lieberman, from the *Columbia Journalism Review,* is next.

TRUDY LIEBERMAN: When I first came to the Whitewater story, I really had no particular involvement in any of the issues other than as a casual reader and television watcher. The one thing that struck me was that there seemed to be a lot of media attention centering on what appeared to be the personal venality of President Clinton, and what I was very curious about at this point was why so much attention was being given to this at the exclusion of some other issues that I felt merited more attention.

At that time I was asked by the *Columbia Journalism Review* to look into what was behind some of the Whitewater coverage, and I began doing that with a Nexis search. The Nexis search was extremely revealing. There was a certain sameness to all of the allegations, a certain sameness to the reporting, a certain sameness to the conclusions—which would lead one to believe that something was behind all of the sameness that was appearing.

There were a number of charges made—accusations, innuendos, suspicions—about what the Clintons did and didn't do that were simply plopped down on the pages of these Whitewater stories without any context, evaluation, or analysis—and sometimes with only the most rudimentary explanation. Various facts were often thrown down as conclusions that seemed to prove whatever point the writer wanted to make.

I think one good example of this was Hillary Clinton's seeking the power of attorney to clean up the Whitewater affair in 1988. This was used widely by many in the media to prove that the Clintons, contrary to their assertions, had been actively involved in the Whitewater development. Other explanations for why she might have been seeking power of attorney never got into the news columns, and so the cause and effect was just simply made without any other possible explanations given. Perhaps her seeking power of attorney had something to do with the fact that she was actually interested in cleaning up the mess and that McDougal at that point was ill and incapable of handling the affairs of the project. The implications, of course, and I think this is the inference the public could reasonably draw, was that somehow the Clintons were lying about Whitewater. That's what one might reasonably assume.

I also began to explore the link between the coverage that was appearing in the press and the involvement of Floyd Brown, of Citizens United. I had visited Citizens United, and one of their personnel, David Bossie, had tried to interest me in writing a story about Lot 7, which was a complicated real estate transaction in which a developer apparently made a lot of money and somehow the Clintons were supposed to have given him something in return. Several weeks earlier, my Nexis search had turned up an *L.A. Times* story that had gone into great detail about Lot 7, but what was striking to me was that the vocabulary used in the *L.A. Times* piece was very much the same vocabulary that Citizens United used in trying to interest me in the piece: the same words, the same themes, the same conclusions, the same documents. Now, if the *L.A. Times* had gotten their story from Citizens United, they did not tell their readers that. Instead, the story talked about "fundamental allegations" by critics whom they didn't name and they talked about an apparent windfall that was raising eyebrows among those examining the Whitewater matter. At that point I began to get suspicious about who these critics were and whose eyebrows were indeed being raised and how the Clintons could be benefiting from all of this.

The charges, the factoids, the conclusions that had been plopped into the stories were often framed in terms of the charges made. "Critics observed," "scandalous odors," "questions persist," "ethically suspect sweetheart deals"—this was the kind of language that peppered much of the coverage of Whitewater that I examined. Again, the implications of all of this, I think, were that the Clintons were involved in some sort of criminal behavior and moral lapses.

I'd like to talk a little bit about using Floyd Brown as a source, and using anybody as a source, because journalists deal with all kinds of sources all of the time. That's our stock-in-trade. And obviously journalists are free to use any kind of source they want, however unsavory or however virtuous. Certainly there's nothing wrong with looking at documents, studies, or any other information a source provides. What's wrong is not to identify the source and—sometimes even more important—the source's political motivation, agenda, and character. What was going on here, I think, is that much of the time the source of the Whitewater data and the source's political agenda were not disclosed.

One of the things that might be helpful in terms of judging the credibility of a source can be applied in this Whitewater matter: How much does the source have to gain or lose by what kind of information is being provided? Citizens United had everything to gain because their agenda and motivations were being spread throughout the press, and I think that's probably what they wanted. Their aim, apparently, was to discredit the President of the United States by attacking his character and somehow implying guilt in various parts of the Whitewater affair. And to a large extent I think the press helped spread that message.

Toward the end of the Whitewater frenzy, around the middle of March, some of the press did begin to identify Brown as the source of the information. *The Wall Street Journal* and the *Chicago Tribune*, for example, and later *The New York Times* ran stories that drew a connection between Brown and some of the information that was being fed to the press. In addition, some of the news magazines were dropping Brown's name in connection with the Whitewater affair. But by this time Brown's message had been spread, and I can't help thinking that the coverage of Whitewater has had some bearing on how the public views Clinton right now.

LAPHAM: For the benefit of people who might not know, Trudy, who is Floyd Brown and what is Citizens United? I mean, what sort of organization is it?

LIEBERMAN: Floyd Brown is the head of Citizens United, which is a right-wing grass-roots organization that lobbies on behalf of conservative causes and I guess gets its money by fund-raising through conservative interests.

LAPHAM: So it's an interested political faction that is providing information.

LIEBERMAN: Yes.

LAPHAM: All right. The next person is Stan Crock from *Business Week*. I have no idea which side he is going to come at this conversation from, but I am looking forward to it.

STAN CROCK: I actually take the view that in some ways Mr. Lyons was too easy on *The New York Times*. He complains that the *Times* omitted stories, omitted a lot of important information. In his *Harper's* article he omitted entirely William Safire's coverage of Whitewater, and let me give you an example of what kind of fodder that would have provided for him. On January 13, Mr. Safire wrote as follows: "Vincent Foster must have been worried sick about his letter of February 28, 1989, to the Federal Deposit Insurance Corporation. In this nine-page letter from the Rose law firm of Little Rock, Ark.—probably among the many papers concealed by the Clintons' subpoena collusion with Justice—Foster made a pitch for the lucrative legal business growing out of the collapse of the Madison S.&L. But nowhere in this document, now under active investigation by the F.D.I.C., is there any mention that the Rose firm had represented Madison when it was open. Foster was asking the F.D.I.C. to hire the firm, in effect, to sue its previous clients, which strikes me as an egregious conflict of interest."

Here's that February 28 letter. It starts off by saying, "The Rose law firm would appreciate the opportunity to bid upon or otherwise be considered for legal services arising in connection with conservatorships and receiverships of savings and loan associations in the state of Arkansas." It is a general request to be considered for any work that the FDIC has to have done in Arkansas. Nowhere is Madison mentioned specifically because the letter was not a request to represent the FDIC in connection with the Madison collapse. Later in the letter is perhaps one of the most quoted sentences in all of Whitewaterdom: "As previously indicated, the firm does not represent any savings and loan association in state or federal regulatory matters." I'm sure you have all seen that quotation. You do not have to be an investigative reporter to have read the rest of that paragraph, which says, "From time to time, we have provided specialized services to some savings and loan associations in such areas as employment discrimination, workout of participation loans, and bankruptcy." It finally says, "Accordingly, while there may be individual transactions or situations where a conflict of interest could arise, we believe that the firm would not be ethically disqualified from serving as fee counsel as generally discussed herein."

It seems to me that's all the notice the Rose Law Firm needed to give to the FDIC. But then how could all of this have happened?

I'd like to make a couple points about that. One is, the White House does have to shoulder part of the blame for putting so many journalists on the trail. Their refusal to hand over documents, their refusal to be candid, the constant changing of stories—some of my colleagues basically were lied to—all of this gets the juices going. It does not excuse getting the story wrong, but it does explain why so many people were on the trail. There is, as Jeff pointed out, and as Gene did in his story, a question of what to do when you have expended substantial resources. The question then is to figure out what story you have: to find the smoking gun when there may not be one, when there may be instead a more subtle story.

The story in Whitewater, it seems to me, was the same story as in the commodities-trading story. In both instances, there was no quid pro quo. In both instances, though, a lot is revealed about the character of the Clintons. Investing in raw real estate, investing in commodities futures, is speculation pure and simple, at a time when a lot of people were speculating and the Clintons were harshly critical of them. What the Clintons were hiding was the fact that they were doing the same thing themselves—perfectly legally, but it revealed a certain hypocrisy. That is the more subtle story. That was a legitimate story. And it's just too bad that the *Times* didn't stop at that point.

LAPHAM: Thank you. Well, we got as far as hypocrisy. But that's fairly common, at least it is in New York. It would not be worth a headline, I don't think, and certainly not a two-day story. Brian Duffy, perhaps you can take us further into what was the story or how much of the story was real.

BRIAN DUFFY: I'll start by saying that I do not know either Mr. Lyons or Mr. Gerth, so I have no particular point of view with regard to either. I would say, though, that I am extremely uncomfortable defending other people's work. The charges that have been raised in the *Harper's* article—of fabrication, fraud—don't get any more serious. They are not terms that I am happy either throwing around or defending, particularly when we do not have the *Times* people here, as Jeff pointed out.

I would have been much more comfortable had the *Harper's* piece singled out me and *U.S. News's* reporting on the Whitewater affair, or Jeff, or Stan, or whoever, rather than single out Mr. Gerth and his reporting in *The New York Times*. I don't see what purpose is gained by making comments about an individual reporter's work when all of us who endeavored to cover the Whitewater matter were possibly guilty of some of the same types of thing that Mr. Lyons raises in his article. I daresay any one of us in this room might have been subjected to the same sort of criticism. To the extent that there is material or mistakes to criticize in the coverage of Whitewater—and there is—I think such an effort would have been better done by examining a broader range rather than singling out one news organization and one reporter.

But be that as it may, I'd like to address what I think is a canard in this discussion: the idea of selective reporting. Put aside for a moment the allegations of fraud and misrepresentation, with which I disagree. "Selective reporting" is itself something of a meaningless term. Just as in a court of law there is no case in which a prosecutor brings in 100 percent of the evidence—it's simply not humanly possible—in any story that you or I report, I daresay the same odds obtain; that is, you don't have the opportunity because of deadlines or because of inaccessibility of sources to get 100 percent of the story.

So I think that perhaps a broader area of misunderstanding is in this notion of selective reporting. Without speaking to the merits of the *Times* reporting, I would say that everyone who endeavored to cover Whitewater was hampered by the facts. The sources, as Trudy pointed out, were not good sources, and they weren't just Floyd Brown. Mr. McDougal's memory was, to put it charitably, faulty. And there were a number of other problems.

The White House, as Stan Crock pointed out, compounded things by misleading reporters, deliberately or not. But just as I reject the assertion of misrepresentation on the part of most of my colleagues who covered this story, I see no basis to charge the White House with deliberate misrepresentation. Fecklessness is a charge that I think can fairly be made against the White House. They did, as Stan Crock indicated, fan the fires of this by failing to be forthright.

In any event, the problems of getting the "full story on Whitewater" were perhaps greater than they were on many other stories of this type. The matter had receded some ways back into the dimness of history. Documents weren't available. So what, then, is selective reporting? Although mistakes were made, I believe they were mistakes that were made because of the reporting difficulties on this story.

And while I respect the allegations made by Mr. Lyons, I would say that they concern a sort of secondary issue in the Whitewater case. The main issue in Whitewater was not the regulatory issue as it involved Ms. Schaffer but the allegations of a sweetheart deal involving the Clintons. Was Whitewater a sweetheart deal? I think a fair analysis suggests that it was. And it is a legitimate area for public inquiry.

With regard to the commodities trading, is that a legitimate area of public inquiry? Well, when the spouse of the governor of Arkansas is involved in a commodities deal—or any deal—as extraordinary as this one apparently was, generating phenomenal profits in terms of the initial capital invested, I think that, too, is an area of legitimate public inquiry. The reason I make issue of these two points is that if the press is going to look into these areas, it ought to do so responsibly and as accurately as possible, but I think the unfortunate inference that could be drawn from this exercise is that the press ought to leave such matters alone. Thank you.

LAPHAM: Well, I assure you I will not draw that lesson from this exercise. My concern is that bad investigative journalism drives out good investigative journalism, and so you've got a Gresham's law operating. And I also think there is a great deal of difference between selective reporting and actually suppressing evidence or making up information or saying something is true when you know it to be false. I mean, I can understand not using A instead of B, but it seems to me a somewhat different procedure to say A *is* B. Perhaps Mr. Hamburger can talk to us about how much of this same kind of reporting appeared in other media, because it was not simply *The New York Times* that repeated some of the allegations that were eventually proven to be empty.

TOM HAMBURGER: What strikes me in this discussion, and in reading Gene's critique of the *Times* coverage, is not so much what it says about *The New York Times* or even about Whitewater specifically but what it says about the norms of journalism, about what we do as Washington reporters every day and particularly in an election year. I think it's time we questioned some of our instinctive responses in the way we go after stories. The Times Mirror Center this year, as many of you know, reported that more than 70 percent of the public surveyed now rate journalists at a lower level than they rate members of Congress and 70 percent reported that journalists are getting in the way of helping the nation understand and solve its problems. Only 21 percent felt that we are a constructive force, that we are helping people understand what is going on.

So what are these norms of journalism that may have led to the media's approach to Whitewater and to Hillary Clinton's commodities investments? These are norms that I think have governed our profession since *The Front Page*, when Hildy Johnson was the main character. The first rule is "Don't get scooped." And the second is "If you do get scooped, don't get left behind by the pack." Eugene McCarthy once likened reporters in Washington to blackbirds on a telephone wire: "When one lands, they all land," he said. "When one takes off, they all take off." The third norm is "Report on conflict." We consider conflict to be news, and we place it ahead of substance on our list of priorities. "Get something new" is another of the norms that sometimes gets in the way of reporting substance.

I think in an election year, when we cover public officials, there are special norms that apply to "Don't get scooped." If you want to do something new in an election year, you look for problems that a political candidate might have had in his or her past. To call such a story a scandal or to justify its presence on page one, we as journalists have to use some extraordinary pyrotechnics. You can't just say Bill Clinton had a questionable land deal; you have to show somehow that he used his public office for personal gain, that there was misuse of the public trust.

When Bill and Hillary Clinton made their original Whitewater investment in 1978, Jim McDougal wasn't involved in the S&L business, nor was Bill Clinton governor. The suggestion that Clinton, the governor at that time, had somehow used the regulatory powers of the state of Arkansas to benefit Madison Savings and Loan was a critical part of propelling this story onto page one and even into the congressional-hearing process. A close examination, though, of the regulatory history of this S&L provided no evidence to suggest that the S&L received benefits by Arkansas regulators, and, in fact, that it is a myth to suggest that it did. We assigned one of our reporters to examine the records of Madison Savings and Loan and of the Arkansas Securities Department. And what we found was evidence that the institution had been regulated appropriately, that Beverly Bassett Schaffer had, in fact, showed regulatory diligence in examining the S&L. And then we called the federal regulator who, as Gene explained earlier, was the one who was primarily responsible for the regulation of this S&L. The records that we found in Arkansas and Beverly Bassett Schaffer's account of her regulation of this S&L were, in fact, accurate. Yet at that time, in March of 1994, no one had contacted this particular regulator, Walter Faulk. *The New York Times* had gone ahead with its story without ever checking whether the regulation of the S&L in Arkansas was appropriate.

LAPHAM: Thank you, Tom. Next, we are going to hear from John Camp, who has followed this story for CNN and is a dean among investigative journalists on television. Perhaps, John, you can also talk about how difficult it was or is to try to present the contrary view of Whitewater against a prevailing wind of wisdom that still wishes to believe in the presence of a large and terrible scandal.

JOHN CAMP: I thought last week in Washington was almost high satire. Most of you know that *The Washington Times* ran a front-page story—"Trooper Recalls Clinton Seeking Loan Help"—about a trooper named L. D. Brown. At the same time this story ran, or the day after it ran, the *Democrat-Gazette* ran two stories side by side: ARKANSAS TROOPER SAID HE SAW CLINTON PRESSURE JUDGE FOR MONEY; and then, right below that, TROOPER DENIES STORY ON SBA LOAN. This is the day after *The Washington Times* story, and these are side by side.

At the same time, *The Washington Post* was running its story, ARKANSAS TROOPER OFFERS PARTIAL SUPPORT TO ALLEGATION OF WHITEWATER LOAN, and it's quoting *The Washington Times* in its story. And then, lo and behold, on Friday we have *The Washington Post* running a correction of its story quoting *The Washington Times,* and you start to wonder what's happening when you see this kind of reporting. *The Washington Times* has not been known as a beacon of high-quality journalism, and yet you have *The Washington Post,* in its fear of being scooped, coming with its own story, then having to correct it.

I was a Johnny-come-lately to Whitewater coverage. I was only drafted into it in March of this year because I am senior investigative reporter on the special assignment staff at CNN. And I went to Little Rock with the belief that there was no story there. That preconceived notion was not based on the fact that Whitewater was not a story but on the fact that I thought all major bases had been covered by the national media: *The New York Times,* of course, foremost among those reporting on the issue. A young producer I had worked with had been in Little Rock off and on throughout the campaign and had assembled two file boxes full of various documents from the Arkansas Securities Department and from the Federal Home Loan Bank.

So I spent a good part of three days doing nothing but reading those documents and reviewing the documentary information that was available about the rise and the fall of Madison Guaranty. And I emerged after three days with a huge dilemma. Was I going to believe *The New York Times* or was I going to believe my lying eyes? And my choice, at this point, was to believe my lying eyes, because the documentary evidence did not support the premise of the initial story in March of 1992. I tried to talk to some of the principals, including Beverly Bassett Schaffer, who, I believe, had been ravaged by *The New York Times* in the course of this—not only in March of 1992 but, unconscionably, in December of 1993, after the Vince Foster suicide. Both in the news columns and in an editorial that followed, an almost direct accusation was made that she had to keep Madison open long after it was insolvent as a payoff for Madison raising funds to retire debt for Bill Clinton.

Bassett Schaffer had never been interviewed on television and had no intention of being interviewed on television. I spent ten hours with her, and the only thing I promised, which she wouldn't believe, was that we would try to bring some context to the story we would do. She ultimately agreed to do an interview.

Gene's story, which I feel is very comprehensive and well done, omits what I consider to be one of the most important pieces of evidence in the entire coverage of Whitewater from day one: the twenty-plus pages of a memo written to Jeff Gerth and delivered some seven to ten days before *The New York Times* printed the story. And if you compare that memo with the body of the story that was written, you will discover there was nothing quoted from that memo. Had that memo been quoted in context, I venture to say, the story probably would not have made the front page of *The New York Times* because it basically undercut the story's entire premise.

This *Times* story basically has influenced everything that has come down the line, such as the idea that this was a "sweetheart deal." I disagree that this was a sweetheart deal. The Clintons signed—and those documents are available—personal guaranties, over $183,000 collateralized by the loan. They were also at risk, and that meant they were at risk individually rather than as a couple. They also were at risk on a $20,000 loan that was used as a down payment. So certainly that was not a sweetheart deal.

This was an era when many World War II veterans were reaching retirement age, and it was believed that there was going to be a great demand for retirement homes and for recreational areas. And many of these land developments were being opened around the country. Most of them were being sold on contract sales, which is arguably unfair to the consumer since you can foreclose on the property virtually without warning. However, there is an argument that it's the fairest thing to the consumer because he is allowed to buy property he otherwise couldn't get if he had to rely on a bank. So there was risk involved.

My great objection to the coverage of Whitewater is that many of the news organizations that used full-time investigative reporters to go look into it have accepted as gospel much of what was reported not only in *The New York Times* but in other major newspapers of record. The *Los Angeles Times* comes to mind.

One particular issue is a story that was run in the same month, March of 1992, which basically said in its lead that Clinton had lobbied favorably for an individual by the name of Dan Lassiter, who had been convicted of drugs and had earned $750,000 on a bond issue by the state of Arkansas.

Well, it turned out—and I understand the *Times* corrected this in a later edition—that Clinton was not lobbying on behalf of Dan Lassiter and the bond issue, he was lobbying on behalf of getting the communications system. More importantly, Dan Lassiter was not the lead underwriter of this bond issue but, in fact, earned only a $115,000 fee as one of three underwriters of the bonds. And this escalated into Lassiter being not just a drug user but a drug dealer who made a million dollars off of bond issues from the state of Arkansas.

This is the evolution of the stories. They gain momentum as they are picked up by other news organizations, and my greatest concern and criticism is: Why don't major newspapers do at least some of their own investigative reporting rather than accept the information that's in *The New York Times,* the *Los Angeles Times,* or *The Washington Post?* I think it's important that we go out and do a little of our own research rather than rely on the research of other news organizations no matter how reputable. Certainly I have a great deal of respect for *The New York Times* and these other newspapers, but they are as fallible as any one of us.

LAPHAM: Maybe we can take questions from people on the panel or anybody from the floor. So far nobody has brought up any real evidence for any scandal, now or then. As far as I know, nobody at the table has suggested that there is evidence of any wrongdoing at all. And that strikes me as remarkable, given the amount of time, space, energy, accusation, suspicion, and allegation that has been carried forward for the last two years. And I'm really disappointed that the *Times* didn't come to answer the questions because the questions are very well framed. The information is solid.

AUDIENCE MEMBER: What reason did they give for not coming?

LAPHAM: They gave no reason. I mean, I didn't talk to them, but the people who called them said that they just hung up the telephone. I'm not sure who the individuals were, but I find that fairly shocking.

CROCK: Well, I was on an investigative reporting panel not long ago with Steve Labaton, who has contributed some of this reporting, and I told him that I was planning to bring up Whitewater as sort of a latter-day Koreagate—I don't know how many people here remember Koreagate—and he said that he would be uncomfortable with that because the *Times* policy has been that the stories speak for themselves. That was the defense.

LAPHAM: This one doesn't speak very sweetly.

CROCK: I would take issue with the very general conclusion that there is no evidence of anything here. I think one potential problem may be that some people who supposedly signed campaign checks at a fund-raiser say they did not do so. There is no politician in Washington who would want Bill Clinton held liable for the veracity of the trail of campaign contributions, though, because they would be cooking their own goose. But there is a constant fear that you might have reached the wrong conclusion: you conclude there's nothing in the Whitewater story, and then you pick up the paper the next day and be embarrassed. We wrote a story raising questions about the whole thing in mid-January, and the only publication I know of that wrote a similar story was *The Boston Globe* the day before we went to press; we've been holding our breath ever since. It is very, very difficult to swim against the tide. Especially with a story like this.

But we pride ourselves on being contrarian. That is another journalistic imperative, and so we wrote that story and it's held up pretty well since, thank God.

LYONS: It's also impossible, as a matter of logic, to prove a negative. I'm not up here to tell you that Bill Clinton hung the moon or that he's innocent of anything that anyone might ever accuse him of. I'm saying: take the stuff in this press package and compare it with what you read in *The New York Times* and you will see what's happened here.

The stories are full of lies, and it is very difficult to conclude that the lies are accidental. If I were going to fault Bill Clinton, I would say you should have taken a pickup truck, gotten every piece of paper pertaining to Madison Guaranty, dumped it on the front doorstep of *The New York Times, The Washington Post,* the Associated Press, and whoever else, and been done with it way back in December.

LIEBERMAN: I would like to ask Tom Hamburger about the difficulty of fighting the conventional wisdom, because *CJR* found that the Minneapolis paper stood out as being one of very few that gave a much fuller explanation of what was going on.

HAMBURGER: While I'm answering that, I also want to answer a comment Lewis made a moment ago. I'm not yet prepared to conclude that there is nothing here. As the congressional hearing opened and Jim Leach of Iowa was saying there may be evidence of a misuse of office, which in the minds of some commentators brought it to an impeachable offense, we thought we should look into it ourselves and see what the record actually showed.

To our astonishment, many other news organizations, and certainly the *Times,* had not fairly reflected the record. But we all deal with wire editors on the desk who say, "The *Times* didn't report it that way!" What do you do? You go back to the rules of basic reporting, which are: review what your sources say, go to the documents, and report it as you see it.

AUDIENCE MEMBER: I'm doing a book on I. F. Stone and dissent in American journalism, and I'm interested in what you said about the whole concept of journalistic norms. I see things every day in the *Post* that we would have been shot for ten years ago. I mean, this concept seems to be sloppy journalism as well as maybe deliberate falsification.

HAMBURGER: I think it's the norms of our business that drive that kind of reporting. And you can see an example of it in the story of Hillary Clinton's commodities trades. I think that's a terrific story. It's fascinating to make this windfall in the commodities market, and it is worth investigating. But Gerth gathered his information and then what did he use to drive it to the front page? He suggested that there was a quid pro quo, that Tyson had received benefits. That part of the story he fudged. It wasn't accurate. Tyson didn't receive extraordinary benefits, as Gerth described in that piece. But that's what moved the story to page one, isn't it?

CROCK: I have one other thing to add about this basically historical amnesia that seems to be a chronic problem. It would have taken one phone call to demolish Jeff Gerth's first story: a phone call to the Resolution Trust Corporation. And you would have asked one question: How many thrifts nationwide were closed down in 1984? Does anybody know the answer to that?

LYONS: I imagine it's none.

CROCK: Well, you're very close. The answer is nine. How many were shut down in 1985? Nine again. In 1986? Ten. But you were left with the impression that everything was being shut down all around this one thrift, and it was left standing because of preferential treatment. Why didn't anybody make that one phone call to the RTC?

AUDIENCE MEMBER: I'm a talk-radio host, and many of our listeners in talk radio think that *The New York Times* is the mouthpiece of the Clinton Administration and the most liberal publication going. And so by the time talk radio got hold of the story, it moved into astronomical directions. I'd like you to comment on what happens in the other parts of the media when a story leaves the written press.

CAMP: Talk radio has been the source of so much misinformation, because it got impetus from *The New York Times* and then expanded into areas that had nothing to do with Whitewater per se. I mean it has taken bizarre twists that are so strange you say, "How does this happen?"

AUDIENCE MEMBER: You said that you thought selective reporting was a canard in the whole story, that prosecutors themselves don't even report 100 percent of the story. And in Mr. Lyons's *Harper's* story he says, "In the post-everythinggate culture, no reporter wishes to appear insignificantly or insufficiently prosecutorial." So is it fair to say, Mr. Lyons, that your complaint about the reportage on Whitewater was not that there was too much reporting but that there was too little selective prosecutorial reporting?

LYONS: Yeah, that's my whole point. I think basically that Jeff Gerth set himself up as a prosecutor, except that it's a prosecutor's job to obtain justice. In this case, I mean "prosecutorial" to simply mean biased. I think that all evidence to the contrary was suppressed.

DUFFY: I agree with Mr. Lyons. I think that the most important decision a prosecutor makes is to decline a case. Where I would be at variance with what was just said, though, is that the *Times* went after it from one angle to the exclusion of other unspecified angles. There are only two basic questions raised by Whitewater. Both are, I think, of legitimate interest and worthy of pursuit. Was it a sweetheart deal? In my opinion, Whitewater was a deal that an ordinary person such as myself, or I daresay most people in the audience, would not have been privy to regardless of the expectations of retiring veterans and all of that. So that's one issue, whether there was a sweetheart deal.

The second issue is whether there was a quid pro quo. Whether as a public official Governor Clinton or Attorney General Clinton did something to benefit a regulatory agency or personnel that cut Madison or McDougal or some other involved party a deal. Both of those issues were worthy of pursuit. So there was grist. I mean, this was not something that was invented out of whole cloth.

The fact of the matter is, even a news organization with the power and influence of *The New York Times* does not have the power or the clout to see to it that not one but two special prosecutors are appointed. Similarly, it does not have the power or the clout that results in RTC criminal referrals. Now, a referral, as most of you know, is only that. It says there may be some violation of criminal law here and these violations may involve the following people. In one of those referrals, at least, the Clintons were named as possible beneficiaries of possibly illegal action. Is that something that's worthy of pursuit? I can't see how you can answer that question in the negative if you are in this business.

AUDIENCE MEMBER: I was a little disturbed by the personalizing of this article against Jeff Gerth. I mean, you said you didn't want to pursue it deeper into the fact-checking, the editing, and so forth at the *Times*, but if you are really going to level this severe indictment against Gerth and the *Times*, I would think it would be very enlightening to know just how all of that proceeded through the *Times*.

LYONS: Well, that's another story. I hope somebody else writes it.

AUDIENCE MEMBER: You're talking about decisions to place stories on page one. But Mr. Gerth doesn't write headlines, and if somebody else wrote the headline, it's not . . . You imply a lot about Gerth's motives at the end of your article.

LYONS: I haven't said a word about Gerth's motives. I don't know what they are.

AUDIENCE MEMBER: You imply that his reporting had something to do with Stephens and Sheffield Nelson. And one other thing. There's a subtext that all these stories about Arkansas culture are kind of flawed in the sense that they come out of this Washington prism and that Washington itself is a fairly corrupt town media-wise. But even if that's true, so what? Is the argument that people from Washington shouldn't be in Arkansas poking into all this stuff?

LYONS: I'll take the first question first. Jeff Gerth's name is on the story. He put his name on it. My name is on the article in *Harper's*. Nobody has suggested that any of the facts in my article aren't true. If they aren't, my name is on it. You can come talk to me about it. You can talk to Lewis, or the editor of the story, or the fact-checker. You know where to go, if you want to pursue it that far. Come to Little Rock and dig into the records, interview people, look at the same records we looked at. Try to figure out how a reporter came up with what Gerth came up with.

CAMP: Gene makes a really important point, because those documents that were constructed contemporaneously in 1984 and 1985 basically go against the premise of *The New York Times* story. I've counted nineteen either factual errors or points of contention in the first story. I did this the day after I went through the records of the Arkansas Securities Department. This information was easily obtained by anyone, and the records were very clear-cut on how Beverly Bassett Schaffer had handled this. That Madison Guaranty had gotten no favored treatment.

LYONS: I'd like to bring up a secondary point. We're all very uncomfortable because we're saying that somebody in our own line of work has done the dirty. We are talking about other people's lives and reputations who have been hurt badly by this. Why are we feeling sorry for Jeff Gerth? Okay. I don't mean to personalize it. I don't know the guy.

HAMBURGER: This discussion is not about Jeff Gerth or his competence as a reporter but about why these stories received such wide currency and why more of us weren't doing more questioning or doing our own independent research.

DUFFY: Well, I think many of us were. I mean, how many of us had reporters in Little Rock? Quite a few, I imagine. And as to there being this sort of slavish rush to follow *The New York Times,* the first Madison story sank like a stone and it was only the conduct of the White House machinery in terms of its response that generated the immense press hunt that followed.

I would also like to go back to an earlier point: I think my understanding of the records with regard to Whitewater is that they are very incomplete. The term "murky" has been used, and I would agree with that. Purely with regard to the regulatory issue, Gene Lyons mentioned the Eighth Circuit opinion, with which I am familiar, but there are at least two laws on the books and one fairly recent memo. So I'm not suggesting who is right or wrong here. I am saying that the record here is not at all as clear as the record might suggest.

LIEBERMAN: It seems that what's going on here is that the Clintons tried to make some money. Neither Bill nor Hillary Clinton came from a wealthy family, so they were trying to make money in land, as many people in the 1970s were doing, and Hillary apparently was very clever in dealing with the commodities market. And I think maybe the same standard was not applied to previous presidents. I don't remember any stories dealing with Barbara Bush and what kind of financial involvement she had or Nancy Reagan or even Nixon in his dealings with Bebe Rebozo. And it seems to me that the standard is different here.

CROCK: I disagree. There were stories about how the Kitchen Cabinet made Ronald Reagan rich, how he got his ranch in Santa Barbara. One way of looking at this, an appropriate way, is that the Clintons were trying to make some money. Another way of looking at it is that some people were trying to take care of them. And it's a very common thing. Probably half of Congress has sugar daddies. I am not suggesting that anything done was illegal, although some of the trading records are, to be charitable, dubious.

DUFFY: That's right, and this goes exactly to the point of the murkiness. There are a lot of very wealthy people in Arkansas, some of whom the Clintons numbered as friends, or at least people they had met and knew socially. So we don't know if the $100,000 Mrs. Clinton made—the precise number escapes me—was entirely due to good fortune or because she read *The Wall Street Journal* or because of her friendship with the general counsel of Tyson Foods or because the profits were allocated to her account for other people who needed tax write-offs. Is that an issue worthy of press inquiry and press investigation? I can't see how you say no to that question.

AUDIENCE MEMBER: With all due respect to the discomfort that's been expressed here in criticizing another journalist's work, I find this discussion a little bit self-indulgent. As Mr. Camp said, everyone jumped on this, and had anyone else been able to advance the story or nail something else into it I don't think we would be sitting here discussing how Jeff Gerth and *The New York Times* are becoming scapegoats on a story that didn't go where we thought it was going to go. Which brings me to my question: What have we learned from this episode, and how is it affecting news coverage at this point?

LAPHAM: I think it has had an effect. I think there is now a tendency to say,

"The press has gone too far. It's too nosy, it's too cruel, it's too mean, or whatever, and let's now be more courtly and more polite." So I do think that bad investigative journalism drives out good investigative journalism, and I think that's the long-term loss from this.

AUDIENCE MEMBER: I once owned a daily newspaper and lost a lot of money. I was an elected official in Florida—I got re-elected six times—and I also headed a major savings and loan. So I can look at all of these things, and what strikes me is that *The New York Times,* the leading news organization, has layers of editors that are supposed to look at what reporters do. And then you see on their editorial page a rather vicious use of the information that Mr. Lyons points out is not very good information, and then Safire takes it a step further. What could possibly be the motive of *The New York Times* in perpetuating this kind of inaccuracy and this kind of vicious attack?

LAPHAM: That goes to the question of motive and we don't have the *Times* with us. I'm sorry we don't, because that is a question that could be asked of [editorial page editor] Howell Raines.

LYONS: I know that we are all prone to self-delusion when we are on a story. But it's hard for me to imagine a reporter prone to this degree of self-delusion. It's hard for me to imagine talking to someone for hours and then writing that they didn't remember anything. I cannot myself imagine convincing myself that that was the right thing to do.

LIEBERMAN: I think it's a danger for reporters to go at their stories just looking for quotes. I don't know how many times reporters have called to interview me about something I've written and say, "Will you please just give me one quote?" I find that's poor journalism.

LYONS: Well, the nameless-federal-officials scam is one that is used very frequently throughout this thing, and I have been unable to determine in my own work who these federal officials are because they are not the people who were in charge of Madison Guaranty or the Federal Home Loan Bank Board or the FSLIC.

CAMP: When I contacted Walter Faulk, who was a senior vice president in charge of regulation for Arkansas S&Ls in March of 1994, two years after the first *Times* story, I discovered that I was only the second reporter in the United States to call and ask him about this. The other was Greg Gordon from the [Minneapolis] *Star-Tribune.*

AUDIENCE MEMBER: Don't journalists have a responsibility and a duty to present verifiable reporting? And if you think journalists should not monitor one another, who should?

LYONS: I certainly have nothing to add to that. I've got a great story for some-body who wants a Whitewater story. It would be a great story for *The Wall Street Journal*. Who is David Hale, the judge who says Bill Clinton made him do it? Check into his background.

CROCK: The *Journal* did that.

LYONS: They did?

CROCK: Yeah, a long time ago. The *Arkansas Times* or *Gazette* did a very good piece. He's been in more trouble as a municipal judge.

LYONS: He was a character in a book I wrote long before any of this took place. In it he made legal rulings that would have shocked an ayatollah. He's got a pile of lawsuits yea high—one from his ex-mistress, whom he defrauded.

AUDIENCE MEMBER: Do you encounter members of the press who bought into the notion that the morality and moral standards of any small, rural Southern state are so inherently inferior to those of a cosmopolitan, urbane New York or Washington that anything that comes out of it must be automati-cally suspicious?

LYONS: Anybody from Arkansas can talk about this for a long time. I've had a lot of conversations with reporters in the last couple of years, and as soon as you start saying, "Well, that sorta is not the way it is" or, "That's not the way it was" or, "You need to talk to so and so," you get the feeling that all of a sudden the conversation turns patronizing and people are thinking, "You're a Clinton whore." Well, what I do is shovel up all my collective works and say, "Here, find all the praise of Clinton in that pile"—which you won't find.

Yeah, I think that there's a certain amount of patronizing stuff that's driven by the media. I have had the experience of living in New England in the early 1970s with a wife from Arkansas, who was treated like a combination of Eva Braun and Daisy Mae Yokum. And we decided to come back South where peo-ple laughed at stuff. I'm sorry for you New Englanders. We like to laugh a lot in Arkansas.

Index

✦

and Anthony Lewis's column,
140–141
and Madison Guaranty, 35, 36
and Jim McDougal, 61–62, 129–130,
160–169
and media, 5n.4
in *60 Minutes* interview, 6
and Sheffield Nelson, 11–13
and Larry Nichols, 13–15
and poultry and trucking industries
in Arkansas, 53–56, 171, 175
presidency of, and Arkansas, 3, 4
in presidential primary season in
1992, 31
and RTC criminal referrals, 74, 82,
210
and "Slick Willie" nickname, 27
statements by, to independent counsel, 121
and Jim Guy Tucker, 88
and Tyson Foods, 50–56, 171,
175–177
wealth and income of, 58
and Whitewater real estate project,
68–69, 70–73, 89–92, 127–129,
155–158, 167, 206
Clinton, Chelsea, 174
Clinton, Hillary Rodham. *See also* "Clinton scandals"
Arkansas career of, 32
and *Blood Sport*, 148–153
commodities trading by, 50, 170–175,
189, 191, 192, 198, 202, 203, 212
corruption potential of, 58–59
and father, Hugh Rodham, 59–60
and Vincent Foster, 7, 63n.4, 103–108
in Jeff Gerth's March 8, 1992, *New
York Times* article, 155–159
Rush Limbaugh on, 7
and Madison Guaranty, 26–27, 35, 36,
43–45, 102–103, 129–134, 137–141,
142, 168
"mystery call" made by, 124
and "Presidential BITCH" T-shirts
and coffee mugs, 122, 123
and Rose Law Firm billing records,
57, 129–134

and RTC criminal referrals, 74, 82,
210
William Safire's attack on, 25–28
and Senate hearings, 117
statements by, to independent counsel, 121
and Susan Thomases, 107–108, 118
and "Troopergate," 23, 60
and Tyson Foods, 51–53
wealth and income of, 58, 62
and Whitewater Development Company, 66–67, 70
and Whitewater documents, release
of, 57, 59–67, 73
and Whitewater grand jury, 127, 131
and Whitewater real estate project,
66–73, 89–92, 90n.13, 97, 127–129,
155–158, 167, 199, 206
"Clinton Chronicles, The" (video),
13, 16–17, 117
"Clinton scandals," 4. *See also*
Commodities trading by Hillary
Clinton; Flowers, Gennifer; Jones,
Paula; "Travelgate"; "Troopergate"; "Troopergate 2"; Whitewater
"scandal"
in Arkansas, 13–29
and *Arkansas Democrat-Gazette*, 10–11
and Australian TV crew in Little
Rock, 22n.14
and "dirty tricks" campaign, 5
and media, 4–9
and Stephens Inc., 19–20
Clinton Watch (newsletter), 192
CNN, 23, 116, 131, 194, 205
Coalition for Peace Through Strength,
The, 13
Coleman, Susann, 17, 17n.11
Columbia Journalism Review (magazine),
41, 134–135, 192, 194, 199
Commerce Department (U.S.), 175
Commodities trading by Hillary Clinton,
50, 170–175, 189, 191, 192, 198, 202,
203, 212
Conason, Joe, 85, 134–135, 152–153
Congress (U.S.). *See* House Banking
Committee hearings; Senate hear-

About the Author

Gene Lyons is a writer and reporter living in Little Rock, Arkansas. He currently writes a weekly column for the *Arkansas Democrat-Gazette* and reviews books for *Entertainment Weekly*. He was formerly an editor at *Newsweek* and has written for numerous publications, including *Harper's Magazine*, *The New York Times Book Review*, *The Nation*, and *The New York Review of Books*. His book *Widow's Web* (1993) is an account of a celebrated murder case in Arkansas. Lyons is married with two sons, and raises beagles as a hobby.

Store near Ft Worth
that does teacher shows
(Commerce?)
TX
Bryston store (Bri-store)
BK store
Wataugh, TX

Education Station Fayetteville
Pam Gilbreath (ship)

Activity Guide to Folktales
citing various AH titles